D1617376

Post-
Industrial
Lives

Dedicated to our Daughters:
Rebecca Anne Hage, Catlin Ishihara Powers,
and Bonnie-Annique Katayama Powers
who have inspired us to worry about the future
and, more generally, to the father-daughter relationship,
which has given us so much emotional pleasure.

Post-Industrial Lives

Roles and Relationships in the 21st Century

HM
101
.H84
1992
west

Jerald Hage•Charles H. Powers

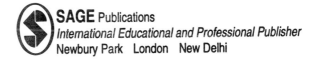

SAGE Publications
International Educational and Professional Publisher
Newbury Park London New Delhi

For information address:

SAGE Publications, Inc.
2455 Teller Road
Newbury Park, California 91320

SAGE Publications Ltd.
6 Bonhill Street
London EC2A 4PU
United Kingdom

SAGE Publications India Pvt. Ltd.
M-32 Market
Greater Kailash I
New Delhi 110 048 India

Printed in the United States of America

Library of Congress Cataloging-in-Publication Data

Hage, Jerald, 1932-
    Post-industrial lives : roles and relationships in the 21st
century / Jerald Hage, Charles H. Powers.
            p.   cm.
    Includes bibliographical references and index.
    ISBN 0-8039-4494-2   (cl)   0-8039-4495-0 (pbk)
    1. Social change.   2. Interpersonal relations.   3. Social roles.
4. Social institutions—Forecasting.   5. Information society—
Forecasting.   6. High technology—Social aspects—Forecasting.
I. Powers, Charles H.   II. Title.
HM101.H84   1992
302—dc20   92-10631
                                                              CIP
92   93   94   95   10   9   8   7   6   5   4   3   2   1

Sage Production Editor: Judith L. Hunter

CONTENTS

PREFACE

Most collaboratively produced books are written by people who either work together or were at one time associated with the same university (Mullins, 1973). This book is different. There has been no overlap in the institutional affiliations of the authors. Instead, we were brought together by a common intellectual style, a body of shared theoretical interests, mutual respect, and a feeling that each of us held different pieces to the same puzzle. Working collaboratively on that puzzle has been an intensely rewarding enterprise. And we hope that our joint effort reflects both West Coast and East Coast sensibilities.

Our initial theoretical attraction stemmed from our shared interest in social roles and our mutual conviction that *role theory*, to use that term in the broadest possible sense, has a great deal of unrealized promise as we enter an era of change in the nature of people's everyday lives, which is, paradoxically, as subtle as it is revolutionary. The growing literature on post-modernism and post-industrialism indicates both its critical importance and its elusive character (for the former, see Bauman, 1988; Denzin, 1991; Featherstone, 1988a,

1988b; Kellner, 1990; and for the latter, see Bell, 1973; Naisbitt, 1982, Naisbitt & Aburdene, 1990; Toffler, 1981). Most of this literature has ignored, however, what the transformation means for everyday life. Furthermore, the literature is dominated by a series of dichotomies that we think are far too simple.

Our effort to provide a more complex perspective reflects intellectual indebtedness to dozens of people. First among them are our respective theoretical mentors, Robert K. Merton, Hans Zetterberg, and Jonathan H. Turner. Hage studied at Columbia University in the late 1950s, where he received the theme of analytical rigor from Hans Zetterberg, including a deep, abiding interest in theory construction and formal theory, and the antithesis of subtle distinctions, including a substantive interest in role theory from Merton. Powers studied with Jonathan Turner at the University of California at Riverside, where he learned that theory is at the heart of science, and that the road to theoretical advance begins with reconceptualization.

Gerald Marwell, too, was an important intellectual stimulus. Together with Jerald Hage, he developed the vocabulary for describing role relationships (Hage and Marwell, 1969; Marwell and Hage, 1970), which is one of the themes of the book. And Ralph Turner led Charles Powers in his early exploration of role theory, giving rise to the work on role redefinition (Powers, 1981a), which is another of the themes unifying the book.

If it is these men who provided us with a set of intellectual problems, it is women—our wives and daughters—who provided us with the solutions. We dedicate this book to our daughters and, more generally, the father-daughter role relationships, in which we have learned about symbolic communication, the key idea in this book.

Hage remembers feeling, the first time he saw his daughter, Rebecca, emotional completeness, a hard feeling to describe, but one so fundamental. And as Rebecca grew during her early childhood, her radiance and happiness nourished the entire family, a family experiencing many hardships and uncertainties associated with movement back and forth between the United States and France, attempting to solve the post-modern crisis of dual-career families compounded by a dual-cultural marriage. But perhaps most of all, Jerry Hage dedicates this book to her because of her enormous skills in reading symbolic communication and in her dedication to using these skills in helping handicapped children.

Powers's daughters are much younger than Hage's daughter, but the emotional sustenance he gains from them is no less intense. Chuck dedicates this book to his daughters for all the joy they bring him, and for two special gifts he hopes never to forget. When Catlin was 2 years old she helped her dad realize that no matter how many "urgent" concerns seem to demand immediate attention, some relationships cannot be put on hold until tomorrow. Catlin's gift has made each day deeper and richer than it would otherwise have been. Bonnie's unfaltering buoyancy in her first months of life helped her dad finally realize the benefits of looking on the bright side. Bonnie's gift has made each day a little more fun and a little more healthy.

Our daughters are inheriting a world that is becoming more complex by the day. And each of their lives is made even more complex by the fact that they are dual-race and enjoy cultural influences from more than one nation. These factors make it all the more fitting that we dedicate this book about complexity and social change to Rebecca, Catlin, and Bonnie. We hope as they grow older they will know that for the 6 years their dads worked on this book, our thoughts were never far from them. Although our ways of showing it are sometimes clumsy, our children are the much loved centers of our lives.

Finally, we want to thank Morris Rosenberg, Sheldon Stryker, Ralph Turner, and Mitch Allen for reading the manuscript and making a large number of critical comments. We have probably not dealt adequately with all of their criticisms, but the book has gained in clarity, subtlety, and range because of their efforts.

INTRODUCTION

Unlike physicists, sociologists keep reading books written by early masters. We still find Max Weber, Emile Durkheim, George Herbert Mead, Vilfredo Pareto, and Georg Simmel, among others, to be of contemporary relevance (e.g., Ritzer, 1988; J. Turner, 1990; Turner, Beeghley, & Powers, 1989). For the period when they wrote, roughly 1890-1930, was a golden age when many new ideas about society sprung forth.[1] It is important that we pause to ask why at that particular moment in time. Why was the golden age of advances in our understanding of society between 1890 and 1930? Why did it not start sooner? Or later? Why did it last as long as it did? Why was it as short in duration as it proved to be?

We think we have an answer for these questions. Weber, Pareto, Toennies, and their contemporaries happen to have lived during the time of the great socioeconomic and political transformation early in the industrial revolution. This first influenced Marx, who did most of his writing in England. Then it touched his sociological counterparts on the Continent as industrialization spread to France and Germany. The concentration of wealth, the rise of bureaucracy, the

1

creation of an extended division of labor, the emergence of anomie, the proliferation of social groups, urbanization, and other changes demanded attention and new theories to explain them. Weber, Durkheim, Simmel, and their contemporaries were on the scene at the time, and were astute enough to note the revolutionary character of transformation that society was then moving through. Sociology emerged as a discipline born of the industrial revolution (e.g., Busino, 1987) and was designed to explain this upheaval.

Our Approach

Our conviction is that **another new epoch is now in the making**. We refer to this, as others have, as the "post-industrial" era (e.g., Bell, 1973), or the movement from a society based on heavy industry to the age of information and high technology (Toffler, 1981). What strikes us is that post-industrialism involves the wholesale transformation of institutional life as we have come to know it—the key to placing this book in its proper context. Others have focused on such issues as the globalization of the economy and the decline of the industrial sector relative to the service sector (Naisbitt & Aburdene, 1985). **Our interest is in understanding the meaning of the post-industrial transformation for our work roles and personal relationships.** We concern ourselves with the everyday world: what sociologists refer to as the micro level of analysis of formal and informal relationships between people.[2]

Not everyone believes that a genuinely **new** order is in the making. Skeptics argue that "post-industrialism" is just a catchy phrase. But we believe there is ample evidence of the sweeping nature of the change now under way, and introduce some new ways of looking at the consequences of that change. Consistent with our attempt to synthesize different theoretical styles and perspectives—especially structural functionalism and symbolic interactionism—we rely upon kinds of evidence that are not normally included in research monographs, taking observations from everyday life, signs of people's feelings about the lives they lead, and information about new family and work arrangements emerging out of people's attempts to adapt to changing conditions. Our style is that of a theoretical essay, much in the tradition of Georg Simmel, where familiar observations are given a new twist by their juxtaposition within a set of theoretical ideas. Hence, this book is not a normal research monograph, but an interpretation. Nevertheless, if we can illustrate how the social world of work and play has changed, then perhaps the average reader will be both more convinced and more aware of these fundamental changes.

It is no accident that the authors of this book are writing from two of the hubs of the new order (Bethesda, Maryland, an area of biotech, and Santa Clara, in California's Silicon Valley, an area of semiconductors and small high-technology firms). For the character of the post-industrial order we will describe is most apparent in areas on the cutting edge of the new technologies that are transforming the nature of roles and relationships. The post-industrial order has not arrived (or even begun to arrive) in many places. Furthermore, not everyone in a post-industrial locale lives a post-industrial life or is at heart a post-industrial person with attitudes, values, perceptions, and capabilities that we shall define as post-modern or post-industrial. But just as the seminal writers at the turn of the century generalized from exceptional cases on the cutting edge of change, notably the British textile industry (e.g. Marx, 1967, Chapters 10 & 15) and Prussian bureaucracy in a hospital (which influenced Weber's theoretical formulations, e.g. 1946, 1968), and projected them into important theses, we have chosen cutting-edge examples to illuminate the future of role relationships in a technology-driven world.

Knowledge and technology have become the dominant social forces shaping society. It is important to note that we are not concerned with how these two intertwined variables affect power and wealth in post-industrial society; that is a topic for another book. Intellectually, this marks a sharp break with Marx, Weber, and other chroniclers of the industrial transformation who were deeply concerned with power, wealth, their workings, and their manifestations. Instead, **we analyze how knowledge and technology are having a profound impact on the nature of face-to-face social relationships and on the character of the social self.** The impact of knowledge and technology is most pervasive in the family and at the workplace, the contexts in which most social life occurs and where real micro-sociological theory should be constructed. Consistent with a symbolic interactionist perspective, we ask how post-industrial role relationships and post-modern selves contribute to the development of new knowledge and the changing of society. Much of our analysis focuses on problem solving, creative research, and their implications for the larger society.

We are far less interested in empirical specifics about individual cases than we are in typifying characteristic forms of social life and social organization; that is, we are self-consciously following the methodology of Max Weber (e.g., 1968, pp. 18-20) in his quest to identify "ideal-types." For example, when Weber (1946, p. 196 ff) identified the characteristics of an ideal-type modern bureaucracy— (a) clear lines of hierarchical authority, (b) units separated by functional specialization, (c) decisions based on the uniform application of clear rules, (d) hiring and promotion based on training rather than paternalism, (e) long-term employment in stable work units, and (f) the maintenance of written records as property of the office rather than the office holder—he was describing a purified analytical model rather than a particular concrete organization. Weber recognized that the correspondence between specific real world cases and ideal-type models will always be imperfect, just as chemists understand that virtually all compounds found in the natural world contain some impurities. But those impurities are ignored when analytically diagramming the compounds. Weber used ideal-types to isolate the distinctive features of the newly developing organizational forms of the late nineteenth and early twentieth centuries.

We employ the same method in our analysis of post-industrial society, and we find striking changes. But rather than perceive, as did Weber, that only one form of bureaucracy was replacing traditional forms of pre-industrial organization, or make the argument of Piore and Sabel (1984) that flexible manufacturing is the new dominant form, or follow the Peters and Waterman (1982) thesis that there is one best organizational form for contemporary businesses to install, our central argument is that post-industrial society is characterized by a great variety of institutionalized forms. Rather than seeing organizational evolution moving from one type to the next, we perceive post-industrial society emerging from at least three types to many more.

At the same time, we can suggest that these many types share important features. The more advanced forms of post-industrial organizations—the inter-organizational network, the joint venture, the small high-tech company, and the profit center in the large high-tech firm—have characteristics that are quite the opposite of Weber's bureaucracy. The distinctive features of post-industrial organizations include: (a) a leveling of hierarchical distinctions, (b) interpenetration of units designed to enhance the integration and maximize the coordination of previously autonomous functions, (c) a dramatic increase in the amount of behavior that is not rule-bound, (d) hiring and promoting people who are creative and have a feel for the job, (e) shifting assignments in and out of flexible work teams, and (f) more widespread access to information within and across organizations (Carnevale, 1991).

It is important for organizations to have more fluid qualities if they are to function under post-industrial conditions, for these characteristics facilitate structural experimentation, decrease response time, encourage adaptive change, and give rise to the great variety of forms we now see emerging.

Conceptual Focus on Roles

Contrasting Weber's ideal-type of industrial organizations with our own ideal-type portrait of post-industrial organizations communicates something of the epic character of changes now in the making. But even more important, although seldom recognized, changes in organizational design are closely paralleled by a metamorphosis in the character of role relationships that link people together. Post-industrial work roles are fundamentally different from industrial work roles. Family roles are undergoing equally dramatic alteration. And with a change in roles, all aspects of a society undergo subtle yet sweeping changes.

There is no more fundamental social science concept than "role" —for roles are the most rudimentary forms of social organization

Table I.1 The Contrast Between Weber's Ideal-Type of Bureaucracy and the Characteristics of Post-Industrial Forms[a]

Industrial Ideal-Type Organization	Post-Industrial Ideal-Type Organization[b]
1. clear lines of hierarchical authority within organizations as whole separate entities	1. leveling of hierarchical distinctions within organizations and blurring of boundaries across organizations
2. units separated by functional specialization	2. interpenetration of units in order to enhance the integration of previously specialized functions, that is, the breakdown of structural components such as departments, occupations, and the like
3. decisions based on the uniform application of clear rules	3. an increase in the amount of behavior that is not rule-bound, but rather is handled by negotiations
4. hiring and promotion based on training, with emphasis placed on intelligence	4. hiring and promotion based on the employees' "feel" for the occupation and ability to work in teams, with emphasis placed on creativity
5. lifetime employment in the same work unit	5. shifting assignment to flexible work teams
6. written records as the property of an office rather than the officeholder or the organization at large	6. open access to information within the organization
7. a few ideal-types	7. many configurations, including small high-tech, joint ventures, profit centers, and so on

a. The word *form*, that is, the combination of technology, structure, and control mechanism, is used in the sense of the population-ecologists (see Aldrich & Mueller, 1982; Hannan & Freeman, 1989).
b. This bears a close resemblance to the famous Burns and Stalker (1961) organic form, but it differs from it in some significant ways as well.

and the most basic building blocks of all systems of social organization (R. Turner, 1990). But the concept has been used in quite different ways by different writers (Biddle, 1979). Some scholars maintain that a role should be conceived of as a package of socially recognized rights and obligations that has an objective existence, separate from actor performance, in the expectations of those not in the role (Merton, 1968). But other scholars argue that a role should be conceptualized as the uniquely individualized style of adaptation by the specific person occupying the position in question, and therefore grounded on individual performance rather than collective expectations (see Biddle & Thomas, 1966; Zurcher, 1977, 1983). Open definitions of roles, such as Biddle's description of roles as "those behaviors characteristic of one or more persons in a context" (1979, p. 393), seem to us to be a little too broad and inclusive, with the result that unnecessary confusion and disagreement arise when people interested in interpersonal dynamics conduct scholarly exchange with those interested in the features of society-wide social institutions such as kinship. Even when researchers self-consciously strive to distinguish these two analytical levels, their work can be inadvertently confusing if no clear terminological distinction is maintained.

Our own strategy for dealing with this problem is to use two distinctly different sets of terminology to refer to the analytically distinct though simultaneous dimensions of relationships. For us, a **role** is a package of broadly recognized rights and obligations that define what would be expected of anyone occupying a given position embedded within a system of social relations. A **role relationship** refers to those rights and obligations commonly taken to define the nature of the tie that links two roles together. And a **role-set** is a list of alter roles with which a given social position is directly linked.

Roles can be thought of as coming in packages that virtually everyone participates in—packages that help people meet basic needs and tend to be associated with a special location in time and space. Sociologists refer to these bundles of roles as **institutions**; kinship and religion are examples. Or we can locate roles within **networks**: concatenated chains of positions that are directly or indirectly linked through exchange.

Note that we conceive of "roles" as having an objective definition that is independent of the style of performance of particular role occupants. But this in no way suggests that we deny the importance of individual performance. We merely call this the "interpersonal relationship" or "role style" in order to avoid confusion. An **interpersonal relationship** consists of those aspects of role performance that are unique to particular combinations of people and would most likely change in the event that the role occupants were replaced (Blumstein & Kollock, 1988). We sometimes refer to this as role style, thus treating the two terms as synonymous and interchangeable. Although we generally prefer the term *interpersonal relationship*, strategic use of the term *role style* will help remind us of the connection between individual behavior and social position, an important point we want to keep in sight. A **person-set** is a list of all the people (as distinct from positions) a person comes into contact with in a particular role relationship. Each of the authors is husband to one person, a father to two people, and a teacher to several hundred people. Person-sets thus differ in size, which, as we will see later, has substantial impact on the propensity for role redefinition to occur.

The distinction between role and interpersonal relationship, or role style, is a pivotal one. The character of both is changing as we enter the post-industrial era, and it is at this level that transformation in the social fabric is experienced most directly and most pointedly in peoples' lives.[3] Each, in turn, implicates a distinct form of **self**, or how one views one's own being as an object.

The crux of our argument is that the most important aspect of change on a societal level is that social roles are transformed at the level of individual people. This is inescapable, because societal change introduces pressures that must be responded to at an individual level. Perhaps the most obvious pressure for role change is **role conflict**, being subjected to contradictory performance demands. A slightly more subtle form of pressure is **role strain** or stress, overtaxing a role occupant with too many demands. Role strain is manifested when people feel they invest too much time in certain roles. A still more subtle form of pressure for role redefinition is **burnout**, which we define as emotional overload. All three kinds of pressure are increasing in post-industrial society and contributing to heightened rates of **role failure**, or the abrogation of some or all of the obligations defined as a part of a role.

Maintaining conceptual clarity will help us better understand the big picture of societal change by examining the ways in which the rudimentary building blocks of social order are being reshaped. For society is literally undergoing a metamorphosis, a transformation from within, as roles change to accommodate new conditions. In the balance of this introduction we briefly sketch how work and family

Table I.2 Definition of Terms

Role: package of broadly recognized rights and obligations that define what would be expected of anyone occupying a given position embedded within a system of social relations.

Role Relationship: those rights and obligations commonly taken to define the nature of the tie that links two roles together.

Role-Set: a list of alter roles with which a given social position is directly linked.

Institution: a system of roles that is being replicated across the entire society, tends to be associated with its own time and place, helps people meet basic needs, and is one that most people in a society participate in at some point in time (e.g., kinship).

Network: concatenated chains of positions that are directly or indirectly linked through exchange.

Interpersonal Relationship: those aspects of role performance that are unique to particular combinations of people and would most likely change in the event that the role occupants were replaced (also sometimes called "role style").

Person-Set: all those people with whom an individual role occupant comes into contact in a particular role relationship with a specific alter role.

Role Conflict: disagreement over the nature of a person's obligations by virtue of his or her occupying a specified role.

Role Strain: the condition that arises when one invests more time in performance of a role than one feels he or she should.

Burnout: the condition that arises when one invests more emotional energy in a role than one feels he or she should.

Role Failure: the abrogation of some or all of the obligations defined as being a part of a role.

roles are being transformed as we move from industrial to post-industrial society. In later chapters we will explore the sociological nuances of this change in detail and, building upon established bodies of literature from sociology, suggest a new theoretical synthesis for making sense out of our social world.

From Industrial to Post-Industrial Work Roles

Our analysis revolves around roles, and much of this book deals specifically with work roles. When you ask people to typify industrial work, they begin by mentioning physical activity. Industrial work characteristically involves high levels of physical exertion aimed at transforming raw material into finished material objects. Our stereotypic notions of factories also conjure up images of a strict division of labor, where goals and procedures are clearly specified, and where each job consists of a narrow range of prescribed tasks (Burawoy, 1979). Punctuality and attendance are emphasized because an assembly line cannot function without workers at all stations. Consequently, workers in these settings have little flexibility in their schedules. They are not given the luxury of staying home from the factory when they feel so inclined or when one of the kids gets sick. By the same token, industrial work is typically restricted to a specific time and place. When the afternoon whistle blows, people go home and leave their work behind. Hence, someone who is a slave to the time clock from 9 a.m. to 5 p.m. is also **free** from 5 p.m. to 9 a.m. (Dubin, 1979).

The characteristic problem of such work—of "industrial" work— is alienation (Erikson, 1986; Garson, 1975). Many workers feel overly controlled, mere appendages of machines, stationed in the open or encased behind windows placing each worker under constant visual surveillance (Foucault, 1977). Although the bulk of the literature has focused on the alienation of blue-collar workers manning factory assembly lines (Blauner, 1964), managers in "gray flannel suits," working in the machine-like bureaucracies of large corporations, can be equally alienated from their work (Harrington, 1958) when it is "industrial" in character. Work, whether at the office or in a factory, can be mindless and monotonous, mastered in a few hours or days and considered boring drudgery within weeks. Work comes to be removed from one's heartfelt concerns, something to be suffered through and forgotten about after hours. That is why many industrial workers complain about feeling "bored to death."

But such complaints are heard far less frequently now than they were a decade or two ago, because work conditions are being completely transformed with post-industrialism. The process at the core of this transformation is automation, what Piore and Sabel (1984) call *The Second Industrial Divide*, as we build machines for those tasks that are most clearly defined, technically simple, and most often repeated. But these are precisely the jobs we associate with industrial economies (Lawrence & Lorsch, 1967). In other words, post-industrial automation destroys the very heart of the industrial order.

What tasks are left for people to perform when mundane, routine, repetitive work is taken over by machines? Nonroutine jobs involving a great deal of mental activity. To be sure, many sorts of jobs fall under this heading. It includes highly technical research jobs involving the development of new products (e.g., making faster computers, finding a cure for AIDS, developing battery-powered cars) or the solution of very complex global problems (e.g., acid rain, ozone destruction, war and peace). It includes occupations involving individual diagnosis and intervention (e.g., working with problem students who fail to respond to a standard menu of learning materials and teaching strategies). The nonroutine job category also includes work involving constant interaction with the public (receptionists, entertainers, and the like). With this variety of post-industrial work options there will be no shortage of work to do in the future, contrary to the worries of those who are concerned about unemployment. At issue is whether the available work force will be well matched with available jobs. Will workers be capable of problem solving in nonroutine jobs? Will they have the requisite education and interaction skills?[4]

If we think of the work opportunities created by a post-industrial economy, we can begin to typify the character of post-industrial work, much as we believe Weber would have done. Confronting work tasks will involve the expenditure of more mental activity than physical activity. **Work tasks will be defined in terms of information gathering, problem solving, the production of creative ideas, and the ability to respond flexibly to new situations or adjust flexibly when interacting with others.** Most unskilled and semiskilled jobs will be replaced with highly specialized occupations requiring at least a college degree. Indeed, we predict that the word *job* will disappear from everyday use and be replaced by the word *occupation*, which provides a neat contrast between industrial and post-industrial work.

Although goals may be specified in post-industrial work settings, exact work procedures—what used to be called the rules manual or referred to as job descriptions—will not exist because the best way to accomplish goals will either be unknown (e.g., how to build the next generation of computer or overcome Jennifer's reading problem) or will be known to depend upon uncontrollable factors that are subject to change, such as the mood, wishes, and even demands of clients.

The new order can produce a great deal of occupational excitement, as depicted in *The Soul of the New Machine* (Kidder, 1979). With many post-industrial jobs, there is a sense of trying to accomplish what no one has accomplished before, or doing something that no one else can do. Because there are no fixed standards or procedures, however, post-industrial workers rarely enjoy the kind of satisfaction that comes from finishing a job in a way that everyone would agree was done as well as it could be done; the idea of "perfection" is going out of style. For this reason, people who are insecure and work best under defined guidelines will suffer some very real discomfort in the post-industrial workplace (Ray & Myers, 1989). Large parts of a post-industrial workday are also spent interacting with other people either in group meetings, on the telephone, or in one-to-one relationships with those who expect individual attention (Kinlaw, 1990). Again, the absence of clear role prescriptions creates social stress and conflict, making role redefinition a pivotal process. For illustrative purposes, in Table I.3 we indicate a number of dimensions on which industrial jobs and post-industrial occupational positions can be contrasted.

As in Table I.1, this schematic device conceals many subtleties. Industrial work was largely unskilled or semiskilled. Professional, managerial, and technical jobs represented a relatively small proportion of the labor force. But in a post-industrial work force, professional, managerial, and technical workers are in the majority. There are many more occupational specialties than before, and the dimensions in post-industrial work are combined in many different ways so that it is difficult to speak of a typical position, in contrast to industrial work, where most of the characteristics applied to most jobs.

From Industrial to Post-Industrial Family Roles

It is easy to focus so tightly on changes in the workplace that one loses sight of other aspects of life. But differences between industrial and post-industrial society will by no means be limited to work roles

Table I.3 The Contrast Between the Nature of Work in Industrial and Post-Industrial Society

Ideal-Type Characteristics of Industrial Roles	*Ideal-Type Characteristics of Post-Industrial Roles*
1. physical activity	1. mental activity
2. transformation of material objects (e.g., picking fruit, smelting iron, assembling toasters, ironing clothes, transporting plywood, selling shoes)	2. information gathering and problem solving
3. roles defined in terms of a narrow range of prescribed tasks and routine activities for which goals and procedures are clearly specified	3. roles defined by goals for which no certain procedure can be specified, consequently involving a relatively wide range of nonroutine tasks
4. time and place for role performance are tightly constrained and there is freedom from role-related concerns when outside that place in time and space	4. the time and place for role activity are not tightly constrained, and people have difficulty insulating one social domain (e.g., family or work) from worries or demands emanating from other domains
5. humans as appendages of machines: machines determine how the work is to be done, how long it will take, and what the finished product will look like	5. people determine how work will be done, how much time will be spent, and what the finished product will look like; machines are tools
6. satisfactory job performance produces a sense of completion	6. satisfactory job performance produces a sense of mastery
7. non-ephemeral aspects of roles resist change	7. roles are frequently and substantially redefined via negotiation and even conflict
8. low interaction rates, even for managers; that is, the role-set is small and contained	8. high interaction rates; that is, the role-set is large and demanding
9. service is a small component of most jobs	9. service is a significant component of many roles

and relationships. The family is always at the vortex of social change (e.g., Degler, 1980).

One way to find out about family life is to ask how people spend their time. Another is to ask how they distinguish a "good" father from a bad one, a "good" parent from a bad one, or a "good" son or daughter from a bad one. A third and more provocative question is to ask how many socially acceptable types of males and females exist in post-industrial society as contrasted with industrial society. We raise all three questions in addition to examining more conventional sources of information about the family.

Family life in industrial societies was characterized by rather authoritarian decision making, gender-specific division of labor, and commitment of significant blocks of time to routine and repetitive tasks. A "bad" parent was, among other things, one whose kids were dressed in dirty, wrinkled clothing. Conversely, a "good" parent was one who kept his or her children's clothes clean and neatly ironed (e.g., Rubin, 1976). The Hollywood movies and TV sitcoms of the 1950s made this emphasis on routine activities, such as washing and ironing, abundantly clear.[5]

But with the coming of post-industrial society, the meaning of "good" parent is being redefined. A good parent is no longer a person who fulfills routine obligations. One must now spend quality time with his or her children, as typified in movies like *Kramer vs. Kramer*. But what is "quality time"? It is the antithesis of industrial family life. It is time spent responding to the uniqueness in your children, and responding to that uniqueness in improvised ways rather than in sterile and preprogrammed ways. And what is a good post-industrial spouse? These days a good spouse is supposed to "listen" to his or her partner and respond to that partner on a deep level. Spouses are now expected to satisfy the emotional needs as well as the physical needs of their partners.

This change in the definition of family roles from the performance of routine physical tasks to "listening," "being responsive," and "giving quality time" came about in part because of the same process of automation that transformed the workplace. Microwave ovens, vacuum cleaners, electric clothes washers and dryers, automatic dishwashers, garbage disposals, lawn mowers, and myriad gadgets have relieved us of the more time-consuming tasks family members used to be confronted by. And just as in the factory, the automation of routine tasks in the home results in a radical redefinition of family roles. Stripped of routine work, family members are left with much more complicated interpersonal tasks to focus on. The role as such becomes less important, and role style grows in importance. There is no limit in quality time tasks. One can always spend more time with the children. Nor are "quality" standards clear. Many feel as though their attempts at quality time could have been better directed.

Post-industrial family life has been transformed in a number of ways that parallel organizational changes in the business world (e.g., Burton, Dittmer, & Loveless, 1986). First, parenting is now more of a team effort, frequently involving not only biological parents but step-parents, members of the extended family, day-care personnel, teachers, psychologists, social workers, and other professional helpers (e.g., Stolz, 1967). Second, raising children is now, more than ever before, a creative act, requiring constant adaptation to the needs of individual personalities and new societal pressures. Third (e.g., Genevie & Margolies, 1987), most parents of both sexes—either in the single-parent household or dual-earner family—work at least part-time. Fewer women remain home, even when the children are young. Therefore, work intrudes and impinges on the lives of children in ways it did not three decades ago, when the typical father worked and the typical mother stayed home (Frey, 1990). Fourth, many people now work at home part-time, either because they work in jobs with flexible schedules that permit this or because they have established their business in the home. While the electronic cottage predicted by Toffler (1981) is not yet quite here, it is true that a large amount of occupational work is now done in the home (e.g., Ambry, 1988). "Telecommuting" has entered the lexicon, which is a sure sign of how far this trend has spread. Fifth, when work tasks involve problem solving—as much post-industrial (alternately PI) work does—people take those tasks home in their thoughts if not their briefcases. One can no longer speak of a clear separation between work and home.[6]

Equally important is that the one "good" mother or father stereotype of the industrial age has been replaced with a variety of "good" archetypes in the post-industrial age. Perhaps this is most visible in the definition of male and female roles. In the industrial age there was a single scale of what was considered desirable masculine and feminine behavior. Now there are a variety of socially accepted "male" and "female" types (Kimmel, 1987). Considerably more diversity is tolerated in every respect. The unifying theme of our book, then, is that work and family roles are being affected by the same forces of automation and advancement in knowledge, with the result that our lives are being transformed from the ground up by the redefinition of basic social roles.

Alvin Toffler's *Future Shock* (1970) argued that the pace of change was accelerating and that we needed to prepare ourselves for the shock we would feel the day the present overtook the future. Perhaps the most interesting aspect of the 1990s is that, despite all the changes that have occurred, we do not find people paralyzed by the arrival of the future. The shock seems to have been most noticeable at the time of Toffler's book, when some of the trends first began to appear. Today, however, the idea of being paralyzed by future shock no longer seems appropriate because people are learning how to cope with the many changes associated with the post-industrial transformation. We are learning how to take role redefinition in stride.

Our Challenge

We give ourselves license to look along the leading edge of post-industrial society in order to glimpse into the future. In the process, we trample on some of the sacred theoretical notions social scientists conjured up while attempting a century ago to describe the development of industrial society. Our discussion of these theoretical ideas is woven throughout the book and suggests a synthesis between macro and micro social theory, which moves beyond the debates that have stymied sociology's growth in recent decades. This synthesis suggests the kinds of individual and structural adjustments we must be willing to make if society is to face up to the social challenges of the twenty-first century.

Chapter 1 begins with the self-evident proposition that the world is undergoing rapid change. The cause of social change, knowledge explosion, is less obvious than the fact that social change has been dramatic. We begin to make the theoretical underpinnings of our analysis more clear in Chapter 2 by explicating how growth in knowledge tends to make roles more complex. That discussion is centered around a dialectic between the processes of rationalization and what we call—for want of a better term—the process of complexification. And we suggest how the mixture of these two processes has changed over time, providing a critical linkage between the macro (societal) level and the micro world of social interaction.

Chapter 3 expands upon George Herbert Mead's symbolic inter-actionism to ask what kinds of "minds" and "selves" will be needed for life in the post-industrial era. Chapter 3 explores the thesis that creative minds and complex selves are needed for successful adaptation to post-industrial society; while Chapter 4 advances the proposition that emotion gains special importance in communication among people with creative minds and complex selves adapting to post-industrial conditions.

Evolutionists and futurologists usually tend to see bright futures, untroubled by peculiarly post-industrial problems. But in Chapter 5 we focus on a fundamental and pervasive problematic in post-industrial society, that of role redefinition. For example, we attempt to explain the rising level of divorce as symptomatic of individuals being unable to redefine their roles and change the nature of the institutional framework of the family in functionally adequate ways. This brings into focus the kind of changes people are being called on to make as we enter the post-industrial era.

Chapter 6 moves to a more structural plane, demonstrating how complexification generates a level of role conflict that makes role change inevitable. And Chapter 7 describes the way in which social organizations will have to be restructured in order to moderate and accommodate that conflict. Our Epilogue concludes by locating these themes within the broader context of sociological theory and by suggesting a research agenda for the future.

Another way to understand the book is as a series of chapters that pose and answer questions. Chapter 1 asks what characterizes the new society, and answers, the knowledge explosion. Chapter 2 asks how roles are changing and finds them becoming more complex. Chapter 3 asks what kinds of people we will need in the future, and concludes that we will need people with creative minds and complex selves to arrive at innovative solutions to difficult problems. Chapter 4 asks how those people will interact with one another, and posits that they will need to communicate on an emotional as well as a cognitive plane. Chapter 5 asks how the social transformation will manifest itself, and suggests it will do so through people redefining their roles. Chapter 6 asks why this is inevitable, and argues that technological change will introduce too much role conflict, role strain, and emotional overload for roles to continue in their traditional forms. Chapter 7 asks what kind of society we will end up with, and posits that role-sets will increase in size and person-sets will decrease in size, resulting in smaller organizations that not only require less time to respond to changing conditions but also tolerate more experimentation and boundary-spanning through networks. And the Epilogue asks what this will mean for sociology, and suggests a new theoretical synthesis offering interactionist solutions to functionalist questions.

The need for more flexible social institutions, complex selves, and creative minds is illustrated over and over again in a variety of ways throughout the book. In the process we synthesize symbolic interactionism with role theory, adding some network theory, theory on emotion, and functionalist concerns. New specialties within sociology are thus united with older perspectives in fruitful new ways. A continual theme is that macro structure and micro interaction are connected at the level of social roles. Observable behavior and subjective mind-sets can thus be best understood within an integrated theoretical framework focusing on institutional roles as the vortex of social change.

Notes

1. This is not to say that there have not been contributions since 1930. Parsons (1951), for example, attempted to push forward a grand thesis. But most sociologists consider the classic works of the early masters to have contributed more. For one who disagrees, see Jeffrey Alexander (1980-1983, 4 vol.).

2. There are as many definitions of micro-sociology as there are social psychologists. Micro does not necessarily mean the individual, but does tend to focus on direct relationships between people. Certainly the character of what are called role relationships is inherently micro-sociology. See Rosenberg and Turner (1981) for an extended review of the nature of a sociological approach to social psychology.

3. The simplest examples of roles are locations in the kinship system. Mother, father, daughter, and son are the names of the social roles in the structure of the family. There are specific rights and duties which define each of these positions in the American kinship system (Wellman & Wortley, 1989), and distinguish the kinship systems of different societies (Sault, 1992). But the role styles played out in any particular family can be quite idiosyncratic. Consider the television family the Simpsons.

4. *Post-industrialization* refers to the transformation of social institutions, especially in the economy (Bell, 1973) or manufacturing (Piore & Sabel, 1984), while *postmodernism* (Featherstone, 1988a, 1988b; Feher, 1987; Kellner, 1990; Lyotard, 1984) is a term used by some to represent the alteration of perceptions, tastes, and values.

5. Even today, one seldom sees men doing the laundry in soap commercials, and the sitcoms have only recently begun to portray divorced mothers or fathers raising children, cohabiting couples, and other examples of contemporary family life, rather than the middle-class stereotypes of the late industrial age.

6. It might be argued that we are describing middle-class behavior rather than the entire society. In part, this is true. We are focusing on what we believe to be the cutting edge. This middle-class hue reflects the fact that the level of education required for most work positions is rapidly rising (Hudson Institute, 1987). Furthermore, the development of mass college education is reshaping the character of the citizenry in PI society. Those without a college degree are increasingly being left outside the societal mainstream—a kind of *lumpenproletariat* of despair and drugs, which is a new and frightening characteristic of post-industrial society. Although we have a large, highly differentiated middle class, a substantial segment of the population works temporarily in unskilled jobs and is increasingly marginalized. Our focus on the former does not mean lack of concern for those who have not "made it" into post-industrial society.

1

THE NEW SOCIETY

Although everyone will agree that the past decade or two have witnessed an astounding rate of change, not everyone would agree that the 1970s and 1980s ushered in a new and distinctly different historical epoch deserving of the label "post-industrial society." It is our belief that contemporary society is qualitatively distinct because basic social *institutions* are undergoing a fundamental alteration in character. By "institution" we mean a system of interrelated roles, which (a) virtually everyone participates in, (b) helps people meet basic needs, and (c) tends to be associated with a special location in time and space. Family, work, education, and religion are perfect examples.[1] Sport might arguably be added to the list. This book focuses on significant patterns of change in the institutional roles that dominate people's lives: work and family roles. Changes in family and work roles in particular provide a clear demonstration of the emergence of a new and qualitatively distinct form of society, a society in which social fabric at the individual level has undergone a fundamental alteration. We begin this chapter by arguing that a new society has emerged. Later in the chapter we ask what the defining feature of this new society is. Explosive growth in knowledge is a partial answer to this question, and the part of the answer that is the starting point for our analysis.

Signs of Role Change

Ogburn (1922) correctly argued that there is a cultural lag, that ideas and values change more slowly than technology. Following from his position, we take signs of wide-scale institutional failure as evidence of the arrival of a new epoch in which there is need for new institutions. Of course, this is not to say that we agree in total with Ogburn. He was wrong to assume that the pace of social development always lags far behind the rate of technological change everywhere. Indeed, social experimentation has been proceeding at an extraordinary pace and is, paradoxically, our second body of evidence of the emergence of a new society, for experimentation suggests that changing conditions compel people to try new adaptive strategies. And phenomenologically speaking, the fact that large numbers of people believe we have entered a new era is a powerful argument that the world has changed, and constitutes our third body of evidence supporting the position that society is now transforming itself in some epic way. Let us now briefly examine three types of evidence suggesting that industrial society is giving way to a qualitatively new and distinct social order.

Institutional Failure

The most dramatic pieces of evidence for a shift in the nature of society are widespread examples of institutional decay. The media is constantly highlighting ubiquitous signs of failure, most notably in the family. Teenage suicide has tripled in the past three decades. Teenage pregnancy kept rising up to the 1980s; although it now appears to be leveling off. The divorce rate has hit 50% in some states, although this rate also appears to be leveling off. To this, one can add rape, child abuse, latch-key children, delinquency, drug and alcohol abuse, and a host of other indications that the contemporary

American family is not functioning effectively. The generation gap of the 1960s seems mild in comparison to the problems that have emerged in the past two decades to challenge the institution of the family. And with more than 20% of American children now living in poverty—largely associated with the low earning power of single-parent families—and considering all the social problems that emerge when large numbers of children are raised in poverty, we can expect social problems to continue mounting for some time to come (Bane & Elwood, 1989; McLanahan, 1985). Equally apparent is the collapse of community in many parts of our cities. The murder rate has continued to climb, and although many of these murders are gang- or drug-related, they do reflect a breakdown in social control. Another major component of the murder rate comes from family violence, which is perhaps the most extreme example of role failure.

When we shift to the economy, signs of decay are less dramatic but just as critical. Manifestations include failure to adopt new technologies, the misuse of new technologies when they are adopted, and lack of innovation (Shaiken, 1985).[2] To make matters worse from an American point of view, the innovativeness of U.S. firms is steadily declining, compared to that of firms in Japan, Germany, France, and Britain (*Science and Engineering Indicators*, 1989). The Department of Defense is increasingly alarmed by an apparent shift in the technological cutting edge in fields like superconductivity and high-resolution television. In both, the Japanese are ahead of Americans in research, patents, and capacity to manufacture products. But Europe will represent a greater threat to American technical hegemony after full economic union in 1992. The Germans are actually the world leaders in exports, with almost $300 billion, in comparison to $250 billion for the United States and $230 billion for Japan in 1987 ("An unstoppable export machine," 1988). Furthermore, France, Britain, and Italy, soon partners in a united Europe, together account for another $400 billion in trade. But perhaps the most provocative indictment of the American economy is that made by the M.I.T. Commission on Productivity (Dertouzas, Lester, & Solow, 1989), which carefully evaluated eight major industrial sectors and found the United States seriously lagging in all but one.

Another dimension of the crisis of competitiveness is found in foreign ownership of domestic commercial enterprise in the United States. It is estimated that 5% of the commercial assets of the United States are now foreign-owned, including everything from RCA television sets (owned by a French firm), to Safeway food stores (owned by a British firm), to Zenith computers (owned by a German firm), and Firestone tires (owned by a Japanese firm). More American companies are being bought by non-American conglomerates each year. In manufacturing, 12% of American capacity was foreign-owned by 1986, with the largest penetration in one of the most advanced sectors, chemicals, where one third of our productive capacity is foreign-owned ("The takeover," 1989). Another side of increasing American dependence is the growing technology gap ("Manufacturing trade gap," 1987). In 1980, imported computer-controlled machine tools claimed only 20% of the U.S. market. By 1986, when $170 billion was spent on imported machines and equipment, the figure was 66%. Even though industrial robots were largely an American invention, 40% of those purchased in 1986 were imported from Japan. It is worth noting that the crisis of competitiveness in world markets is now so great that the American political elite has moved it near the top of its political agenda.

If the trade deficit is the symbol of macro institutional failure in the economy, the budget deficit is the symbol of institutional failure in the political sphere. The budget deficit reflects much more than just a difference in values between a Republican President and a Democratic Congress; it is also a tangible sign of the fiscal crisis of the state (O'Connor, 1973). Do we raise taxes or cut programs? Can anyone in Washington set the priorities necessary to make responsible decisions when confronted with difficult choices? Lacking such priorities, the United States has proved unable to deal with new problems, which are reaching crisis proportions. Public education is a prime example (Paulos, 1988). Dropout rates remain very high. Standardized test scores like the ACT declined dramatically after 1970. Knowledge about fundamentals, like geography and math, is appalling (Rutherford & Ahlgren, 1990), and even many college graduates lack sufficient understanding of cultural traditions to participate in meaningful dialogue with people outside their own narrow circles of friends (Hirsch, 1987). But perhaps the biggest failure of the American educational system at the secondary level is that it is geared only to producing graduates who go on to college. It has shown very little concern for the training of students in technical and vocational courses. The absence of this kind of training helps explain part of the dropout rate—few courses and little encouragement for children who like to work with their hands—and part of the failure of the economy—an absence of technically skilled workers.

Matters are further complicated by the fact that contemporary problems are interwoven in ways that make them seem almost intractable. For example, failure on the education front leaves many people without marketable skills and, therefore, all but frozen out of the labor force. A recent study ("Impending U.S. jobs disaster," 1989) estimates that many students lack the reading ability they will need to function, and will be unqualified relative to future needs. Without meaningful employment they may be unable to keep their families intact, which takes us right back to problems associated with divorce and children being raised in households with incomes below the poverty line (Sidel, 1986).

The point of this book, however, is not to harp on everything that is going wrong in the United States and other countries swept by change, such as Britain. Although many of the problems we face appear to have reached crisis proportions, we see them as signs of transition. If the analysis presented in later chapters of this book is correct, they will not continue to escalate indefinitely. Attempts are being made to solve them, and over time more complex institutions will come into existence to replace decaying ones. As that happens, social problems will diminish in intensity, although they certainly will not disappear.

New Institutional Forms

We view the widespread experimentation with new family and work arrangements as an additional sign that we are in a period of institutional transition, when the very fabric of society is being transformed. Experiments currently under way may not, in the final analysis, offer the best solutions to vexing problems. But the fact that people are replacing traditional definitions of role responsibility with new designs is prima facie evidence that old institutional arrangements are no longer functional.

The most dramatic examples are the many new forms of family that have been labeled and identified (e.g., Furstenberg & Spanier, 1984). Among other new designs we have witnessed are the spread of serial monogamy, cohabiting couples, single-parent families, multiple-parent families, never-married single people raising adopted children, dual-earner families, and job-sharing spouses. At the same time, the dual-person career (Papanek, 1973)—a single earner, usually a husband, implicitly or explicitly requiring full-time job-related support services from a spouse—has largely disappeared.

Current statistics on "traditional" families are presented in Table 1.1. In families with both parents present and with children under 6 years of age, more than one-half of the women work. This proportion rises to more than two-thirds with children between the ages of 6 and 17.

The most reasonable conclusion to draw from this data is that the "traditional family" is no longer the norm. For better or worse, new family forms are replacing it. Change of this sort is not ordinary in character; it is epic in its very nature.

Meanwhile, the world of work is also undergoing dramatic change. Job prescriptions are being relaxed (Naisbitt & Aburdene, 1985). Symbols and rituals are being used to de-emphasize rather than highlight status differences between superiors and subordinates (Kidder, 1979). Cooperation rather than competition is now a viable model for organizational success. And work teams are coming to be viewed as temporary rather than permanent (Peters & Waterman, 1982). Most of these changes can be summed up under the theme of "small is beautiful." It may be difficult to demonstrate, but it is our belief that the small high-tech company, the small high-tech profit center within multidivisional companies, and the joint venture will become the archetypal organizational forms in post-industrial society, in much the same way that the large corporation came to be the symbol of industrial society a century ago. This theme will be explored further in Chapter 7.

Table 1.1 Three Types of Families, by Presence of Children and Working Arrangements, 1989 (Numbers in thousands of families)

	Presence of Children		
Type of Family	*No Children Under 18*	*With Children Ages 6 and Under*	*With Children Age 6-17*
Married-couple families	27,167	11,540	12,316
Percentage with only husband/father employed	14.2	38.0	23.1
Percentage with only wife/mother employed	8.3	1.2	2.9
Percentage with both spouses/parents employed	40.6	52.9	65.7
Percentage with other combinations (no one employed or different family members employed)	36.9	7.9	8.3
Families maintained by women	4,470	2,639	3,883
Percentage with the woman employed	50.5	48.1	71.0
Families maintained by men	1,795	378	710
Percentage with the man employed	64.4	82.0	83.5

SOURCE: From *The Social Organization of Work* by Randy Hodson and Teresa A. Sullivan, calculated from U.S. Department of Labor, Bureau of Labor Statistics, 1989b, "Employment and Earnings Characteristics of Families First Quarter 1989" (news release, April 28). © 1990 Wadsworth, Inc. Reprinted by permission of the publisher.

It is worth noting that the most important changes are sometimes the most subtle, and this is a case in point. The two major social institutions in which peoples' lives unfold, the family and the workplace, are rife with experimentation. But why now? The current rate of experimentation in fundamental social institutions convinces us that **contemporary social change** is distinguishable not only for its rapid rate, but for the fact that it **is shaking the tree of society at its institutional roots—our most fundamental interpersonal ties at work and in the family**. The bulk of this book will focus on the epic transformation of work and family roles that marks this particular point in history. But before moving ahead, let us mention a third body of evidence which convinces us that the present change is epic in nature.

Recognition of Change

People instinctively recognize that changes are afoot. The popularity of such books as Toffler's *The Third Wave* (1981) and Naisbitt's *Megatrends 2000* (1982), which describe large-scale social change, provides striking evidence pointing to this. These books have sold millions of copies, remaining on the best-seller lists for months on end. Their continued success demonstrates that their argument, that society has experienced some fundamental shift, resonates well with a large segment of the educated population. We do not believe these books about basic social change would be popular unless they captured an important underlying truth.

Evidence of the birth of a new order can also be seen in the keen interest that many people have in radical solutions to existing problems. Again, the titles and sales figures of books are evidence. Ouchi's *Theory Z: How American Business Can Meet the Japanese Challenge* (1979) sold more than 300,000 copies as businessmen and businesswomen searched for new ways of running their companies. *In Search of Excellence* (Peters & Waterman, 1982) and *Reinventing the Corporation* (Naisbitt & Aburdene, 1985) sold even more copies. These books are not romance novels, pulp detective stories, or science fiction/ fantasy. Nobody reads them for escape. The readership for these books is made up of thoughtful, well-educated people with serious occupational responsibilities who sense that fundamental changes are in the making and are trying to make sense of those changes by unraveling their complexities.

The seemingly fragmented array of facts and figures presented in the first pages of this chapter can be easily summarized around a few basic points. We have entered what appears to be a new period in history. Old institutional arrangements are failing. People are in search of viable new solutions to distinctly modern challenges to work and family. And a large number of people intuitively recognize that a qualitative transformation is taking place in the work and family roles that make up the central fabric of society. Hence, we are convinced that a new society, a post-industrial society, is coming into being.

Few would deny that widespread change is under way. And most people would grant the argument that basic family and work roles are changing in the process. But less obviously, we believe that **the knowledge explosion is shaping this transformation by setting the parameters within which work and family roles are changing**. We will explore the broad contours of the knowledge explosion in the balance of this chapter, then begin a detailed theoretical analysis of its impact on social roles in Chapter 2. For this reason, Chapter 1 may strike some readers as containing two themes that are not closely connected: (a) traditional institutions are on the wane, and (b) roles are becoming more knowledge-intensive. The connection between these two themes, hinted at in this chapter, will be the explicit subject of Chapter 2.

The Growth of Knowledge

A fundamental force shaping the contours of contemporary change in social roles is the knowledge explosion, especially as it is reflected in research and development, automation, and the spread of higher education. As a conceptual starting point for examining the character of role change in post-industrial society, it is vitally important to understand how research and development, automation, and higher education have come to reflect the different manifestations of late-twentieth-century knowledge growth.[3] For us, **research and development involves the creation of new knowledge or the extension of old knowledge in novel ways; automation is the implanting of knowledge into machines, and education is the implanting of knowledge into minds.**

Reconceptualizing Knowledge

Knowledge is a **multidimensional** force, and some explanation of our use of terms is necessary. Knowledge can take its form in sophisticated scientific theories, as in nuclear energy, or in craft knowledge, as in a French restaurant. This means knowledge can be invested and applied in a multiplicity of ways. Common usage of the term **technology** to describe physical apparatuses like tools or machines tends to obscure the importance of the methods and techniques associated with the use of those tools and machines. A tool can be as simple as a scalpel, yet the technique for its use can be amazingly knowledge-laden. Likewise, when people use the term **education** in everyday language to apply to only certain kinds of schooling, it obscures the fact that individuals develop a range of valuable talents in a variety of ways. We prefer to use **education** as a generic label for human capital investment of all types, so that we don't overlook the fact that considerable knowledge is involved even in relatively simple craft-like technologies, such as selling cars or providing baby adoption services. It is this holistic sense of knowledge, involving not only the creation of new knowledge but the implanting of knowledge in machines and minds, that is central to our understanding of post-industrial society.[4]

In Table 1.2, we suggest how knowledge is implied in four distinct components of hardware, software, skills, and ideas (Collins, Hage, & Hull, 1988). We can think of these components as either tools, techniques, training, or theories; or we can describe them as machines, methods, minds, and models. The two descriptions together—machines and tools, techniques and methods, training and minds, theories and models—provide a more complete image of how knowledge impacts on society. Rather than separate research, technology, and education, we should see these as aspects of the same fundamental process, namely the growth in knowledge.

Distinguishing between different kinds of knowledge can help us appreciate the significance of the fact that knowledge is concentrated in different places within different kinds of organizations, and thereby better understand the radical character of change as we move into the post-industrial period. A computer-assisted machine is quite sophisticated, but its operator may be relatively unskilled. Or a classroom teacher may use nothing more than chalk and a blackboard, but bring to bear all kinds of knowledge when teaching his or her students. Generally, organizations that process people rely more on knowledge embedded in skills and models, while manufacturing has until recently tended to simplify the human component by embedding knowledge in machines and assembly-line organization (Blauner, 1964).

Table 1.2 The Interrelationships Among Knowledge, Technology, Education, and Kindred Concepts

	Knowledge Component			
	hardware	*software*	*skills*	*ideas*
the "t" word	tools	techniques	training	theories
the "m" word	machines	methods	minds	models
generic term	technology	application	education	research

The post-industrial growth in knowledge manifests itself in a variety of ways, including the growing importance of research and development (one of the primary places where knowledge is now created), the expansion of automated manufacturing (one of the primary new ways in which knowledge is implanted in machines—Piore & Sabel, 1984; Womack, Jones, & Roos, 1990), and the spread of mass college education (one of the primary ways in which knowledge is now being implanted in minds—Meyer & Hannan, 1979). The consequences of these trends have received surprisingly little attention, considering the fact that improvement in what economists would call human capital is perhaps the most fundamental change afoot as we move into the PI era. There is also a collective level to the impact of knowledge in organizations where machines and individuals are organized together to produce products and/or provide services (Hage, 1980; Perrow, 1967). Theories about how to motivate workers (Theory X and Theory Y, reinforcement theory, and the like) fit into this knowledge category.

What we are arguing, then, is that the knowledge explosion tends to take three different forms as we enter the PI era: (a) research and development, where knowledge is created; (b) flexible manufacturing automation, where knowledge is implanted in machines; and (c) higher education, where knowledge is implanted in minds. Chapter 2 develops the point that these three manifestations of knowledge growth are shaping the development of institutional roles, especially work roles, which are qualitatively different from earlier role types. But before moving on to that portion of our argument, let us consider for a moment not only how important research and development, flexible manufacturing automation, and higher education have become, but also how these trends express themselves in contemporary society.

Research and Development
as a Domain of Knowledge Growth

Bell (1973) emphasized the growth of services in his important book on PI society. But the most critical change has been in the production of new knowledge, as manifested in research and development. Post-industrial society is not so much a service-oriented society as an innovation-oriented society (Cohen & Zysmen, 1988): a society where many more people than ever before are engaged in problem solving, in inventing new ways of approaching problems, and in applying knowledge creatively for the development of new products and the delivery of new services (Toffler & Toffler, 1990).

The growing importance of knowledge creation is revealed by research expenditures. Starting in 1975 (which we date as the true beginning of PI society—2 years after the publication of Bell's thesis), American businesses began increasing their research and development (R&D) budgets between 4.5% and 5.5% per annum beyond the rate of inflation. What is most striking is that this increase did not abate until the late 1980s, not even during the recession of 1982 (*Science and Engineering Indicators*, 1989). Although the pace of R&D in the United States has slowed considerably in the past few years, we are convinced that the overall pattern signals that increasing numbers of businessmen and businesswomen understand that their main competitive strategy must be the creation of knowledge in the form of new technologies and innovative products and services. In the short time since Bell published his book, there has been a quadrupling of the money (constant dollars) spent on research in the United States, and the global competitors of the United States have been doing even more. Britain, France, Germany, and Japan (considered for the moment as an aggregate) now surpass the United States in expenditures on nonmilitary research (see Figure 1.1). Furthermore, other countries, most notably Italy and Korea, have also been rapidly increasing their R&D budgets.

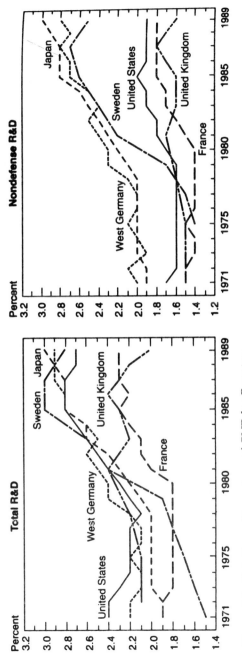

Figure 1.1. R & D as a Percentage of GNP, by Country

Note: Some data are estimates

The percentage of GNP (Gross National Product) that is being allocated to nonmilitary research is telling because it reflects societal commitment to the creation of new products and technologies. During the past two decades, Japan and Germany have been consistently spending a greater proportion of their GNP on nonmilitary R&D than the United States. They now each allocate about 2.5% of GNP for this purpose, whereas the United States allocates only about 1.9%. France has moved even with the United States, and Italy now allocates about 1.5% (*Science and Engineering Indicators*, 1989). This variance makes more of a difference each year because all of these nations are outstripping the United States in terms of economic growth. Indeed, we would argue that the problems of American competitiveness stem in large part from a neglect of nonmilitary research. Bell (1973), of course, did not discuss the R&D efforts of other countries since the United States so dominated research in the 1960s. But this is no longer true and is an important factor to consider when trying to make sense of the contemporary world.

Japan and France have gone so far as to develop national strategies of international competition based on developing new products and technologies. Their focus now concerns super-fast computers, biotechnology, and other joint industry and government endeavors. Similarly, Americans are now working on changes in U.S. tax laws to encourage greater investment in research and development. Washington is also altering its antitrust laws to allow for much greater cooperation among large American firms in what has come to be defined as an international race for new technology. And the United States is beginning to emulate Japanese practices by stimulating joint efforts in R&D by government and industry.

The current events in Eastern Europe and the Soviet Union should only accelerate the amount of money spent on civilian R&D as major weapons-development programs wind down. The integration of Western Europe, the unification of Germany, and the disintegration of the Soviet Union could lead to an explosion in economic growth in Europe, requiring even more R&D commitment in the United States for the country to stay competitive. So much has been made of the costs of German unification that observers have ignored East German technical and scientific potential. Unification should result in East Germany's receiving enough material capital to harness its human capital and stimulate the development of a number of new products. The size of the newly integrated European market will also be an enormous stimulant for investment.

The crux of our argument here is that the rules of competition have changed (Hage, 1988). In the future the most competitive producers will be the most innovative rather than the cheapest. This means that the producers enjoying the greatest success in research and development will also enjoy the most commercial success. Hence, initiatives to create new knowledge and develop new and better applications for existing knowledge will necessarily be the watchwords of the post-industrial order. They will inexorably drive the future. As we will see in Chapter 2, this sets the tone for role change in PI society. But in order to understand how that tone is translated into action, we have to consider the ways in which knowledge is presently being implanted in machines and minds.

Growth in knowledge is fundamentally altering the nature of competition. Increasingly, products compete on the basis of their innovativeness, including technology and styling. Indeed, quality and innovation are now more important in the marketplace than price. The dizzy pace of technological change in the computer industry is only one example. Competition in the marketplace now depends on rapid product innovation and consistent product/service improvement. As a result there is increased emphasis on new product development, and product lives have shortened considerably. New technological advances occur at an ever faster rate, which in turn translates into the more rapid creation and disappearance of businesses. The rise and fall of Genentec, Osborne, Atari, and other companies is increasingly becoming a pattern in many lines of business: rapid growth of firms developing one innovative new product, followed by rapid decline if the promise of continued innovation goes unrealized. Wang is a recent example. Even the largest companies find themselves being jolted by technological advances that make some of their product lines obsolescent. In response DuPont and General Electric have sold a number of formerly important industrial product lines —dyes from DuPont, and televisions and home appliances from General Electric—to make themselves more "lean and mean."

An important lesson is that small firms often find it easier to adjust to the demand for rapid product innovation and the contingency of shortened product lives because they can be more flexible. Much of the business administration literature traditionally argued that larger firms have the best chances of surviving in hostile environments (see Aldrich & Auster, 1986; and Hannan & Freeman, 1989; for competing views). But given the turbulence created by international competition, large firms such as General Motors, International Harvester, U.S. Steel, and even IBM are finding it difficult to adapt.[5] It is no accident that the new Saturn plant has very few working ties with General Motors. Saturn is independent by design in order to encourage flexible response to the marketplace. Thus, the need for flexibility has important consequences for the way we approach automation.

Flexible Manufacturing Automation: Implanting Knowledge in Machines

The small high-tech firms, the small profit centers in large high-tech firms, and joint ventures are three of the new organizational forms that have developed in response to changing conditions. What characterizes this new generation of organizations is an emphasis on adaptability and rapid implementation of new ideas (Carnevale, 1991, p. 51). And most of these organizations are distinguishable by the fact that they implant knowledge in machines differently from the way old-style firms do. This is done under the banner of "flexible manufacturing." Flexible manufacturing involves a high degree of automation, reducing the need for unskilled people who feed material into machines. But it also involves the frequent reprogramming of machines to accommodate small production batches of customized versions of a product line. This, in turn, requires a much more highly skilled, albeit much smaller, work force.

Flexible manufacturing has important implications for the nature of roles. Computerized automation systems currently coming on-line are fundamentally altering the character of blue-collar work (Shaiken, 1985).[6] In recent years, the key impact of automation has been the elimination of a large number of unskilled and semiskilled jobs, especially in assembly-line work in the automobile and household appliance industries. The number of production workers in these industries has declined by half since 1975, and outgoing unskilled and semiskilled workers have been replaced by a smaller number of highly trained professionals and technical specialists performing qualitatively different roles (P. Collins, 1991).

This process has gone more quickly in Japan than in the United States. A comparative study of 35 flexible manufacturing systems in the United States with 60 in Japan in 1984 ("New challenge," 1986) found that the Japanese plants had an average of 40% engineers, whereas the Americans had only 8%. Those numbers are very important because they suggest a different kind of workers to meet the requirements of a different kind of work, workers who will master machines rather than be controlled by machines. It suggests a workplace in which machines perform mindless routine tasks, and humans devote their time to problem solving and implementing innovations. Again, this will make for a very different kind of society than that described by Max Weber. This is a new society in which we are not only accelerating the search for new ideas but also rapidly accelerating the rate at which we implant knowledge in machines. This necessarily transforms people's roles.

Education: Implanting Knowledge in Minds

Parallel to the expansion in R&D and automation, there has been exponential growth in higher education. In a little less than one century, the United States, much of Europe, and the other developed countries of the world have moved from universal primary education to something approaching mass college education (Meyer & Hannan, 1979). When at least one-fourth of the population receives degrees from accredited colleges or universities, it is clear that there has been a significant departure from earlier times when a university education was reserved for a small elite (*U.S. Statistical Abstract*, 1990). Although it is true that there are big differences in the quality of education students receive at various kinds of universities, the fact remains that society is very different when the average level of education moves from 6 years of formal schooling or less—from, say, bare literacy—to something more like 16 years of formal education.

There has been a massive increase in the total stock of human capital in our society. This, like the other manifestations of knowledge growth, has far-reaching implications for social and economic life.[7]

In many ways the quality of education is being upgraded as well, especially in fields like engineering. The amount of information contained in textbooks is certainly becoming more dense and compacted. And occupational specialization, which has traditionally been used as a strategy for minimizing information and activity overload, now operates much more slowly than the accumulation of new knowledge. Consequently, professionals must develop the capacity to absorb more information relevant to both work and life, which in turn creates a need for more theoretical synthesis. Proliferation of journals (Bell, 1973) is a concrete manifestation of the knowledge explosion.

These trends make a college degree even more important than it was in the past. For example, males with a minimum of 4 years of college had less than 3% unemployment between 1970 and 1988, except for the recession year of 1983, when it reached 3.4%; in 1988, the last year for which figures are available, it was 1.6%. In contrast, male workers with less than a high school diploma have experienced 10% or more unemployment, except in the beginning of the decade, when it was 8.2%. The rate in 1988 was 10.1% (U.S. Statistical Abstract, 1990, p. 397). The figures for women are comparable and show the class-differential impact of automation. Those figures also suggest that the occupational structure is undergoing massive change.

Speaking broadly, the proportion of occupational categories that are knowledge intensive is expanding rapidly while the number of less knowledge-intensive occupational categories is on the decline. The portion of the labor force in professional and technical specialties, where occupational specialization is the greatest, will continue to grow rapidly as more individuals graduate with college degrees and as more unskilled and semiskilled workers are replaced with flexible machines (see Table 1.3). The pace of knowledge growth is so fast that we must implant more knowledge in minds even as we are implanting more knowledge in machines.

Even the lack of reported growth in the professional and technical occupations between 1980 and 1988 supports the trend toward greater occupational complexity. Job reclassifications moved a number of technical workers, such as computer operators, into clerical job categories, an example of upgrading in the level of skill we expect people to have.

It should also be noted that broad occupational categories understate the amount of specialization that is occurring. For example, up until 1970 most sales jobs (51%) were in retail sales and were relatively unskilled. By 1986 only 23% of all sales workers were employed in retail (Hodson & Sullivan, 1990, p. 325). The most rapid growth has been in specialized sales (e.g., computers, business services) where college degrees are frequently required. Even more telling is growing specialization in clerical work. Increasingly, the nonspecialized clerk is being replaced with highly specialized record keepers, perhaps best symbolized by the medical records librarian. This is a point Daniel Bell (1973) missed in his analysis two decades ago. College degrees are now required in many occupations that previously did not require diplomas.

There is another generally overlooked dimension to skill upgrading. Rapid growth in knowledge not only makes products obsolete, but also means that human capital depreciates quickly. It is estimated that the knowledge of a physician is outdated within 5 years after leaving medical school. Indeed, how could it be otherwise with the introduction of 500 new drugs each year? The pattern in medicine is repeated in one field after another. The more money is invested in research, the more rapidly existing information, knowledge, and even theories and models, are replaced with even more sophisticated and complex information, knowledge, and theories. As a personal example, in sociology, the authors have had to retool their methodological skills about every 5 years. In the 1950s, methodologically sophisticated people used cross-tabs and percentages. Next came bivariate correlation analysis in the late '50s and early '60s, soon to be followed by multiple regression in the late '60s, and then path analysis in the early '70s. About that same time factor analysis replaced Guttman scaling as the major approach to the problem of index construction. The introduction of structural equations (mid-1970s) was quickly followed by the development of pooled panel analysis and log-linear techniques (late 1970s). More recently, methodologists have been trying to perfect time series techniques and

Table 1.3 Occupational Distribution of the United States Labor Force, 1900-2000

Occupational Group	1900	1930	1960	1970	1980	1986[a]	2000[a,b]
White-collar workers	17.7%	29.4%	43.4%	48.3%	52.2%	54.1%	55.9%
Professional, technical	4.3	6.8	11.4	14.2	16.1	15.5	16.8
Managers, administrators	5.9	7.4	10.7	10.5	11.2	9.5	10.2
Clerical workers	3.0	8.9	14.8	17.4	18.6	17.8	16.6
Sales workers	4.5	6.3	6.4	6.2	6.3	11.3	12.3
Blue-collar workers	35.9	39.6	36.6	35.3	31.7	26.9	24.0
Craft and kindred	10.6	12.8	13.0	12.9	12.9	12.3	11.7
Operatives	12.8	15.8	18.2	17.7	14.2	14.6	12.3
Nonfarm laborers	12.5	11.0	5.4	4.7	4.6	[c]	[c]
Service workers	9.0	9.8	12.2	12.4	13.3	14.8	16.5
Farmers and farm workers	37.6	21.2	7.9	4.0	2.8	3.2[d]	2.6[d]

SOURCES: 1900 and 1930: Hauser (1964). 1960, 1970, & 1980: U.S. Department of Commerce, Bureau of the Census. (1981). 1986 & projected 2000: Kutscher (1987). From *The Social Organization of Work* by Randy Hodson and Teresa A. Sullivan. © 1990 Wadsworth, Inc. Reprinted by permission of the publisher.
[a]Data for the 1986 and projected data for 2000 use new occupational codes that do not correspond exactly to the codes for previous years.
[b]Projected data.
[c]This code was not used after 1980. The new code, "operators, fabricators, and laborers," is reported as "Operatives."
[d]Includes forestry and fishing workers after 1980.

event history analysis (Allison, 1985). Simulation strategies are the next logical step (Hanneman, 1988; Powers & Hanneman, 1983). One can repeat this example in specialty after specialty. Those who do not learn the new ideas, models, or techniques are gradually bypassed or outperformed by others.

Economists do not discuss human capital decay, but it is one of the most interesting and pivotal characteristics of PI society. Companies must not only retool machines, they must also retrain people. IBM is an example, spending some 7% to 8% of its sales dollars on continuing education. Micro-electronics and other developments are clearly revolutionizing the workplace, its jobs and its roles (see Forester, 1985, for many examples). For the continual production of new knowledge is not only changing the occupational distribution in the labor force; it is also changing the content of occupations. The world of work is becoming much more knowledge intensive, requiring that individuals constantly update their knowledge. Human resource managers must find ways to stimulate people to continue learning both on and off the job.

Although not the subject of this book, these changes raise the specter that Marx's fears about capitalist society will come true. The technological elimination of unskilled and semiskilled jobs means that a great many people will be caught in a world of despair, lacking marketable skills or hope for the future. That translates into what Marx referred to as the **lumpenproletariat,** an underclass of unemployed or marginally employed individuals living under dire circumstances and surviving by whatever means possible. Growth in that underclass represents a challenge that governments have thus far been unable to meet.

Conclusions

This chapter has been brief and to the point. Not only is change proceeding at a rapid pace, but there is also reason to believe it is revolutionary in character, transforming our most fundamental social institutions: work and family. The most convincing pieces of evidence that contemporary change marks an epic juncture are the general breakdown of traditional institutional forms; widespread experimentation with new types of family ties and work arrangements; and pervasive signs that people are searching for new ways of making sense of their circumstances and are willing to try even radical solutions in an effort to combat newly emerging social problems.

Knowledge explosion is one of the defining qualities of the era. The most obvious contemporary manifestations of this knowledge explosion are a quantum leap in research and development where knowledge creation occurs, the accelerated implantation of knowledge in machines through automation for flexible manufacturing, and the accelerated implantation of knowledge in people through expanded higher education. Starting in Chapter 2, we will examine how these manifestations of the knowledge explosion set the parameters for role change; for the creation of knowledge and its implantation in our lives, either in machines or in people, are determining the changing character of work and family roles as we enter the post-industrial age.

Notes

1. We are discussing micro institutions; that is, institutions at the role level. Parallel to these are macro institutions, such as the polity, health and welfare, and the system of science.

2. The dynamics of automated production are quite different from those in old-style mass production. Gains from the new machines can only be achieved with a skilled work force (Carnevale, 1991).

3. Knowledge growth has contributed markedly to the collapse of centrally planned economies controlled by single parties. But in this book our emphasis is on the less dramatic changes that have unfolded in the United States during the past two decades.

4. Given the general public's association of knowledge with science, we appreciate the fact that our definition may cause some readers difficulty. Yet, we believe this is the sense in which Bell (1973) employs the term, and it provides important conceptual foundation for the balance of our book.

5. As we go to press, General Motors appears to have barely halted its slide in sales. International Harvester is now defunct, and U.S. Steel has little steel business left and has changed its name to USX.

6. CAD/CAM, NCI, and FMS are examples of the computerized automation systems now coming on-line.

7. Why this very dramatic increase in a brief span of time? In the United States part of the reason might be the G.I. Bill, but this does not explain the worldwide trends (Meyer & Hannan, 1979).

2

FROM RATIONAL
TO COMPLEX WORK

The objective of this chapter is to offer a dialectical theory about the evolution of social roles.[1] Long-term change can be viewed as a composite of two contending forces that shape the way in which knowledge is embedded in activity. For want of better terms, we call these forces the processes of (a) rationalization and (b) complexification. Both processes influence the way in which social life is constructed. And a shift in the relative importance of these forces recently occurred. In this chapter we ask: How are work roles changing as we enter the post-industrial era? Our answer is that they are becoming more complex. In Chapter 3, we will generalize this analysis to roles of all types, including family roles.

Stages of the Industrial Revolution

In Chapter 1 we reported on the knowledge explosion. In this chapter we want to understand the impact that knowledge growth has on the countervailing processes of complexification and rationalization, which shape social roles, and we want to explore how these two countervailing processes currently articulate with each other. We see history as an unfolding in an evolutionary sequence in which each stage is defined by a change in the relative importance of rationalization and complexification. Rationalization and complexification are always at work in society—only the relative preponderance of the two shifts—and that change in preponderance is influenced by knowledge growth (Chapter 1).

In Table 2.1 we have located the stages of the industrial revolution, beginning in England with the creation of a textile industry capable of producing clothes at low cost. This first stage was propelled by rationalization—investing more knowledge in machines and organizational design so that unskilled workers could produce great quantities of clothing and other products. Technology "deskilled" work in all of the early key industries, such as textiles, ironworks, railroads, telegraphy. Occupational roles were simplified as craftsmen were replaced by machine tenders, often women and children hired at low wages. The process of rationalization inspired much of Marx's (1967) as well as Weber's (1946) thinking about the industrial revolution[2] and deskilling became the popular way of characterizing the effects of industrialization. What is important to recognize in order to understand this process is that it was predicated on embedding increasing levels of knowledge in machines precisely so that workers could function effectively without much knowledge or experience.

The second stage of the industrial revolution saw the emergence of brand-new industrial sectors based on the inventions of the period. The chemical industry, the telephone industry, and the electrical industry were brand-new additions to the economy, born out of growth in scientific knowledge. These did not develop out of existing industries, but rather were new "add-ons" to the economic infrastructure.[3]

Only with the second stage of the industrial revolution did we see the introduction of some complexity in a few industries (Landes, 1969). For example, the chemical, telephone, and electrical appliance industries created their own research and development labo-

Table 2.1 The Stages of Industrial Revolution

Complexification	Rationalization	
	Low	High
low	agrarian revolution	first stage of the industrial revolution
high	post-industrial revolution	second stage of the industrial revolution

ratories. The link between science and the production process was therefore relatively strong. Jobs in these industries tended to be relatively complex, and became more complex over time. The Germans, in particular, placed a heavy emphasis on hiring technically trained workmen and engineers in these industries. So complexification, we would argue, was an important process during the second stage of the industrial revolution. That is, a number of jobs were growing in complexity. Some complexification notwithstanding, however, rationalization continued at a rapid pace during this second stage, most notably in automobiles, rubber tires, flour, matches, elevators, meat packing, department stores, and food stores (Chandler, 1977), especially in the United States.[4]

It is important to note that the development of these new second-stage industries meant the creation of whole new occupational roles. The advent of motion pictures, for example, gave rise to some entirely new jobs—camera operator, sound technician, darkroom technician, projectionist—and to modified versions of roles found in the theater—director, writer, producer, lead actress, supporting actor. More novel were the development of research occupations in laboratories associated with firms like General Electric and DuPont. The second industrial revolution was also the period when professionally trained non-owner managers entered the scene, especially in those industrial sectors that had a link to science. And as the scientific laboratories of second-stage industrial firms developed novel products, they also created new markets, such as the home appliance market. This meant that specialized managers, sales personnel, transportation experts, marketing specialists, and so on had to be added to the corporate headquarters, for each new market required new occupational roles (Chandler, 1962).

In the third stage, which we refer to as the post-industrial stage, a whole new series of industries is being added to the economy: software, bio-tech, robotics, and advanced materials are among the major new industries to date (Freeman, 1982; *Science and Engineering Indicators*, 1989). In each case we are witnessing the addition of a new industrial sector to the economy, rather than the differentiation of an existing industrial structure into more units. In this respect the PI transformation is similar to the second industrial revolution. But the process of complexification is more in evidence now, and rationalization is less so.

The post-industrial stage of industrial development has not occurred equally in all sectors of the society. It has appeared more rapidly in some sectors than others. In order to determine whether a sector has entered this third stage, we can use two of our indicators from the previous chapter: the proportion of money spent on R&D and the proportion of the labor force that is professional and technical.

Industries can be easily ranked on the basis of the proportion of their sales dollar involved in R&D. First-stage industries spend almost nothing on R&D, second-stage industries spend between 1% and 5% of sales dollars on R&D, and third-stage industries spend in excess of 5% of sales dollars on R&D. At least until recently, about 75% of corporate nonmilitary research has been performed in some 20 large multinational companies (Freeman, 1982), indicating that the stage-three PI transformation has a long way to go before making itself felt throughout the entire economy. But R&D is gaining in importance everywhere. One of the most interesting examples is the automobile industry, where the impacts of both the energy crisis and the pollution crisis are forcing a revolution in engine and drive systems via the introduction of electronics and miniaturized computers. As a consequence, General Motors' research budget grew from less than 1% to more than 3% of sales dollars during the 1980s. We also see this at work in France, Japan, and Germany, with the development of high-speed trains. These trains represent a totally different technology, one requiring a large investment in R&D and a highly skilled work force.

But while large firms account for the bulk of the expenditures, the real driving force of PI is the small high-tech firms. There are approximately 6,000 software firms in the United States, but only slightly more than 100 of those are large firms, employing at least 500 people. Of the 26,000 high-tech firms that have been counted, 24,000 are small (*Science and Engineering Indicators*, 1989, p. 363). And we believe smaller firms have been undercounted. The visibility of Boeing, IBM, Microsoft, and other big spenders tends to obscure the importance of small high-tech firms in our society.

A second indicator of upgrading is an increase in the proportion of professional and technical personnel. As expertise increases within a sector, there is a fundamental change in the distribution of personnel. Occupational distributions within industries tend to have a great deal of inertia (Stinchcombe, 1965), so when they do change, that is compelling evidence that fundamental alterations have occurred. In the previous chapter we reported projections about the United States' occupational distribution in the year 2000. Here, our point is that high-tech firms, universities, hospitals, and other post-industrial organizations will account for most of the jobs in the American economy by the turn of the century.

The point is that the level of investment in R&D and the makeup of the occupational structure of the industry allow one to determine which industries are post-industrial and which are not. Understanding what the PI transformation means for work roles requires that we more closely examine rationalization and complexification.

The Process of Rationalization and Concomitant "Deskilling"

Before moving on, it is worthwhile to discuss rationalization in greater depth, as a counterpoint to the analysis of complexification that follows. Rationalization, the tendency to streamline and simplify which relies on knowledge being implanted in organizational processes or machines, was recognized by both Marx (1967) and Weber

(1922) as one of the defining characteristics of the industrial age. The term itself comes from Weber, who regarded the drive for rationalization as the engine of early twentieth-century social change (Weber, 1923). The process of rationalization involves, in varying degrees, codification of procedures, mechanization of work, simplification of tasks, and routinization of work flow. In all its forms, rationalization has the consequence of simplifying roles.

The clearest expression of Weber's view on this subject is in his discussion of rational-legal authority and bureaucracy, where he stresses that the best way to minimize problems is through the codification of rules, prescribing the behavior of "offices," what we more broadly label "social roles." Earlier, in the introduction to *The Protestant Ethic and the Spirit of Capitalism*, Weber (1958) also stressed the importance of codifying rules so that it is easier to control behavior—implicitly by teaching people how to behave in roles.

The rationalization process involves a number of different and quite separable components. The first element, the one stressed most by Weber, is codification of rules. Codification of rules means that formal scripts come to define the flow of activity for a role. The advantage of codification is that the experience of each employee or civil servant can be recorded within an organization's memory. Every time a serious problem arises, a rule can be made to prevent its recurrence or to minimize the damage done if the problem does occur again. Codification of experiences not only reduces the amount of time needed to plan responses if a problem repeats itself but also reduces the amount of time needed to train replacements when hiring new staff. Codification also reduces previous experiences to a set of basic principles, making them easier to internalize, while also conveying something of the spirit of an organization to its new members. This is not unlike the codification of grammatical and spelling rules, which makes it possible for an individual to learn language more quickly. Nor is it unlike the development of a musical scale or the creation of the Roman code of law, examples used by Weber in his preface to *The Protestant Ethic and the Spirit of Capitalism*.

It is important to note that in this case, increased learning does not result from the introduction of new knowledge, but from the recognition of better ways of organizing what is already known.

This is a crucial insight. When codification occurs, experience is being used to make work more simple and hopefully more efficient. Only in a very limited sense is something new being added, which distinguishes rationalization from its countervailing process of complexification.

In addition to codification, the rationalization process can assume a number of other forms, some of which Weber barely touched on. Mechanization is often overlooked as a dimension of the rationalization process. Yet, machines are introduced precisely because they can perform repetitive tasks much faster and with less fatigue and error than human beings. During the first stages of the industrial revolution, machines substituted for human beings. Machines did not represent additional knowledge per se, but were simply more efficient than people at performing a given range of tasks (Landes, 1969).

Parallel with mechanization was the advent of what has come to be called "deskilling" (Braverman, 1974). Put simply, the first industrial revolution involved a great deal of job simplification. By rearranging the work process so that machines did part of the work, remaining work tasks were broken up into smaller, more routine, more readily prescribed bits. This simplified manufacturing was important because it helped to achieve high volumes of production at low cost (Chandler, 1977; Perrow, 1979). The classic example is Ford's development of the assembly line for the production of automobiles (Chandler, 1977). Ford's assembly line did not result from the addition of new scientific knowledge about mechanics or electronics. Ford simply recognized that enormous gains could be made in productivity by pulling a chassis along a track, thereby rearranging the work flow and limiting the variety of tasks executed by each worker. Indeed, the improvement was fivefold (Chandler, 1977).

Rationalization is usually understood in terms of the deskilling impact of machines on industrial workers, but bureaucratization represents the same deskilling process for managers. Codified rules provide predictability. They make it possible to process more people faster and with less effort by standardizing procedures, thereby reducing opportunity for the exercise of discretion or initiative. As Blau and Scott (1962) argue, and Blau and Schoenherr (1971) demonstrate, rules circumscribe the decisions of managers. Weber stressed this idea in his discussion of the limits placed on monarchies by the development of administrative bureaucracy.

The rationalization process occurs in a variety of ways, but can be usefully summarized under the themes of codification of procedures, mechanization of work, simplification of tasks (including deskilling), and routinization of work flow (see Table 2.2). Using these strategies it becomes possible for an agency or firm to handle larger volumes of work with smaller numbers of employees, which constitutes a substantial gain in productivity.

Thus, the rationalization process is defined not by the addition of new knowledge, but by the recognition of better ways of arranging work. This is in sharp contrast to complexification, which is driven by the accumulation of additional knowledge and the adding in of more demanding activities.

The Process of Complexification

The impact of complexification on occupational roles is the exact opposite of that of rationalization, for machines don't always simplify or replace roles. Their introduction can also be associated with the creation of new occupational specialties and the addition of new activities to existing roles. (Indeed, this is the more interesting impact of the computer.) The growth in knowledge relevant to roles means that more and more skills and education are required of the typical worker, which necessitates ongoing learning. It also means constant change in the definition of roles (a pivotal subject in later chapters).

Few people have a genuine understanding of how radically roles are now being transformed. Most observers are so enamored with the concept of rationalization and the enticing notion of deskilling that they remain oblivious to the fact that leading sectors of the economy are becoming more complex over time. This is of special concern to us because we believe **complexification will be the prevailing pattern of social change in post-industrial society.**

Instead of proceeding forward on the basis of a simple set of codified rules (the rationalization model), complexification is associated with

Table 2.2 Aspects of Rationalization and Complexification Applied to Occupational Roles

| | Basic Processes | |
	Rationalization	Complexification
Mechanization (technology)	simple machines	sophisticated instruments that yield better information for workers to act upon
Codification of Rules (or emphasis on scripts) (techniques or behavior)	many specific rules and little room for human agency	few specific rules and a great deal of room for human agency
Routinization	standardization of procedures and little need for information search	emphasis on customized response and great need for information search
Skills (training)	reduction of the number of roles, and deskilling of remaining roles	proliferation of specialized fields and upgrading of skill levels required for most roles
Primary Performance Criteria	efficiency, quantity, or large volume	innovation, quality, customization, personalized service

the addition of new activities to existing roles and the creation of new locations in the social structure. For example, in the previous chapter we observed that growth in knowledge is reflected in the development of new products and that these imply new activities for many existing social roles, as well as the creation of many brand-new roles.

The point may be banal, but it is critical. Not only did the invention of the automobile create traditional manufacturing jobs, it meant the development of many new kinds of work associated with the service sector. This can be seen in the proliferation of gas stations, garages, and automobile maintenance functions, such as muffler repair.

Furthermore, new technological developments have, especially in recent years, added activities to existing roles. It is no longer enough to understand points and plugs. A good automobile mechanic must now have at least a rudimentary understanding of computerized electronic ignition. And mid-level corporate managers who try to survive with a dictation machine and avoid electronic mail find that they quickly become isolated. Thus, one can easily see how the computer has added new activities to familiar roles, with the consequence that occupations are becoming more complex, and requisite skill levels are increasing.

The addition of new knowledge is the driving force behind the complexification process (Chapter 1). As research and development expands we learn more, and this new knowledge makes itself felt in several ways. Frequently it leads to the discovery of previously unrecognized problems. The area of medicine provides good examples of this. We are continually discovering new diseases as well as learning much more about already recognized diseases, and this additional knowledge is being added to the total of known information that physicians are expected to master or at least have at their disposal.

One response to expansion in requisite medical knowledge has been specialization, encouraging people to master a greater volume of knowledge covering a more narrow area of inquiry (Parsons, 1966). Another response is extension of the prime knowledge acquisition years via seminars, short courses, books, journals, and the like (for an extended discussion, see Hage, 1974).[5] A distinctive characteristic of modern times is that practitioners of every occupation with a significant knowledge base must keep learning. **Rather than rationalization, which results in deskilling, the opposite process comes into play; namely, role occupants must acquire more knowledge so that they can recognize and respond optimally to individualized circumstances.** Each discovery represents an expansion in required knowledge, and therefore greater options and more complexity. To continue with our medical example, each new drug contains protocols relative to proper usage and side effects.

We should also think of this on a theoretical level. All occupational roles have a base of knowledge, though they vary in how extensive that base is. The more deeply rooted in science a given body of occupational knowledge is, the more rapidly that knowledge base changes. Logically, this also means that the more knowledge-intensive professional, managerial, and technical specialists are seeing the behaviors in their occupational roles change faster as the knowledge explosion progresses further. This necessitates continued learning and role redefinition, or else poor role performance. Moreover, with the passage of time a higher percentage of the adult population is employed in the rapidly changing professional, managerial, and technical fields.

The creation of new knowledge marks an important difference between the logic of industrialization and the logic of post-industrialization. With complexification, more activities are allocated to social roles that already perform a wide range of tasks. This is in marked contrast with rationalization, in which duties are subtracted until we are left with roles defined by one simple task that is endlessly repeated (Zuboff, 1984). Both processes can be found at any given time, but rationalization has been replaced by complexification as the dominant trend in PI society. The addition of new knowledge sometimes results in the elimination of some activities or duties from existing roles. The polio vaccine largely eradicated one whole area of treatment. But in recent years the addition of knowledge has generally involved the recognition of two new problems (or problematic issues) for every one that is solved. New knowledge leads to the recognition of new kinds of clients and customers. In turn, technologies are developed to teach, treat, handle, or supply these additional clients and customers, further expanding the responsibilities of role occupants.

This pattern is perhaps best demonstrated by the development of a special class of machines that are best labeled "instruments." We draw a distinction between instruments and other machines used directly in the production process. While most machines are used to **replace** labor, and are therefore conduits for rationalization, instruments add to the number of tasks being performed—they expand the amount of work being done. One sees this most clearly in health care instruments, such as the C.A.T. scanner, which allows medical personnel to collect new kinds of information, making diagnosis more involved and leading to more individualized treatments. The importance of instruments is that old roles accumulate additional activities and encounter a wider range of variable exigencies. They are made more complex because a greater number of factors are made problematic as we gain more and better knowledge. Roles thus become more complicated as new instruments are introduced.

Instruments of measurement provide added ways for role occupants to probe and collect information about their environment, reminding us that information search is one of the defining characteristics of roles transformed by PI complexification. This is perhaps most noticeable in the area of basic scientific research, but it has analogies in the production of drugs, chemicals, airplanes, and other medium- and high-tech products. What instruments do for us is speed up or slow down physical, biological, psychological, and sociological processes so that we can see and comprehend them. Similarly, the number-crunching power of supercomputers allows us to perform analyses faster and employ the results of our research earlier. Instruments aid our senses and our ability to reason. In PI society this kind of machine—the instrument—is becoming more and more critical.

Economists have placed so much emphasis on the tendency of firms to replace labor with machines that it goes largely unrecognized when upgraded equipment increases the skill levels needed by technicians and professionals. The addition of laboratory tests in the modern hospital is perhaps the most striking example. The introduction of new equipment often requires the addition of new occupations, specialists to operate that equipment and assist in diagnostic activities.

Social roles literally expand and contract under the dual processes of rationalization and complexification. But at this particular technological juncture, complexification is the predominant trend. This fact, which is a direct outgrowth of the knowledge explosion (Chapter 1), must be understood if one is to make sense of the PI transformation. Routine jobs that have to be done frequently, and for which we can precisely prescribe straightforward procedures, are perfect jobs for robots and are made redundant with automation. Meanwhile, other jobs are being made more complex both by our improved ability to collect information about a plethora of variables and by our increased understanding of the ways in which those variables influence one another—knowledge that requires individualized rather than mass production and servicing.

The Balance Between Complexification and Rationalization

The process of complexification is not well understood. But there are three essential components that can help shed light on complexification of roles. The first is that the accumulation of knowledge results in an expansion of the professional, technical, and managerial sectors of the labor force (see Table 2.2). Second, organizations specialize to deal with the specialized markets that develop as our knowledge base increases. The growing number of small high-tech firms, profit centers in large high-tech firms, and joint ventures is evidence of this. Finally, greater periods of time are spent acquiring specialized occupational training. As will be argued later, this has an impact on people's tastes, values, and market preferences.

Meanwhile, as the sophistication of the production process moves to the level of reprogrammable machines in flexible manufacturing (Chapter 1), the number of unskilled workers in society rapidly declines (see Figure 2.1). Together these processes explain why we observe more people in professional and technical occupations and why these occupations are becoming more complex over time. Meanwhile, the number of unskilled jobs is on the decline, which means that opportunities for those without skills are disappearing. Raising the human capital of those who have been or are in danger of being left behind poses one of the most serious challenges societies will face as they undergo the post-industrial transition. A PI society that easily discards people will be a PI society that fails the test of international competition.

It is true that occupational specialization reduces both the number of activities associated with a given job and the length of training required for that job by limiting what one needs to know in a particular position. That is one of the manifest functions of structural differentiation (Parsons, 1966). But knowledge accumulation and attendant pressure for complexification have been occurring even faster. And this is why it is so important not to confuse structural differentiation with the process of complexification. As machines eliminate routine activities (Mann & Hoffman, 1960; Mann & Williams, 1960; Walker, 1957), roles are gradually redefined to have a focus on nonroutine

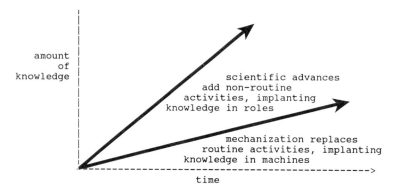

Figure 2.1. The Impact of Machines on the Definition of Activities in Social Roles. Adapted from Lawerence and Lorsch (1967).

issues characterized by uncertainty. Machines also create new roles. The overall consequence is more task effort. This process was described several decades ago by Lawrence and Lorsch (1967) and is included in Figure 2.1, but few people have made the connection between the knowledge base of the occupation, the introduction of labor-saving machines, and the transformation in the nature of the role-related activities that are left over.

Surprising to say, the consequences of the adding of labor-saving machines are just as apparent in the family. Time-consuming, routine activities—like dishwashing, canning, and ironing—either have been replaced by machines or made irrelevant with the introduction of new products, such as permanent press fabrics. More difficult and less codifiable activities, such as socializing children, consequently claim more of our concentration and redefine what family roles mean, even if labels like "father" stay the same.

The accumulation of knowledge is also producing what might be called the Chandler (1962) effect, that is the increasing specialization of managerial units to deal with the increased specialization of products and technologies. Like everyone else, managers and administrators experience limits to their cognitive abilities. This is what Chandler (1962) argues in his famous discussion of the decisions to divisionalize DuPont, General Motors, Standard Oil of New Jersey, and Sears Roebuck. The contemporary manifestation of this tendency has been the emergence of many small high-tech organizations; the creation of new profit centers, that is, the subdivision of large firms into even smaller units than a division; and the creation of joint ventures when joint expertise is necessary.

All of these changes in the nature of management shift the proportion of firms toward the small high-tech end of the continuum and reduce the number of old-style bureaucratic organizations found in the economy. A major implication is that the effective workplace is becoming smaller (Granovetter, 1984). In short, there is a limit to the number of exigencies and the amount of uncertainty a work unit or control system can cope with and still operate with an acceptable degree of efficiency (a lesson even the Russians now seem to have learned). The creation of small workplaces, with the average now less than 300 employees, means an entirely different kind of work environment. Most people will know everyone in the workplace, so interpersonal relationships will have more play.

Complexification and Market Change

Carnevale (1991), in his monograph for the Department of Labor, *America and the New Economy*, argues that the new consumer values are convenience, customization, variety, quality, and reasonable cost. Left unanswered is what has produced this change. We believe that a partial answer is to be found in the extended periods of increasingly more specialized training that are a part of the knowledge explosion and the complexification process.[6] College education leads to an exposure to a wide variety of ways of thinking about the world and an appreciation of its complexities. With this comes a deeper appreciation of the interdependence of seemingly unrelated factors. Travel, which is another form of education, has the same impact. It offers exposure to alternative cultures, and therefore alternative ways of doing things as well as ways of viewing things. Education, formal or informal, teaches that the world is complex and that there are no easy answers. It teaches people to think about complex problems from alternative perspectives and to perceive creative solutions.

Staying in school to finish a college degree followed by a professional degree also requires that we defer gratification. This lengthens our temporal horizons, which in turn leads us to recognize the problems of durability, longevity, and long-term operating costs (e.g., "buy cheap, buy twice"). We become more aware of long-term quality. We become more willing to pay a higher initial price for a product that is better suited to our needs. Thus, we buy more expensive but more energy-efficient, durable, or design-suitable lightbulbs, dishwashers, house paint, and a host of other products, or we spend more money on homes or clothes in an effort to find what best satisfies our tastes and fits our personalities so that we will feel comfortable with it longer.

There is a very large literature indicating that education, travel, and reading—three alternative modes of learning—contribute to shaping people who are more open to and more capable of innovation, the subject of the next chapter. Furthermore, these three modes tend to be mutually reinforcing. People with more education also tend to travel and read more. For the consumer, these changes in cognitive structure mean a whole new set of values. Post-industrial men and women prefer innovation and customization. The marketplace itself is thus radically transformed. A college-educated consumer tends to demand customization, quality, and innovation, while a high-school-educated consumer tends to expect standardized products and quantity relative to price.

This movement toward customization in America has an ironic historical and cultural twist. One of the major differences between the cultural values prevailing in America and those traditionally found in Europe has been the American preference for procuring the largest possible quantity at the lowest possible price. It was this preference, just as much as America's large internal market, which facilitated the growth of mass production in the United States (Chandler, 1977). By the end of the nineteenth century the American economy was dominated by large-scale organizations engaged in high-volume production of relatively low-cost, low-quality goods.

Low quality has been a time-honored tradition in American manufacturing. Home construction offers a clear example of America's love affair with size over quality. Home builders make all kinds of obvious tradeoffs in quality of materials and workmanship to maintain some control over prices, while at the same time maximizing square footage. This is not dishonest or fraudulent, merely a response to consumer demand. Indeed, many mass-produced goods could only have been brought into production in a country like the United States, where there was relatively little concern for quality. As long as things worked in some basic way, people made do. This element of American values, coupled with America's huge size, created the mass market that was a precondition for the rise of big business at the end of the nineteenth century. But this is changing. For example, many Americans are growing dissatisfied with chain bookstores, which offer little variety outside the standard fare available in other chain stores and are manned by employees who don't have wide-ranging knowledge of what is available in print.

Of course, demand for some products remains standard, so there is little need for product differentiation. Cigarettes fit this mode in both Europe and the United States. That is why they are produced in large quantities with little product differentiation. In contrast, both Europeans and Americans stress distinctive taste in cigars, and, as a consequence, cigar making has remained a craft industry on both continents.

Clothing is an entirely different case and one that shows cultural difference. Clothes are produced in much larger and less differentiated batches for the American market than for the European market. Americans accept mass-produced suits and dresses, but Europeans generally opt for more quality and customized design. As a result, the tradition of tailors has continued in Europe to this day, whereas it has largely disappeared in the United States.

But people are changing, and post-industrial America is leaving the mass market behind as consumers demand the latest gadgets. This is a built-in mechanism for the "prosumer society" in which people seek out individualized products and services (Naisbitt, 1982; Toffler, 1981). We are leaving behind a "mass society" and replacing it with a customized society, with a few exceptions such as the hamburger and French fry industry, in large part because of increased and more specialized education, propelling differentiation in tastes and discouraging complacent acceptance of things that are not to one's taste or well suited to one's particular needs (McQuarrie, 1991).[7]

Parallel with the concern over customization is the demand for service that grows when a populace is well educated. People are so fond of using the phrase "goods and services" that it obscures the current trend for all goods to have a service component. Increasingly, the manufacturers of goods are recognizing that their customers demand service along with those products. Many companies now have toll-free hotlines that can be used by unhappy customers. And it is increasingly common for advertisements to contain a lot of information about the kinds of services provided with a product. Certainly, Peters and Waterman stress (in their book *In Search of Excellence*, 1982) that the customer is king in successful companies. The more that service is emphasized, the more responsive people are to different needs on the part of customers, and the more interactive the conduct of business becomes, which introduces additional elements of job complexity.

Conclusions

In Chapter 1 we suggested that growth in knowledge is a defining characteristic of society. This results in a long-term shift in the occupational structure toward the predominance of nonroutine jobs requiring substantial training and jobs having problem solving as their principal task. Hence, most work roles are becoming more complex, and this complexification is reshaping the nature of PI society in ways that are quite unlike the rationalized restructuring that characterized much of this century. It involves the addition of new industries, new public sectors, and new scientific disciplines. Most important, it adds new, less routinized activities to existing roles. Of course, countervailing tendencies always exist. The process of rationalization has not completely stopped, but it is no longer the dominant force shaping contemporary society.

In industrial societies large populations with low education levels generate markets for standardized products at low cost. As education increases, consumer values shift toward customization, quality, and innovation. This provides markets for a steady stream of new and adjustable products and services, and changes the rules of competition. Speed of change and innovation become paramount, further accelerating the pace of complexification.

We have moved beyond the typical discussions of social roles in a number of ways. First, we have connected the larger macro social processes of complexification and rationalization to micro-level social roles. Second, we have emphasized occupational roles, ones that are not normally discussed in role analysis. Third, we have identified a number of critical dimensions—the number of activities, level of education required, amount of codification—that allow us to test the implied hypotheses in this chapter. Fourth, we have connected technology or the use of machines to role behavior, an aspect that is almost totally ignored in role analysis. We have, furthermore, given this a post-industrial twist by discussing the rise of instrumentation as a different kind of machine. Finally, we have elaborated both the push and pull of various causal mechanisms for the processes of complexification and rationalization, including the ways in which these processes shape and are shaped by market changes.

In Chapter 3 we begin to explore the implications that complexification has for the micro world of face-to-face interaction. We will argue that complexification fundamentally transforms the character of social interaction and, by altering people's everyday experiences, creates a social world that molds a new and different kind of citizen. Chapter 3 will argue that the age of complexification is a time for people with creative minds and complex selves.

Notes

1. Collins (1988) has criticized evolutionary theories in sociology for their tendency to assume that progress is inevitable. This problem is reduced by the introduction of dialectics involving conflicting trends.

2. There have been many discussions about Weber's types of rationality stemming from his mature work. A seminal idea in his earlier work (e.g., 1905), the definition of rationality as simplifying codification, is sometimes lost to view.

3. The process of "add-on" has been lumped together with "structural differentiation" by Parsons and others (e.g., Parsons & Platt, 1973; Smelser, 1959). But this

does not accurately describe what was happening at the time. The differentiation of social institutions, occurring as a long-term process: for example—the separation of the military from the monarchy, the emergence of the nation-state, the creation of a police force, and so on (Tilly, 1975)—involved the development of new social units to specialize in the performance of functions that had previously been performed, but by units with more far-ranging responsibilities. This would seem to be conceptually very distinct from the phenomenon that occurs when scientific breakthroughs spawn qualitatively distinct new industries.

4. Space does not allow us to explain the difference between countries except to note that the process of rationalization was much more dominant in the United States because its larger market was composed primarily of working-class people who wanted standardized products. Europe, because of the relative importance of the aristocratic class and *haute bourgeoisie*, retained its preferences for quality and specialized products, resisting the rationalization process to a degree.

5. Although some sociologists (Smelser, 1959) have discussed the process of structural differentiation, Parsons and Platt (1973) seem to us to have come closest to accurately gauging the role of knowledge growth in qualitatively transforming the nature of society.

6. One way of dealing with the accumulation of new knowledge and increasing sophistication of technology is to expand the length of training required to enter each profession. But this is not always practical, given the upper limit on cognitive power (Simon, 1957), so there is a tendency to expand the number of occupational specialties. Yet another response is more and better theoretical synthesis, allowing individuals to better cope with the problem of information overload.

7. The fast-food industry is in part an adaptive response to the tensions in dual-career families and the stress of those involved in high-tech work. The desire for convenience, even though it suggests standardization, can coexist with the desire for customization, reflecting our argument about increased variety and complexity of self (Carnevale, 1991).

3

CREATIVE MINDS
AND COMPLEX SELVES

The knowledge explosion is transforming the nature of society, and this is nowhere more clear than in the economy. Change is the watchword of the day (Chapter 1), and innovative response to shifting conditions is the litmus test of business success (Chapter 2) as we enter the post-industrial era. But this has been said in some form before. We now seek to pose a series of questions to help us better understand the PI transformation. Our question for this chapter is: What kind of people will society need in order to meet the PI challenge? The answer is people with creative minds and complex selves.

We begin our exploration with a reference to one of the seminal works of sociology, George Herbert Mead's attempt to explain how society is possible. People learn interaction skills that enable them to adjust to others (Mead, 1964). Mead went on to describe the kinds of "mind" and "self" characteristic of America at the beginning of the second phase of the industrial revolution. This was a natural subject for him to embrace, since he believed people's mental make-ups are shaped by their social experiences (Wells & Marwell, 1975), a theme also found in Parsons (Parsons, 1967; Parsons & Shils, 1951). Thus, he implicitly posed but never answered the question: What kinds of minds and selves are needed for which kinds of societies? Following Mead's logic, we will ask what kind of people are needed for a PI world. Our answer is that the PI era will be an age for creative minds and complex selves. The exigencies of PI life will help shape people into more creative and complex beings. And speaking functionally, social systems of the future will need more creative and complex citizens in order to operate effectively.

We begin this chapter by exploring what Mead said about the mind and the self. We will then describe how minds and selves are changing in subtle yet fundamental ways. Our thesis is simple: Complex institutions, specialized markets, complex occupational roles, and other institutional arrangements in PI society require both complex selves and creative minds to function.

Basic Framework

This chapter flows logically out of an examination of Mead's work and an extension of his concepts. So we will begin with a discussion of Mead's ideas in their own context, as a way of laying a foundation for our own analysis of contemporary trends.

Mead on the Mind

For Mead, "mind" connotes the cerebral quality that sets human beings apart from animals: the ability, based on a limited number of **acquired interaction skills, to adjust our actions in light of the behavior and actions of others.** The first of these requisite interaction skills is the ability to communicate with gestures. Humans share this first skill with most animals. Dogs, for instance, clearly communicate with body language and growls. Indeed, such communication is often quite intense and can elicit dramatic responses, such as aggressive posturing or submission. Even newborn babies have the capacity to communicate with gestures. Their cries send clear signals to others in the environment. Yet, at least at first, infants' use of gestures is imprecise. A newborn's cry is a general appeal that sweeps the environment, rather than being aimed at a particular person or requesting a specific action. The gestures of a newborn have not yet attained the "conventional" form characteristic of a language. Thus, the meaning of an exchange between growling dogs, or between a baby and a caregiver, is entirely embedded in the interaction itself (Mead, 1964, pp. 55-56).

Acquisition of language is associated with the development of "deep" mental structures influencing how people generalize (Chomsky, 1965). This is an important component in our analysis, for we will argue that **the deep structures that people use to map out their lives are changing with the post-industrial transformation**. For as we suggested in Chapter 2, people do not just have different kinds of jobs; they must have different minds in the most fundamental sense. This thesis is consistent with a well-established body of research on the relationship between occupation and worldview, which has found that people in jobs characterized by considerable autonomy come to value personal initiative, while people in jobs that are narrowly constrained or closely supervised come to value conformity to external authority. Thus, the kind of work one does fixes the mental framework on which the individual constructs, maintains, and reformulates his or her reading of and attitude toward the rest of the world (Kohn, 1977; Kohn & Schooler, 1973).

The second acquired skill Mead associates with "mind" is an ability to take the role of the other; that is, being able to determine what the other person will do. Mead argues that the very existence of complex social life is predicated on the assumption that human beings can somehow ascertain what other people want to achieve and how they are likely to act (1964, p. 89). A task as simple as walking down a street requires constant use of role-taking skills to navigate: to detect in advance the time at which, as well as degree to which, others are likely to change course and speed. People who never develop good role-taking skills are likely to be forever out of sync with everyone around them, and are likely to make a hopeless mess out of their lives (1964, p. 109).

Mead's first two characteristics of "mind"—(a) the capacity to use conventional gestures that symbolically represent situations other than the one immediately present, and (b) the ability to take the roles of others—are each prerequisites for Mead's third quality of mind: (c) imaginative rehearsal. Imaginative rehearsal is the ability to think ahead and consider alternative courses of action in light of different scenarios (1964, pp. 90-91).

Many of the structured games children play foster the development of this third skill. Baseball is a good example. Multiple players interact, each occupying a different role. Each player learns to expect other players to do different things at different times. For instance, a runner on first base can be expected to behave differently from the pitcher. Differences in behavior can also be predicted as circumstances change. A runner on first base can be expected to behave one way if a high fly ball is hit and another way if a bouncing ground ball is hit. Games in which children learn to apply clear rules to a narrow range of scenarios work for socializing children to the demands of an industrial age. But it is our feeling that people in the future will need to be more creative, building new rule systems to regulate relations with others, rather than learning existing systems of rules, a theme we will return to after discussing Mead's treatment of "self."

Mead on the Self

Mead regarded self-concept as **the ability to view oneself as an object**, that is, to make judgments about the kind of person one is and to modify one's behavior accordingly (Mead, 1913). It was in this light that Mead introduced concepts of the "I" and the "me," sometimes rather misleadingly referred to as the unsocialized and socialized selves. Mead was acutely aware that people can be spontaneous ("I"), and considered such behavior to be evidence of an inner self. But people are also self-conscious ("me"). Even if we allow ourselves to be spontaneous for a time, we eventually adjust our behavior in light of the responses of others. For instance, many people tell improper jokes when they are straining to be funny, but generally stop when they notice that others disapprove (1964, p. 175). For Mead, self-concept emerges out of interaction with others. He was greatly influenced by Charles Horton Cooley (1902), who suggested that the way people respond to us forms a "looking-glass reflection which shapes the opinions, assessments, and fears we have about ourselves" (Mead, 1964, p. 138). This position has been confirmed by a long series of empirical studies (e.g., Katz, 1988; Miyamoto & Dornbush, 1956; Snyder, 1987). The "self" is thus a subjective sense one gains of one's own essential character and worth as a human being (e.g., Juhasz, 1985).

Scholarly treatment of self-concept has not always been consistent, either in Mead's work or in the works of contemporary social psychologists (Rosenberg, 1979). There are times when Mead discusses self-concept as a relatively stable and enduring configuration of attitudes and response patterns, which a person carries from situation to situation and which predisposes the individual to respond to the world in predictable ways (e.g., Mead, 1964, pp. 140-144).[1] At other times Mead discusses transitory aspects of self, assessments of our performance that might influence us in an immediate situation but which we are unlikely to retain as more permanent portrayals of our being. Though he discussed the self at great length, **what is missing from Mead's "self" is the answer to the question of what kinds of selves are most appropriate in what kinds of society.**

Since Mead's time, a good deal of additional research on self-concept has been conducted (e.g., Rosenberg & Turner, 1981), but none of this work considers that different properties of self might be more adaptive in one historical epoch than in another. As we will argue, successfully negotiating the demands of post-industrial life will require people with complex selves who are comfortable maintaining multiple identities. People will need to be more in touch with their own feelings and less responsive to the looking-glass of social pressure. Mead might have described this as a movement in the direction away from "me" toward "I."

Post-Industrial Society and Mead's Problematic

What kinds of selves and minds will be needed for a successful life in PI society? The knowledge explosion is making for a diverse world in which people are increasingly aware of interdependence and contingencies (Chapter 1). Roles are changing in the process;

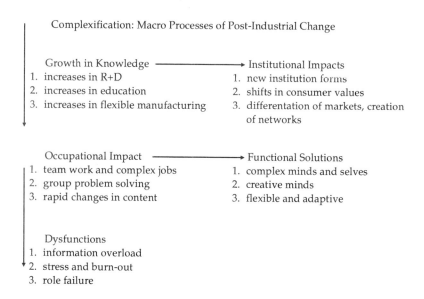

Figure 3.1. Post-Industrial Society and the Problematic of Mead

these changes manifest themselves with special clarity in the world of work, where routine activities are being taken over by machines, and the roles that remain are made more complex by the addition of tasks involving information search and decision making in the face of uncertainty (Chapter 2). The balance of this chapter argues that people will need creative minds and complex selves to meet expectations associated with PI roles. Our argument is diagrammed in Figure 3.1.

A profound implication of our analysis is that there is a shift toward problem solving and creative work in most social and economic roles. This shift transforms our occupational roles and reverberates throughout all other spheres of activity. Its impact on social relationships is developed in subsequent chapters. For now we only observe that problem solving has grown dramatically in importance, and with it decision making. This means role scripts are outmoded, and **the ability to engage in fluid relationships, creatively recast social roles, and invent new forms of social institutions will be the defining sociological characteristics of the PI era.** As Figure 3.1

points out, the alternatives are role failure, information overload, and burnout, discussed at greater length in Chapter 6.

The crux of our argument in Table 3.1 is that institutional arrangements affect the quality of role performance. Sophisticated new technologies necessitate that we have people with creative mind-sets who are linked together in institutional arrangements which encourage and nourish that creativity. But in Chapter 1 we provided ample evidence of the failure of traditional institutions to adapt to changing conditions. Institutions are not being transformed fast enough or in ways that are appropriate, given the changing environment, and role failure occurs as a result.

As the rate of technological change and product innovation accelerates, role improvisation will become the watchword. Learning how to negotiate appears to be an absolutely central element of success. **In industrial society the emphasis was on learning rules that make situations unambiguous by making them standardized. In PI society the emphasis must be on transforming rules in order to individualize cases.**

One of the shortcomings in Mead's work is his failure to explore the ways in which societies with different structures must socialize their children differently in order to insure that they will develop the skills necessary for navigating prevailing forms of social structure. Epoch-specific socialization may, for example, explain the phenomenal popularity of baseball in America earlier in the century. Baseball is a highly scripted game. Adjusted responses to unfolding conditions are quite predictable. A person paying attention to the game can confidently predict what every player on the field will do if, for example, a fly ball is hit. Baseball emphasizes learning rules, not being creative (Gelber, 1983). By contrast, it is far more difficult to predict what will happen as the ball goes into play in a game of basketball or soccer, sports that are growing in popularity as baseball wanes. Basketball and soccer are faster moving games that not only allow for more scenarios but also constrain players less in their selection of scenarios. These games require more complex imaginative rehearsal and more fluid adjusted response, and players need better interaction skills in order to accurately read opponents. They are games that offer more room for innovative responses and creativity. Consequently, they more accurately reflect the kinds of lives adults now lead (Gelber, 1991).

Our argument seems simplistic. Children should play the kinds of games that cultivate the social skills and sense of self that they will need as adults. But this raises all kinds of questions with radical implications. How do the social skills required for life in a post-industrial society differ from those required for life in industrial society? And how might we best prepare our children for life in PI society?

From Industrial (Intelligent) to Post-Industrial (Creative) Minds

Mead stressed intelligence as the key quality of the mind for industrial society. But we seriously question whether this is the quality of mind that is most critical in PI society. If the capacity to invent new products and imagine alternative scenarios is at the core of PI existence, than intelligence is no longer the critical factor. **The true PI "mind" must have the capacity to imagine scenarios that have not occurred, to envision new ways in which relationships and patterns of social organization can be restructured.** These are attributes of creativity, not intelligence.

What is creativity? Or more profoundly, what is the difference between industrial minds and PI minds? For us, these questions represent the keys to a theoretical understanding of PI society.

There are at least two different qualities of mind we need to consider. The industrial age places emphasis on **intelligence:** the ability to manipulate symbols according to a learned system of rules. The current stress on test-based intelligence is so ingrained that it is easy to lose sight of how much it dominates our thinking. Success from the outset is governed by learning rules. We judge our toddlers by how rapidly they learn our rules and how willing they are to employ them. Children leaving preschool are tested to see if they are "kindergarten ready" by assessing the rules they have learned—primarily social rules but also a few rules governing their use of grammar and their organization and integration of facts. Later, children are tracked by the skill with which they memorize and the tenacity with which they adhere to new rules, especially spelling rules, grammar rules, math rules, and rules of comportment. Those children who most consistently demonstrate the ability to learn and the willingness to apply rules in elementary school are the kids we place on the college prep track in high school, the kids we place on a trajectory to become tomorrow's leaders. We test for rules again by using the SATs to determine admission to colleges of varying quality, with examinations like the LSAT and GRE for admissions to graduate and professional schools, and with board exams for admission into the professions. Yes, indeed, we have national systems of education and occupational placement, which ensure that responsible jobs are filled by people who are very intelligent: very adept at learning and very consistent at applying rules.

There is nothing wrong with intelligence. It is better to have than to be without. However, another kind of mind appears to be more appropriate for PI society. This is the **creative** mind. In contrast with intelligence, creativity involves the ability to either invent new symbols or modify and combine old symbols in novel ways. Existing measures of creativity are not very refined, which suggests that educators have not considered it very important relative to intelligence —a serious mistake.

Research by Getzel and Jackson (1968) indicates that, beyond a certain minimum level of intelligence, there is very little correlation between intelligence and creativity. One standard creativity test is to give an individual a symbol, such as an umbrella or a car, and ask how many different things it represents. The more symbols that are perceived, the more creative the individual is presumed to be. Thus, creativity involves the ability to perceive many different meanings in the same symbol. Another aspect of creativity is the ability to see connections between different symbols. This is essential for the development of hypotheses or for recognizing patterns. What we call "new insights" typically involve recognizing connections that others have missed. This may seem to be a simplistic description, but most advances in both science and art rest on the discovery of patterns or connections that predecessors have not seen.

The real key to creativity is problem solving. Problem solving is the ability to bridge the gap between what is and what one feels ought to be. Problem-solving skills include the ability to recognize and define problems, invent and implement solutions, and track and evaluate results (Carnevale, 1991, pp. 110-113). Once creativity is defined this way, we appreciate how commonplace it is—and how fundamental.

Unfortunately, our thinking about creativity is too closely tied to cultural images of recognized geniuses like DaVinci, Edison, Picasso, Einstein, Mozart, Galileo, and Diaghilev. Instead of dwelling on geniuses, we would be better off if we recognized that everyone has problem-solving abilities and spent our time thinking of ways to raise creative faculties across the whole population. A creative citizenry will be central to success in the PI era. If countries are to be competitive they must be first with innovations and inventions, and first in improving products and services. A few Einsteins and Picassos will not be enough. The entire population must be transformed so that everyone, or at least most people, exercise more creativity than they do at present.

The Universality of Creative Thinking

Creativity seems to be a capacity of mind that most people possess, but our cultural beliefs and social structural arrangements often discourage its expression, prevent its development, or blind us to its presence. The average person does not feel creative. Instead, he or she regards creativity as the province of art and science, even though a great deal of artistic and scientific activity is routine and unimaginative. At the same time, most of us overlook how much creativity ordinary people exercise every day in performance of their roles.

Demands for creativity are increasing steadily. And these demands have transformed many occupations. For example, instead of applying a single "correct" teaching approach, we now define "good" teachers as those who seek out different pedagogies for different students, problem solving to discover how different students learn and experimenting with a full spectrum of approaches in order to better meet the distinctly different learning needs of each individual student. Creativity is a greater part of the role than ever before.

Being creative doesn't require winning the Nobel Prize. Creativity simply involves the introduction of new behaviors in roles or new activities in role relationships. And everyone does this to a degree. At issue is how to nurture creativity so that it is expressed more freely and more often, since it is clearly needed and expected, as a part of normal role behavior now more than in the past (Mohr & Mohr, 1983). This indicates a subtle but very important change in the way people think. Room for creative modification rather than precise duplication has become a part of our deep structural mind-set. It is something we are increasing more comfortable with and actively seeking out. A performer playing classical music is, by definition, playing something old. But we also expect the musician to modify and interpret as well. We assume there is room for innovation because we take for granted that the composer left certain things ambiguous, allowing for interpretation within a framework that we recognize as the classical original. PI people generally do not want to hear something exactly the way they heard it before. That rankles us on a deep structural level, marking an alteration in the way in which people look at the world. We demand something that is simultaneously new and old, a sign of our growing comfort with dualism. Thirty years ago the average audience didn't want to hear interpretations. They preferred "golden oldies" in their unaltered state. To use a different example, creative interpretations of the national anthem were once thought of as unpatriotic, whereas they are now usually viewed as expressions of patriotism.

Again, creativity is all around us. For instance, clinicians exercise it in deciding if and when to apply techniques and procedures, and in deciding how those techniques and procedures should be selectively used or modified for maximum impact for a particular client. And recent developments in the delivery of social services are illustrative of an increasing team orientation, as clinicians pool efforts to meet the complex and individualized needs of clients. In the 1970s it was common to find welfare agencies wastefully duplicating effort in some areas of need while ignoring others. A family might find, for example, three agencies capable of providing food stamps, but no help in locating appropriate counseling to deal with special problems. Case management evolved in the eighties, with a central resource person accessing a full range of service providers to offer complete yet unduplicated care for people in need (a theme developed more in Chapter 7).

Creative problem solving is most easily demonstrated in the PI family where parents constantly discuss how to handle difficulties raised by their children as they grow. What do you do when your children exclude other children from friendship groups, or when they themselves are excluded? What do you do when children turn off to a particular teacher, which often involves turning off to school and to learning in general? Keeping both practicality and values in mind, does a parent promote safe sex or no sex at all? Can children have parties with alcohol, and if so, at what age? The list of problems to solve has grown as the rules governing child, adolescent, and young adult behavior have been swept away.

Our discussion of many kinds of innovation suggests the universality of creativity in the human species. In science, the discovery of new concepts and the creation of new theories are illustrative. In sports, the development of new strategies is analogous to improving scientific theories through successive approximations. In art, the development of a new expressive style, whether in painting, sculpture, music, or theater, is another equivalent. The unskilled worker who envisions a better way of doing his or her job is no different at the heart of it from a scientist in search of a better theory, or an artist exploring new modes of expression. All that differentiates them is the area in which the discovery occurs, not the magnitude of the discovery from the standpoint of our definition of creativity. Unfortunately, our understanding of creative processes has been hindered by our tendency to give disproportionate emphasis to extraordinary examples of creativity. If we instead focus our attention on problem solving in everyday life, we will see that creativity is ubiquitous.[2] There are, of course, differences in creative talent, enormous differences in the creativity of different physicists, biologists, economists, schoolteachers, policymakers, social workers, parents, and so on. But everyone has the innate potential to be creative in his or her role enactment. Differences emerge because some organizational or institutional environments are better at nurturing creativity than others.

Although we think of great inventors who transformed material objects, such as Thomas Edison, as being creative, we tend not to perceive institutional inventors in the same way. Certainly, Henry Ford developed an enormously important institutional form when he perfected the assembly line, as did Alfred Sloan when he introduced a divisional structure at General Motors. Institutional inventors of the past included educators such as Charles Eliot at Harvard University and Robert Hutchins at the University of Chicago, as well as Jane Hull in social work, and Clara Barton in nursing, to name just a few. Such institutional inventions are rarely the products of a single mind. They are team products.

Institutional inventions frequently come into being because of the efforts of many people working over a period of years, gradually changing the rules, roles, and network interconnections making up an organizational setting. The managers of the Pennsylvania Railroad during the nineteenth century and the managers of General Electric in the early years of the twentieth century showed great creativity. And yet, it is impossible to single out any one person as having inspired change (Chandler, 1962, 1977).

In PI society, developing creative response is frequently a collaborative activity. This is apparent in the way people talk about things. We discuss team sports, team treatments, team teaching, ensemble acting, quality work circles, commissions, and task forces. Even when we focus on cultural products such as articles in scientific journals, collaborative effort, once the exception, is now becoming the rule. For example, the number of scientific articles with four or more authors has jumped in recent years from 15% to 31% of all published articles worldwide, while single-author articles declined from one third to one fifth. The more instrument-intensive the research area, the more collaborative the research enterprise tends to be. The percentage of articles with three or more authors is above or near 50% in clinical medicine, biomedical research, chemistry, and physics, but only 8% in mathematics (*Science and Engineering Indicators*, 1989). Consequently, much of our attention should be on creativity as an organizational or group attribute.

Organizationally Stimulating Creativity

Everyone is capable of being creative, and almost every PI social position will require creative enactment as an element of successful role performance. But there are enormous differences in creativity between people, even when we restrict our comparisons to people in the same role. Why is the average person not more creative? Our answer is that industrial society has smothered, rather than nourished, creative minds.

In the literature on innovative organizations, one can find a number of themes that help explain why industrial people are not more creative in their roles and relationships. First is the importance ascribed to rank differences. People give more credence to the possibility of higher ranking role occupants being creative, and at the same time ignore the creative ideas of lower ranking persons. Yet line personnel are often in the best position to know how to improve the work process because of their intimate familiarity with production problems. Managers with an industrial mind-set tend not to tap the creative energies of people in subordinate positions, in part because rank differences inhibit communication (Blau & Scott, 1962; Ronken & Lawrence, 1952). Yet, if those in higher ranking roles ask for the advice or counsel of subordinates, they usually discover how creative and insightful lower ranking persons are. This was the great discovery of the Coch and French (1948) experiment in a pajama factory. When seamstresses were given a chance to express their ideas, it turned out that they were filled with them, substantiating the position that some organizational cultures inhibit the expression of creativity while others encourage it (Perrow, 1979).

Comparative research on Japanese and American firms suggests that Japanese workers make, on average, 10 times the number of suggestions that American workers do (Azumi & Hull, 1986; Azumi, Hull, & Hage, 1983). This shatters the myth that American workers are more creative than those of any other nation, and that the Japanese only know how to copy. Japanese managers recognize worker insights as a resource and use a variety of techniques to stimulate the flow of advice and ideas from line workers. Again, the evidence is that organizational culture regulates the flow of creative juices. In reviewing research studies, Hage (1980) found that centralization and stratification diminish levels of innovation. People working in stratified bureaucracies tend to develop a mind-set that Janis (1972) calls groupthink. Everyone learns to think in the same way and to ask the same questions. Everyone mimics the attitudes and thinking of their superiors. Gradually, the creative centers of the mind atrophy like unused muscles. The less often synapses fire, the more spark it takes to ignite them, and the more often glimmers of creative insight get lost.

Formal role scripts are a second inhibitor of creativity, although not necessarily as great. Opportunities for creativity are eliminated to the degree that roles are specified and tasks are rigidly defined. While the role occupant may have creative ideas, some roles offer little opportunity for experimentation.

What organizational characteristics promote innovation? The range and richness of human capital present in a given setting, a mix of occupational specialties or of people with higher education, seem to encourage expression and development of ideas. As noted in Chapter 1, this is one reason we see a lot more creativity in PI society.

Diversity of background and experience is also essential. The world is complex and growing more complex all the time. Organizations need people with a diversity of perspectives to better comprehend this complexity. With a greater range of perspectives, especially opposing perspectives, new opportunities for synthesis and for creative adaptation to environmental pressures present themselves. When members of a diverse work force communicate well and work cooperatively, organizations can respond creatively to changing conditions.

Teamwork is also an essential part of our imagery about creativity (Larson & LaFasto, 1989). As noted before, most of today's major innovations are essentially team products (Pelz & Andrews, 1966). Teams created synthetic leather, the computer, and the Concorde. Most committee meetings in organizations involve group decision making, and creative outcomes are almost always collaborative efforts. This is especially true when the decision is to create a new output to satisfy an unmet need. Design and deliberation extend over time and involve the input of many people (Hage, 1980, Chapter Four). R&D is a long, arduous road from the embryonic inception of a bright idea to the delivery of a finished product or the provision of a useful service (Ronken & Lawrence, 1952) and often involves the input of hundreds or thousands of people. Furthermore, in contemporary work teams, the roles of the expert, worker, and leader keep alternating among individuals (Carnevale, 1991, p. 107).

The many lines of analysis explored in this section are unified by a single theme: The future will demand people with creative minds. We need people who can innovate, who can envision novel new ways of approaching problems, especially in team settings. In the next section we argue that changes in self are called for as well. PI situations call for complex selves.

From Industrial (Dominant) Selves to Post-Industrial (Complex) Selves

We can understand better what is meant by a complex self if we contrast it with models of the self that were employed by an earlier generation of social scientists. In David Riesman's *The Lonely Crowd* (1961), part of the thesis is that nineteenth-century pioneers had to be inner-directed men and women as a consequence of living on the frontier. The Horatio Alger myth symbolized all the virtues of the inner-directed person, especially the capacity to struggle against adversity. Inner-directed individuals—people like Edison, McCormick, Morse—made the nineteenth century an age of discovery. The inner-directed self was prominent on farms and in small businesses, giving rise to the myth of American individualism and industriousness, a very different flavor from European culture (Landes, 1969).

But Riesman's real interest was in the personality type that seemed to prosper in the large corporations that came to dominate the twentieth century (Chandler, 1977; Landes, 1969). This was the corporate manager, the outer-directed individual, the person who borrows standards and values from others. Sloan Wilson's (1955) book, *The Man in the Gray Flannel Suit*, described how people in the executive suite conform to the standards that are set for them by others. Gray flannel personalities want to be like everyone else, or perhaps like everyone who is materially just a little better off than they are. Thus, Chandler and Wilson were describing role style, the way in which people enact and perform their roles. Conformity in attitude, behavior, taste, and spirit was the norm, the ideal, reflecting the impact of rationalization.

The occupational role for the man and the housewife role for the woman were key and important ingredients of the self and self-esteem (Rosenberg, 1979). And what of the working class and of minorities? In this era of mass society, when a great deal of emphasis was placed on conformity, little variation was allowed across occupational roles, especially those at the bottom of the occupational hierarchy. Gender roles were quite rigid. The housewife role was highly standardized with tight role scripts. Minorities were almost defined as nonpersons, with roles that were even more submissive than the ones defined for middle-class women. In all these cases both unidimensionality of self and clear location of one's self within a hierarchical system of domination were key. **Industrial selves feel most comfortable when there is a sense of certainty about who the self is and where the self sits in relationship to other selves, and all the feedback one receives about the self is consistent.** People with this kind of self-concept fit perfectly in the bureaucratized industrial society. For industrial personalities, self-actualization comes from completing tasks, while for PI personalities self-actualization comes from mastering problems.

But simple dichotomies of the self, like Riesman's, are losing their value with the passage of time.[3] For in the era of small high-tech companies, one needs to be both inner-directed and outer-directed. New organizational arrangements, group problem solving, and research and development are becoming more important. To be successful in these activities, **one needs the capacity for independent thought and the simultaneous ability to work well with other people of different backgrounds.**

An analysis of current public opinion polls, especially regarding political attitudes, appears to document the development of more complex selves. Young college-educated professionals hold far more complex views of the world than did members of the previous generation. They see themselves as more liberal on political issues and civil rights but more conservative on economic issues.

Research on ethnic identity also confirms the growth in complexity of self. The standard thesis from Durkheim (1964) to Deutsch

(1953) was that modernization leads to the breakdown of regional and ethnic loyalties; but at present there appears to be a resurgence of ethnic identity (Alba, 1990). Individuals are proud to be Italian, Polish, Irish, or Bantu. Perhaps the symbolic importance of the television miniseries *Roots*, about the African-American heritage, was not that African-Americans watched it, but that so many whites did. Implicitly, whites learned that they, too, had lost their roots and should actively work to recapture them. This is not a reversion to tribalism, events in Eastern Europe not withstanding.[4] It simply means that complex selves find it natural and appropriate to maintain several identities at once.

The rise of interracial marriages is another indication that more complex selves are coming into existence. The case of Eurasians— offspring of marriages between people of Asian origin and people of European origin—is especially interesting. Eurasians tend, in our experience, to identify themselves as Caucasians and as Asians at the same time. They also identify themselves as Eurasian, or something both new and different from either group of origin. Hence, the self comes to be made up not only of a number of old identities, but also of an entirely new synthesis (Nakashima, 1991). There is nothing inconsistent or schizophrenic in this. Indeed, it is our argument that complex selves are best adapted to the demands and conditions of PI society. That is why society should no longer try to mold each individual into a standardized version of the same "ideal" person. Complex selves are too individualized to match an archetype.

Even parenthood takes on a different character, and a more professional-client character, in PI society. Of course, mothers and fathers have always been part teacher, therapist, doctor, welfare worker, and counselor. But now more than ever before, being a parent brings people into regular and sustained contact with professionals from outside the home, and sometimes makes the parent an auxiliary for the outside professional. Baby-sitting co-ops and on-site day care provided by employers are other good examples of recent efforts to draw the family and nonfamily caregivers into closer cooperation.

Equally important is the issue of flexibility or adaptability of the self. The complex self is more likely to be adaptive precisely because it is capable of moving in more than one direction. Multiple identities not only reduce the sense of failure if we do poorly in one area, but also give us the capacity and emotional strength to move into whole new adventures (Thoits, 1983). Redefining a job or a marriage role, for example, necessitates flexibility and adaptability in one's sense of self.

Perhaps one of the most common examples of a redefined role and role-set occurs when two people live together. This produces a whole set of ambiguities. Do you call your partner's parents "mom" and "dad"? What contact should the parents of the respective partners have with one another, and what should the nature of their relationship be? Just what are the duties and obligations of the partners to one another? The role-set becomes even more complicated when the couple lives with one parent or set of parents.

Another excellent example of role redefinition occurs when relationships break up. What obligations do former spouses have to one another? What is the role of noncustodial parents? What happens to the grandparent role if your child gets divorced and does not retain custody of your grandchildren? What should the nature of a "step" relationship be? And how does the redefinition of these pivotal roles impact upon the self?

The number of types of identities a person has are important (Stryker, 1990), but to our knowledge, no one has adequately described the melding of different identities into the kinds of complex selves that we believe are becoming common—selves that can entertain different identities simultaneously, take apparent contradictions in stride, and accept periodic shifting of their relative social positions without reacting defensively. While a number of theorists (for a major review, see Rosenberg & Turner, 1981) have commented on how social statuses, membership groups, and even personality types can invoke identities, the assumption has been that only a few, or perhaps even only one, identity dominates a person's conception of self (Stryker, 1980, 1990). Most previous writers have attempted to isolate dominant identities, contexts in which one or another identity becomes central, or ways in which a central identity is maintained (Heise, 1979). We, on the other hand, want to suggest both that the core self is becoming more complex and that the idea of the flexible self is needed to replace the notion that whatever identity is most

Affective Social Roles	gender, age, family, religion, friendship
Work Social Roles	occupational roles, whether white-collar or blue-collar; roles in organizations that are other than occupational
Leisure Social Roles	roles in voluntary associations, spectator roles, roles in leisure-time activities, and so on
Cultural Social Roles	community roles, ethnic roles, racial roles, nation-state roles

	Expressive	Instrumental
Formal roles	Leisure social roles	Work social roles
Informal roles	Affective social roles	Cultural social roles

Figure 3.2. The Social Roles in a Complex Self

salient in a situation is all-prevailing. For **people with complex selves can look at situations from more than one point of view, and can therefore be more creative in envisioning solutions to problems and more effective when enacting those solutions cooperatively with others.**

Complex sense of self or identity can be based on at least four types of affiliation. First, there are gender, familial, religious, and friendship roles, what Ralph Turner (1978) would call the basis of the impulsive or affective self. Second, there are the work roles, which we discussed in Chapter 2. Third, and long overlooked, there are leisure-time roles, such as club memberships, involvement in sports, and life-style activities. And fourth, there are the roles people occupy that correspond to various collective identities, such as race, ethnicity, and nationality (Deutsch, 1953; Inkeles & Smith, 1974; Sofranko & Fliegel, 1977) as outlined in Figure 3.2.

A complex self can entertain different identities with equal salience simultaneously, and has the ability to handle change in

the definition of social roles and their corresponding identities. High self-esteem in PI selves emerges from being able to effectively handle changes in the definition of social roles. This is in sharp contrast with industrial selves, for whom esteem comes from script-like performance of roles and a sense of occupying a clear place in a hierarchy. Role failure is most likely to occur where there is an absence of complexity or flexibility of self among people who must deal with changing conditions.

Recognizing Complex Selves

We make four fundamental assertions about the nature of the self in PI society. First, post-industrial people expend more effort in the *construction* of self than in the presentation of self. Construction of self flows from participation in problem solving and the role redefinition associated with problem solving. We see this in dual-career families, in quality work circles in high-tech companies, and in task forces designed to solve community problems. This is consistent with our argument that Blumer's (1969) image of society, based on continual reconstruction of social roles, has grown more appropriate over time. Even with ascriptive characteristics such as gender, the PI self tends to personalize the meaning of the attribute rather than projecting some script-like definition of the "macho" male or "perfect hostess" female. Second, PI people move away from a single core self and assume a more complex configuration of self-conceptions and identities. Third, self-judgment is therefore less dependent upon performance in any particular sphere and, as a consequence, the entire process of self-appraisal is less critical. Fourth, since social identities are constantly being redefined and recombined, self-esteem based on evaluations of others is less important and is being replaced by a sense of efficacy in dealing with change, in being flexible and overcoming problems.

Changes in family life exemplify this transformation. In the past, and especially prior to the Second World War, the rigid association between familial self and work self and the lack of leisure time meant that women were mothers and stayed at home, and fathers worked and had little involvement in the raising of children. But the tight connection between work and family has broken down, thanks to rapid growth in the number of college-educated women; to the feminist movement opening up more employment opportunities for women; to inflation in living costs, which has forced more women into the work force; and to developments such as telecommuting, which have enabled more men to stay close to home while working (Fleming, 1989). These forces have added a work identity to women's conception of self and have legitimized child care by men. The concept of dual-career families thus celebrates an expansion in the self—in the conception of what gender means—for both men and women. The gender roles of both men and women are becoming more complex, and much greater diversity of gender roles is tolerated.

Family roles are becoming more complex for a variety of reasons. To begin with, more American families are transcultural. This means that more people have experience in confronting different identities, view themselves as having membership in the group of origin of one's spouse, and experience formation of different identities. Identity change is also inherent in the development of multiple families via divorce. It is telling that the word "step" is being dropped from our active vocabulary. Unlike the past, we now accept stepmothers and stepfathers as really being mothers and fathers. Moreover, we do this without abandoning a sense of affinity for natural relatives. For the first time, we accept as fact the idea that children can have more than one mother and more than one father; children in these arrangements can now have multiple role models. Multiple role models provide a variety of options for children to follow in becoming men or women, husbands or wives, balancing career and family, and so on.

The premise of symbolic interactionism, that creative individuals can construct their own lives, is now finally being achieved. And there is a movement toward much more complex definitions of self, because people now typically hold a wider array of statuses. In the dual-career family, for example, both men and women are attempting to be actively involved in their careers and in their families, a far cry from the separation common two decades ago. Another example is the single-parent family, where the parent tries to combine the role responsibilities of both the father and the mother and has an occupational role as well. This is probably the ultimate in complexity. The dual-career and single-parent families are, after all, now the two most common types of families (see Chapter 1), so they offer the perfect theater for understanding the experimental arrangements people are creating as they adapt to new conditions.

Extensions to the Established Literature

Our treatment adds to the established literature in a number of ways. Two of those will be briefly highlighted before we move on.

The Complex Self Versus the Situational Self

A number of writers in the classical literature have argued that different selves are relevant in different situations (Stone, 1962; Stryker, 1980). We would argue that for post-industrial men and women the various selves are being activated at the same time. This means there is more complexity of self.

The old thesis of the situational self is easy to explain. People were thought to adopt a particular identity or status as defining the self in a specific situation. For example, it may be the affective self at home, and the instrumental self at work. During the day, some would say people rotate selves systematically as needed in industrial society. But with the arrival of post-industrialism, increased complexity of self is needed. To be successful in a PI workplace it is necessary to simultaneously remain conscious of all one's selves in order to be able to look at perplexing situations from different points of view.

Managers and professionals have desks with pictures of their families or of favorite leisure-time activities that allow them to reenact fond memories symbolically. Unfortunately, this whole dimension, the number of times during the day that we think about our other roles and the relationships they encompass, has never been studied, but we feel it is an important aspect of the complex self. Similarly, the number of telephone calls has been growing exponentially because they allow us to "reach out and touch someone," an accurate slogan, even if it sounds a little trite. Car phones are especially interesting from this standpoint. The implications of the telephone for both role analysis and the self have not been appreciated. This is a case where technology makes a complex self more possible, allowing the inter-penetration of nonwork contact during the workday. The reverse is also true. We can more easily maintain contact with work while we are on vacation, or can have work concerns interrupt family activity at home. Separation of work and family is a thing of the past, which makes for a great deal of role conflict that can best be accommodated by creative minds with complex selves (Chapter 6). Technologies thus allow for much greater flexibility in interaction and force people to juggle and intersperse the demands of all the social roles they occupy, which requires a complex self.

The Leisure Self as an Important Addition

One place to observe the growing complexity of the self is the arena that is usually ignored the most, namely the choice of leisure-time activities. Leisure time was never considered very important in industrial society. Nor have sociologists thought about the choice of how we spend our leisure time as an important way of expressing and nourishing the self. But in PI society it is precisely that. The average vacation in France is 5 weeks. Four weeks is no longer uncommon in the United States. This allows us to pursue the activities and inter-ests that are "really us," even if we have never done them before. It lets the "real me" come out. Leisure time becomes another kind of occupation, pursued with the same intensity as work life.[5]

Leisure activities become whole styles of life, as, for example, any-one who has been a motorcyclist, boater, camper, scuba diver, or backpacker knows. What is especially interesting to us is the impact of technology on a number of these activities. Boats, for example, can have a greater array of sophisticated equipment than most non-boaters would imagine, including navigational devices developed for the Strategic Defense Initiative (President Reagan's "Star Wars" program), which precisely locate position by triangulating from not one but an entire system of orbiting satellites. Each activity can also have its own uniform, and these uniforms are often quite expensive. Many activities rest on coordinated activities among large numbers of people, such as Civil War reenactments. Others bring people together for activities that are communal in their essence, such as poetry reading.

Organized spectator sports provide another source of identification for people. Being a fan of the Redskins or the Dodgers or the Celtics can absorb people for 6 months a year. From Little League on up, team affinity provides many people with the strongest sense of emotional bonding they have with the broader community. Spectator sports also provide opportunities for seemingly mild-mannered people to express controlled rage. Fitness clubs provide another kind of identity and emotional release.

This is not to say that leisure is rampant. Americans enjoy less discretionary time now than they have in years. Reduced discretionary time is especially noticeable among professionals and managers. Work stress has become a very common problem in the United States. And more than a few Japanese suffer **karoshi,** literally working themselves to death at a young age (ka-ro-shi: excessive-work-death). However, working harder to produce more is counterproductive in a PI environment. And it is counterproductive for everyone: for the individual and his or her family, the organization for which that person works, and the clients ultimately consuming products and services. For just as quality customization requires creative solutions to individual problems, creative problem solving requires time to think in settings where one is not too deeply mired in conventional approaches. This means leisure time, when the deeper recesses of one's subconscious can rotate a situation on its various axes and ponder new approaches offering the prospect of better solutions. The knee-jerk organizational reaction to competitive failure is to have workers do the same thing but more of it, tending to produce workaholics. But workaholics tend not to be creative. PI workers need meaningful periods of leisure time to be creative and, consequently, useful.

Another reason why the leisure self is so important is that it provides an opportunity to counterbalance the stresses associated with PI work. The handling of large numbers of people with diverse expectations places considerable stress, emotional and otherwise, on postmodern men and women. Leisure activity provides the counterbalance (Freudenberger, 1981).

Finally, leisure activities allow the impulsive self much more opportunity to come out. As much as we emphasize the amount of choice involved in family and in work, the reality remains that these roles impose responsibilities and constraints, even if they are co-determined. Leisure activity is much freer and less restricted, and therefore the impulsive self can more easily be articulated. We stress the importance of Turner's (1978) idea of the impulsive self because we believe that it allows for the expression of emotions and for emotional repair, which help prepare people for effective symbolic communication, a theme developed further in Chapter 4.

Conclusions

We have answered Mead's question about the kinds of minds and of selves best suited to post-industrial society. The answer is creative minds and complex selves.

Creativity is not limited to geniuses, but is inherent in all kinds of problem-solving work. Since success in a PI environment is contingent on innovation (Chapter 1), and people's roles are being transformed accordingly (Chapter 2), it is time that we consider how to stimulate and nourish creativity across the society at large. We can encourage the expression of creativity with less hierarchical organizations and fewer role scripts. And we need to nourish the development of complex selves: people who have multiple identities that they can invoke simultaneously in order to comfortably approach a single problem from several different perspectives, and people who are comfortable with contradictions and have resilient egos that are not easily threatened.

Ours is really a functional theory. Societies will need to produce citizens with complex minds and creative selves in order to be prosperous in the PI era. But adapting to PI conditions is more than a matter of the minds and selves of individuals in isolation. It is also a matter of what happens between people, the subject of the balance of this book. For creative outcomes tend to be the products of teamwork among people who bring diverse talents and perspectives to bear on common problems. This only works if people are able to communicate effectively. However, effective communication is very difficult to achieve in diverse groups. It requires listening to underlying feeling tones as well as substantive content. Hence, emotional communication is a critical ingredient in PI success. This ingredient is the subject of Chapter 4.

Notes

1. This conceptualization is very similar to Manford Kuhn's concept of "core" self (Kuhn, 1960; Kuhn & McPhartland, 1954).

2. Blumer's (1969) main theme is that society is constructed by individual people engaged in face-to-face interaction, rather than prescribed by some unseen external force. Although Blumer's analysis seems to us to have been essentially inaccurate when applied to industrial society, we believe that PI society will prove to be almost exactly as Blumer described: a society in which reality is created by people, and social structure is molded within and arises out of relatively fluid interaction of people exercising agency.

3. Many of the old dichotomies that sociologists use to describe the emergence of industrial society are no longer applicable. The coming of the industrial age has been described in terms of a movement from rural to urban (Redfield, 1941), from *gemeinschaft* to *gesellschaft* (Toennies, 1963), from expressive to instrumental roles (Parsons, 1951). We would suggest that complex selves contain both parts of these pairs. PI people are capable of having both kinds of social relationships, living in both kinds of worlds, and feeling comfortable with both kinds of identities. Successful adaptation to future conditions will increasingly be predicated on the ability to view the social world from a variety of perspectives.

4. Events in Eastern Europe would seem to suggest otherwise. However, Eastern European nations have yet to enter the post-industrial era.

5. And sabbaticals ranging from several months to a year in length are no longer the exclusive province of college professors. Even some blue-collar workers are now entitled to periodic sabbaticals, and we expect this trend to spread much further. People doing post-industrial work need to be replenished.

4

EMOTION

We began Chapter 3 with a question: What kinds of minds and selves will people need in post-industrial society? The answer is that people will need creative minds and complex selves in order to deal with the heightened demands for innovation and personalized response that are attached to PI complexification of roles, and the demands for customized products and services and individualized treatment. Our question for Chapter 4 shifts the focus away from changes within people to what happens between people. In this chapter, we ask: How will people need to interact in post-industrial society? The answer is that people will have to learn to read emotion, to "hear" feeling tones.

Rapid technological change and role complexification require that people be adaptable and flexible. And the growing demand for customized products and services places new stress on innovation and teamwork among people from different backgrounds. This means that in the future people will require more acute interaction skills. In particular, people will need to develop better listening skills in order to make teamwork operable under conditions of diversity. In a word, symbolic interaction is the key to success in a PI world.[1]

Table 4.1 Interaction Skills Necessary for Smooth Functioning in Adult Life

Skill	Initial Acquisition
ability to read conventional gestures	forced interaction of infants with parents (e.g., feeding)
role-taking ability	unstructured play (e.g., peek-a-boo)
ability to evaluate one's own actions (e.g., embarrassment)	consistent reward and punishment from parents
imaginative rehearsal, adjusted response	structured play (e.g., baseball)

In this chapter we build further upon George Herbert Mead's insights by suggesting emotions as a solution to a number of problems that emerge in symbolic communication between people facing PI role demands. Communication of feeling tones provides a way of understanding how we accommodate PI demands for intensely personalized interaction and innovation-oriented cooperation among people from different professional and social backgrounds.

Interaction Demands of the New Society

Mead was both fascinated and perplexed by the fact that society is made up largely of unrelated individuals with different goals who nevertheless interact in meaningful and coherent ways. In short, Mead asked how it is possible for society to even exist. His answer is that society becomes part of the individual during the socialization process (e.g., Mead, 1964, pp. 152-164). Children move through a series of developmental stages in order to acquire the requisite social skills to be productive citizens. On the developmental road to becoming adults, children learn conventional gestures (in forced interaction, such as feeding), acquire role-taking skills (in unstructured play, such as peek-a-boo), learn to assess their own performance (e.g., feel pride or embarrassment, acquired when parents provide consistent reward and punishment), and learn how to imaginatively rehearse and adjust responses simultaneously with a multiplicity of other role occupants (in structured games like baseball).

Mead argued that the acquisition and use of interaction skills allows people to enjoy some flexibility in their lives without destroying the social fabric of their surroundings. That is, people can find ways of altering behavior and changing relationships without threatening the coherence of interaction in extended social networks. Adults are able to accomplish this feat, as Mead discovered, because of their acquired capacities for role-taking, imaginative rehearsal, adjusted response, and reading conventional gestures. Indeed, those individuals who have the greatest difficulty maintaining their relationships with others—people who are labeled "deviants"—are often persons who lack well-developed interaction skills (Pitt & Hage, 1964).

We believe that the need for well-developed interaction skills grows more acute by the day (Carnevale, 1991, p. 104). Some of the reasons for this were made explicit in the first three chapters; others will be developed later. Following are the basic points. (a) As the pace of technological change increases, people change roles more often, and this requires adjustment. (b) As technology releases people from more routine activities, roles focus more on problem solving, which requires that people be able to "read" clients in order to ascertain what their problems are. (c) The more advanced technology becomes, the more progress we make in overcoming small, disciplinarily narrow problems. Consequently, we spend more time addressing interdisciplinary problems with people from different fields who speak different disciplinary languages, with all the communication problems that entails. (d) Demand for customized products, services, and personalized attention means that scripts must be supplanted by individualized treatment. (e) The breakdown of traditional institutions throws even the most clearly defined roles of the past open to renegotiation. (f) The deconstruction of occupation, department, hierarchy, and even organizational boundaries means that the scripts in jobs are being replaced by high amounts of interaction and role redefinition.

To sum up, our central argument is that in PI society the growth in knowledge, the process of complexification, and the appearance of more creative minds with complex selves will call on people to be much more responsive to others, much more interactive. On the other hand, the widespread breakdown of traditional institutions, and the role failure associated with that breakdown (e.g., the high divorce rate), suggest that communications skills have failed to keep pace with intensified demands for fluid interpersonal exchange. In other words, the minimum level of interactive competency required for an adult to function effectively in industrial society is not sufficient for effectively navigating the social waters of PI society. If technology is constantly changing the definition of occupational roles and family roles, and if the relationship between work and family is also being altered, then roles have to be redefined, expectations have to change, and interaction patterns must be reconstituted. Since all of these redefinitions have to be negotiated, symbolic communication is critical. These are key ideas in the symbolic interactive framework we are building our argument upon.

This line of analysis about the impact of complexification on roles is tied to a seemingly obvious but ultimately profound question. **Will citizens of post-industrial societies typically be interacting with other people like themselves or with people who are different from themselves?** We think the answer to this question is "very different." Diversity is the watchword for the future and must be for success in an age of global interdependence. Not only are we interacting more with people of different cultures because of travel, but our universities, businesses, cities, and politics are becoming internationalized. So is our marketplace, as a greater number of American businesses are purchased by foreign owners, and as a greater number of American firms use foreign labor or foreign components. More blue-collar workers and white-collar employees are now and will be working for foreign bosses who have different cultural traits. In sum, different peoples are brought closer together by globalization. Even in the absence of globalization, workplace diversity would increase because complex problems demand team-generated multidisciplinary solutions, requiring that people with different backgrounds and talents be drawn together. And social diversity would increase by virtue of the fact that complex selves tend to like people who differ from themselves. Among people with industrial mindsets, "birds of a feather flock together"; but among complex selves, "opposites attract." The arrival of PI society thus offers a possible explanation for the substantial increases we have witnessed in interracial and cross-cultural marriages in recent years. All these factors work to increase the diversity of contacts each person experiences, and this in turn requires heightened interaction skills if people are to cooperate effectively and avoid misunderstandings.

These trends add impetus to the growing importance of symbolic communication. It is in this light that we need to rethink one of the central ideas in symbolic interaction, namely the place of symbolic communication in making society possible. This idea, which has been so attractive to many, lies at the heart of Mead's analysis. But what new interaction skills will be required of people as we move into the PI era? Emotion is, we would argue, the key to effective communication in an environment in which everything is in flux. It is what makes the coherence of PI society possible, and must therefore be the centerpiece of any effort to apply Mead's perspective to the analysis of contemporary conditions.

Emotion: The Nonverbal Channel

A large number of researchers working in the symbolic interaction tradition have looked at the problem of emotion. More recently the sociology of emotions has emerged as a legitimate area of study in its own right (Kemper, 1978), as indicated by the creation of a new section on emotions within the American Sociological Association. Peggy Thoits (1989), in a broad review of the sociology of emotions, notes that there has been considerable work on the shaping of emotions, including work on their biological bases. Other recent work has looked at how children learn emotions: "emotional socialization." David Heise (1979) has developed a theory of affect control, arguing that people orchestrate their encounters with others in order to promote emotional stasis by reaffirming one's sense of self, a very industrial but not a very PI thing to do. Randall Collins (1981) similarly notes that emotion pervades interaction because the outcome of every social encounter can be seen as an evaluative statement on the self. But to our knowledge, the emotional content of symbolic communication has not been stressed, only the emotional flavor of outcomes. This seems to us to be the wrong way to approach the subject.

For our purposes, symbolic communication consists of two channels: a verbal or cognitive channel and a nonverbal or affective channel. Both channels are necessary for the kind of effective communication that we have argued is essential in a PI world characterized
by intensified interaction oriented toward the generation of innovative breakthroughs.

When we speak of different channels of communication, we are
suggesting that both information and feeling are being transmitted.
The bulk of symbolic interactionist analysis has focused on gestures
or symbols as informational rather than as feelings. Yet we suggest
that in PI, the latter becomes increasingly important if we are to be
creative (Chapter 3), negotiate roles (Chapter 5), and interact in complex networks or role-sets (Chapters 6 and 7), all of which require
that people accurately and rapidly appreciate the symbolic meaning
of what is being said.

Of course, it is true that emotions are stated verbally, such as "I
like you" or "I love you." But the true symbolic meaning of these
verbal statements, we would argue, is revealed not in words but in
the tone, glance or look, the gestures, the spontaneity, and other nonverbal cues that let us know the sincerity of the statement. Sincerity
is an important precondition for nonexploitive communication
(Habermas, 1968, 1984). Our argument is that sincerity is signalled
nonverbally for those who read the cues and is therefore quite measurable. The inner meaning, which is so important in symbolic communication, is added on the emotive, nonverbal level. It provides
an anchor in the otherwise free-floating imagery of symbolic interaction, for comparing what is said verbally with what is said nonverbally allows us to judge sincerity.

We can become much more adept at "speaking" the language of
feelings if we learn how to concentrate our attention on this second
channel of communication. The trick of translating, for us, can be
reduced to two very basic but also very important interpretive rules:

1. The emotional level on which interaction occurs is distinct and separate from the informational content of communication. Emotions are
   usually expressed on the nonverbal level, including tone of voice, gesture, and body stance, as something other than information content.

Table 4.2 The Emotional Messages in Conversation and Their Impact

Emotional Message	*Emotional Consequence*
1. Importance to speaker	Motivation of listener
2. Truthfulness of speaker	Detection of impression management versus discernment of sincerity
3. Specific feelings	Release of negative emotions, affirmation of self
4. Feelings of speaker for listener	Sanction (reward or punishment) and sense of belonging to the relationship

2. The most important affective points communicated are: (a) the importance, from the standpoint of the speaker, of what is being said; (b) whether the speaker believes what is being said; and (c) the feelings of the speaker for the listener.

Each of our interpretive rules is a simple insight and is explicated below.

Locator Messages

Separate from the informational content of an exchange, there are three of what we call **locator messages** on an affective plane (see Table 4.2). We regard these three locator messages as the core of affective communication, and **as central to the work of building the trust people need to sustain role relationships that are not governed by scripts** (e.g., Bellah, Madsen, Sullivan, Swidler, & Tipton, 1985). They are: (a) How important to the other person is the subject of the communication? (b) Is the other person being truthful? (c) Does the other person express affinity for us and our position? The idea that emotions act as a signal function is not new (Thoits, 1989). What we offer as new is the specification of the variety of signals being conveyed in each conversation.

These messages affect our propensity to act by determining the depth and nature of feeling we are likely to have. That is, they can motivate or demotivate.[2] This focus on motivation is central to our understanding social phenomena. Motivational energy is generated in situations that include people, confirm a positive sense of self, and engender trust and security about a person's continued acceptance (J. Turner, 1987).

Although Mead noted a basic distinction between verbal and nonverbal behavior, he largely ignored the nonverbal, emotive channel. Indeed, we accept his position that most of the informational content exchanged between human beings is communicated with words. But the most powerful and evocative symbolization occurs at the nonverbal level. Too much attention has been focused both on the far-flung array of symbols that people can exchange verbally and on all the problems of deciphering them. In contrast, we argue that it is more important to understand the limited number of identifiable and highly important messages communicated nonverbally, for these are the signals that either motivate us into action or deactivate our interest. The first and perhaps most critical emotive signal is the degree of importance of what is being said. If the speaker demonstrates feelings about what he or she is saying, then the listener is likely to respond affectively as well as cognitively. We sense the importance of the message and conduct ourselves accordingly.

Closely related to the issue of importance is the second signal, whether the speaker really believes in what he or she is saying. A good illustration is the "Joe Isuzu" ads of the late 1980s. On one level, the commentator makes a set of statements that read like facts. On another level, body language and inflection let us know whether the informational content is true or false. In the "Joe Isuzu" ads, the Japanese auto manufacturer Isuzu ran a series of television commercials featuring a 40-year-old car salesman who made verbal claims about the car, which his tone and body language "said" were patently false. The Joe Isuzu commercials are prototype PI advertisements because they frankly call attention to the presence of two channels, one verbal and the other nonverbal. Slapstick comedy was characteristic of the industrial age. Double-message humor will be characteristic of the future, which suggests a good deal about how minds and selves are changing (Chapter 3). Irony is a more complex form of humor for the more complex minds that emerge in more complex times.

When we verbally say something is important or true, but indicate the opposite nonverbally, we create a serious interpretive problem for the listener. Psychiatrists appreciate this all too well and rely upon discrepant nonverbal messages to alert them to "lying." A special form of this pattern is the double bind. When you are given contradictory messages about what is appropriate or expected, you are likely to fail regardless of how you perform (Bateson, 1972). Parents who tell their children that grades are not important, yet secretly wish for exceptional school performance, illustrate the importance of understanding that there are two levels of discourse. A different kind of example is that of the shy teenager who tells his mother he is taking a girl to the school dance, only to have the mother respond: "Did you tell her you can't dance?" The result of a double bind is to undermine the person's confidence and leave him or her in limbo. It demotivates and erodes social bonding.

Still a third signal is how a speaker feels about his or her listeners. Feelings of affinity are rarely communicated directly with words. Instead, they are conveyed with tone and body language suggesting the quality of interpersonal feelings, as well as with references to events that indirectly and subtly indicate the degree of intimacy the audience is supposed to feel with the speaker, or by manipulating cultural symbols that cast the perspective within which audiences are being encouraged to frame topics under discussion.

Being able to discern two levels of communication—the verbal cognitive and the nonverbal emotive—means that we have built into our theory an important way of discovering the other person's perception of truth. The nonverbal level lets us know when people are truly committed to what they are saying or doing, which Habermas (1984) regards as essential to the kind of humanistic communication as equals that will allow people to build a better social world.

We have focused on relational messages communicated on an affective plane. Is it important to the communicator? Is he or she being honest? What affinity does the communicator have for the audience? Next we ask what more specific feelings a communicator has about a topic.

Specific Feelings

Sociologists who study emotions have tended to focus on the specific content of the feelings (Thoits, 1989). Scheff (1979) assumes that individuals must release negative emotions, such as grief, fear, anger, embarrassment, and boredom. We agree with this assumption and believe that if the expression of negative feelings is suppressed, positive feelings will be undermined—in other words, the blockage of negative affect causes problems.

The most dramatic examples of blocked feelings erupting into violence are rape and serial killing. While these terrible transgressions have many causes, and we do not want to diminish the complexities involved, one common theme is the inability of some individuals to receive emotional gratification in their role relationships. Violence provides a kind of emotional high for some people whose emotional communication with others is blocked.

Despite **differences** in the ways in which a particular emotion may be expressed in diverse cultures, including occupational and organizational cultures, emotions themselves are **universal**. Feelings such as grief, anger, fear, happiness, and the like are within all people's everyday experience. And while the cultural and even personality specifics of emotive expression can be quite disparate, they nevertheless help us decipher the universal language of emotion.

The inner feelings themselves are universal—joy, pain, fear, happiness, anger, and the like. And since emotions evoke physiological processes in the body (Kemper, 1989), they can be "read" or felt by others, even in cross-cultural situations. We can "pick up" feelings, even if we are not always certain about precisely what is felt by the other person. If we were unable to do this, there would be little opportunity for true cross-cultural communication.

There seem to be relatively few content emotions that are central to affective communication. These sort themselves out in people's minds as semantic differentials. The three pairs that strike us as pivotal dimensions of emotional communication are:

contentment	anger
confidence	fear
happiness	sorrow

These are basic or primordial emotions, which can be combined in various ways to reflect other kinds of emotions (Kemper, 1989).

Some caveats are in order. Expressions of basic emotions differ from culture to culture. In England, when someone is really angry, he will lean forward in his chair. In France, the same person may wave his fist. The expressiveness of the gesture should not be confused with the degree of emotion involved. It is not necessarily the case that the Frenchman is more angry than the Englishman. The degree or importance of the emotion can only be understood against the cultural backdrop, and also the personality background, for some people are more expressive than others, just as some cultures are. When we say someone is **really** upset, we mean the nonverbal communication is more intense than normal for that individual, indicating an extreme score of importance.

Impression Management

Sincere, emotionally open communication is not to be taken for granted. Many people attempt to control the nonverbal level of their communications, so that it does not give away their emotions (Goffman, 1967). This is the emotive dimension to Goffman's impression management. But impression management is hard to maintain on an emotive level when there is sustained contact between people who are good at reading emotion. And the act of impression management, when feelings are managed, undermines social bonds and works against the person engaging in Goffmanesque behavior. The fact that Goffman's work was so popular suggests to us that dishonest or incomplete communication was normative for industrial society. PI movement toward more open and honest communication marks a change of deep significance.

Impression management, literally trying to project an inaccurate impression of oneself to others (Goffman, 1959), was the quintessential approach to interpersonal relations in the industrial era. In school we tried to look smart, in bars we tried to look cool, at work we tried to look competent, and with everyone else we tried to seem powerful and in control. Admit it: We all tried to manage those impressions, which is to say we engaged in deceit, because the images people tried to project were seldom entirely accurate.

Post-industrial people with creative minds and complex selves are less concerned about how they look in every situation or exactly where they place in terms of status. PI people also develop better interaction skills, allowing them to judge sincerity on an affective plane. This unmasks managed impressions. Well-developed second-channel communications skills help to trip up even the most skillful impression managers, for even if we can control our words, we have a difficult time controlling the physiological reactions that serve as a base for nonverbal expression of our feelings. Thus the expression of feelings, the nonverbal communication channel, provides a way of discerning how much people are manipulating their presentations of the self and packaging of issues. It is a medium for honest communication.

The unmasking of managed feelings does not happen automatically. Indeed, sociologists have been slow to recognize the nonverbal channel because it is almost subliminal. Most people take the verbal for granted and do not pay attention to the other dimension until misunderstandings arise. If the second communication channel were easier to read, the study of emotions would have emerged much earlier in the development of sociology.

Evaluating the feelings of others is not easy, but three interaction mechanisms can help. The first is accumulation of experience with a particular person across time. The more experience we have with an individual, and the wider the range of settings from which that experience is generated, the more likely we are to be able to read their feeling tones. Collins (1981) has observed that cognitive meaning is given to events retrospectively. We suggest that the meaning assigned events depends upon the nonverbal channel and a repetition of experiences related to an individual. Only slowly can we sort out our readings of the feelings of others, interpret what has transpired, and decode the cultural and personality quirks that give shading to a person's nonverbal behavior. Previous experience with a person allows us to better assess the "truth" or sincerity of what he or she says by reading nonverbal cues.

A second mechanism is counting the number of times people seek to control feelings—theirs or ours. The more aware we are of people attempting to control feelings, the more suspicious we are, and the flatter our own feelings become.

A third mechanism builds upon Scheff's (1979) insight that people have a need to express negative emotions. Impression management usually means the outward suppression of negative emotions. Unexpressed, they accumulate and manifest themselves in vindictiveness and other ugly responses. We would argue that the absence of the expression of negative feelings is another implicit or indirect indicator of impression management, and thus a lack of sincerity.

Among sociological theorists, Jonathan Turner (1987) recognizes the importance of affect in building trust as a motivation force, and Bradley (1987) insightfully analyzes the place affect occupies in the process of redefining relationships over time. Bradley notes that transforming social relationships requires an enormous mobilization of energy. Communion based on affective communication overcomes conventional barriers to role redefinition and imbues people with the energy required when one seeks new ways of arranging ties with others. And that communion also helps us develop more complex selves (Aron & Aron, 1986).

Freudian Slips

There is a self-corrective in social interaction that helps true feelings be expressed. As we interact with people we know well, nonverbal slips occur. Sigmund Freud's concept of the Freudian slip was a verbal slip, not a nonverbal one. We propose broadening his idea to include both verbal and nonverbal messages that lead us to recognize when people are not committed to their statements, in essence, when they are being dishonest. Since nonverbal reactions are harder to control than verbal ones, nonverbal slips occur more often.

When do these unintentional slips occur? Existential philosophers have described moments of crisis when the truth of our position is dramatically revealed to us. For example, Camus's *The Stranger* (1988) describes the moment when an existential man, who has killed for no reason, suddenly sees the world as it truly is moments before his execution. This is an extreme example, but it illustrates a very common category of events, namely role failure. When we fail in roles and admit this to ourselves, not just cognitively but emotionally, a sick feeling comes into the pit of our stomachs. It is at this point that we have a meaningful opportunity to reconsider the direction of our lives and change our behavior. If, on the other hand, we assume no responsibility for some role failure, then we will continue to repeat the same error.

Another avenue for our discovering what people believe most fundamentally is in the nonverbal emotional slips we make when we are off guard during a crisis. In everyday interaction, moments of truth will occur when our real principles and our cherished assumptions about life surface. We may choose to suppress verbal expressions of those feelings in order to avoid conflict; but the signs are relayed in second-channel communication to anyone who is tuned in to that channel. And awareness that the person in the other role is being less than fully open and honest with us has a weakening effect on the relationship.

The capacity to "read" both levels of discourse—the rational verbal and the emotional nonverbal—is critical for a whole series of activities (Chapter 5). It is needed to construct meaningful relationships, to bring order out of the chaos of social interaction, to build teams, to think creatively, and to solve problems. It lies at the heart of the "how" of negotiated process. Emotions allow for the expression of new ideas that are fundamental for creative problem solving. And they allow for effective symbolic interaction, which is needed to make teams work, to renegotiate roles and relationships, and to handle large amounts of social interaction. Of course, the very technology that is transforming relationships and making affective communication more important also poses barriers to affective communication. Reliance on electronic mail and the most common forms of telecommuting cut down on second-channel communication, a problem that poses new sociological challenges in the workplace.

Being able to successfully renegotiate role relationships so central to everyday life in PI society requires that we be able to understand the feelings of role partners, feelings that will not always be expressed verbally. By detecting fear, anger, or sorrow, we learn what is negotiable and what is not negotiable. American negotiators from the State Department have frequently misinterpreted silence as agreement in their negotiations with the Japanese, not fully recognizing that silence is common to many cultures as an emphatic way of saying "no." Silence is also a way of saying "no" among a number of Native American groups. Regardless of the culture or language, an emphatic "no" is more often communicated by gesture or inflection than by word, including inactivity when action is expected. Such gestures are easily learned, but the "listener" must have an emotive or non-verbal road map in order to read them.

Along with Freudian slips, we might also mention a very special class of social interactions, the symbolic act. This is the gesture that takes on special meaning because it marks a change from some norm or past state. Peace offerings in the midst of hostility fall into this category. A husband may not participate much in housework; most do not. But if he tries to do so, it becomes an important symbolic gesture to the wife and says a great deal about his feelings regarding the marriage.

This also has everyday implications. The interaction demands that come with more complex roles require that people develop better communication skills, accurately read emotions, and understand the critical importance of symbolic acts. We "sit up and take notice" of discrepancies from past norms because in periods of flux, they can cause a breach in relationships. That is, they tend to symbolically challenge the ways things have been done in the past, which can call the status of the entire relationship into question (Garfinkel, 1967). Symbolic acts of this sort can be volatile junctures. The emotions that end up being expressed in the heat of the moment tend to feed on one another and determine the future direction of the relationship. Both deviation from a usual pattern, and what is signaled after a disagreement or conflict, are exceedingly important because they frequently result in a recasting of the emotional disposition between people, which precipitates the redefinition of the role relationship.[3]

The Growing Importance of Emotions

The creation of a section on emotions within the American Sociological Association was no accident. It reflects the increased interest

in feelings as a topic of research. We believe interest has grown because emotive communication is of growing importance in a changing PI world. In a more complex world people have to spend more
time in problem solving. Much of this problem solving involves
time spent with people who are different from us occupationally,
culturally, or otherwise. So our communication skills need to be more
acute. To be effective, we need to use nonverbal and emotive communication as well as verbal and cognitive communication.

There are also a number of other factors at work promoting affective
communication. Television and more recently video, among the major
socialization agents of this generation, have sensitized viewers to
the nonverbal aspects of communication. While radio forced people
to concentrate on voice alone and thus was largely cognitive, television allows us to see the nonverbal gestures and thus gives us un-
conscious data about symbolic interaction and symbolic acts. Furthermore, television has brought into our homes different kinds of
people, so that our knowledge of many different kinds of personalities and cultures has also broadened. It should not be forgotten that
the first generation raised on television, those born in the late 1940s
and early 1950s, was the generation of the sixties. One of this generation's complaints about society was its plastic conformist quality.
Part of the message of the 1960s was a revolt against impression
management and the suppression of feelings. While Woodstock, communal living, and love children may now strike us as extreme, the
fact remains that their common theme was the importance of being
genuine, spontaneous, and free in expressing one's feelings.

The growing importance of feelings has also transformed gender
roles. One sign of more complex gender roles is the idea of the sensitive male as opposed to the "macho" male. And a dramatic sign
of the new legitimacy for emotional expression among men is the
growth in the wildmen movement, started by Robert Bly (*The New
York Times Magazine*, 1990). The coming of age of the sensitive male
is important because it allows males to express emotions, which, in
turn, makes for more effective symbolic communication. As men
become more in touch with their feelings, they can more easily take
the role of the other and be more effective team members.

How far we have come in the destruction of impression management is exemplified in the recent Gulf war. Soldiers reported being anxious and having fears about battle. It was a far cry from the macho behavior of Rambo. There was less public reporting of emotional states 20 years earlier, when soldiers were expected to put on a brave front, at least during the initial years of Vietnam.

When we perform certain activities and find ourselves enjoying them, we have discovered an important ingredient of our self. If we are in touch with our feelings, we can sense which roles are compatible with our self. But if we have been playing routinized roles and engaging in impression management, we are not likely to be in touch with those feelings and we may make wrong choices about who we are and what we should do.

There are a number of ways in which we can discover what our true self is. We can listen to ourselves in conversations. If we are reflective, we will note that in some conversations our total being is involved. When this occurs we should recognize that something deep inside us is being tapped. Sustained enthusiasm is another sign that we are making choices consistent with who we really are and what we really want. It is also the case that role partners point out problematic aspects of the fit between self and our pattern of activities. If we listen on a nonverbal level, they give us insights via nonresponses to statements we make, questioning looks, and other cues signaling that they think we misperceive our own basic needs or the match between those needs and our activities and commitments. Thus, symbolic communication on an emotive level becomes critical in the search for one's identity and destiny.

Being in contact with one's feelings does not guarantee perfect judgment. People make mistakes. The issue is how quickly we learn from them, if at all. It is here that feelings are so helpful. Feelings are signposts to the discovery of the self that can be decoded if we reflect on the activities that bring us a sense of gratification. Maslow (1954) suggests that self-actualization is the highest human need. We agree, and believe the complex selves that will be characteristic of postindustrial society will find the highest level of actualization, will receive the greatest amount of emotional gratification, when being creative and responsive to the needs of others. While efficacy for

industrial selves came from task completion, efficacy for complex
PI selves comes from mastery over problems.

Conclusions

Descartes's famous dictum, "I think, therefore I am," in PI society
needs to be altered to "I feel, therefore I am." Descartes was concerned with the rational proof of existence, with mind, while our
concern is with the discovery of affect, with the self. The discern-
ment of our individual identity is no less difficult a task than the
philosophical proof that we exist. And just as Descartes looked for
some assertion that appeared to be self-evident, we want to make a
similar argument about the discovery of self. We believe that feelings lie at the core of the choice of self and the construction of role
relationships. Our most fundamental point is that heightened levels
of emotive communication are essential because societal change
necessitates role redefinition; customizing roles can only be accomplished in an environment of interpersonal trust, and interpersonal
trust is predicated on emotional communication and commitment.

In our proposed linkage between the post-industrial institutional
transformation toward greater complexity and the need for greater
skills in negotiation, expressing emotion, and being creative, we have
in effect combined a form of functional theory with symbolic interactionism. **Post-industrial society has a set of prerequisites for success at the micro level that make the symbolic interactionist framework particularly opportune.**[4]

We thus conclude that our view of symbolic interaction and its emphasis on feelings allows us to unite the existential literature with
the sociology of emotions. Impression management, common and
perhaps necessary in industrial society, has become dysfunctional.
Being in touch with our own unsuppressed feelings, and being open
to feedback from others, provide critical mechanisms for the ongoing construction of the complex self an individual will need for life
in PI society. The pursuit of extrinsic rewards rather than intrinsic
gratification results in alienation—an unharmonious commitment
to social roles that ignore what we really are and deny what is right

for us. This is one example of the role/person misfit described by Ralph Turner (1990). To cover it up, many people engage in impression management, but this is to cleave to an inappropriate industrial adaptation to the PI world. What people should do, instead, is redefine the role relationships in which they find themselves to better fit their own needs. This is the subject of Chapter 5.

Notes

1. One might ask why we have chosen symbolic interactionism, rather than social exchange theory or some other branch of social psychology, as a micro foundation for our work. First, symbolic interaction deals with a broader class of social interactions. Not all relationships are exchanges of resources, but emotion and reading of gestures are common to all. Second, symbolic interaction is compatible with a perspective on social roles. The ideas of taking the role of the other, negotiated order, role failure, and the redefinition of roles are critical in understanding how post-industrial society impacts on social life at the micro level.

2. Other studies have touched on the point that in every conversation, the affective importance of the individual is being communicated. Randall Collins (1981) has suggested the emotional importance of belonging, but has not indicated the mechanisms by which this occurs. Sacks, Schegloff, and Jefferson (1978) explore the ways in which conversational discourse is constructed to display sensitivity toward the various participants in a conversation. But few other ethnomethodological studies try to isolate the axes of affective communication as we do here. Nevertheless, the recent burgeoning literature on semiotics focuses on the double channels of communication or on affective meaning. Much of discourse analysis looks at texts from a cognitive perspective, even if it is multidimensional. For example, Foucault has explored the symbols of power in architecture, in discipline, in madness, and the like, but not the symbols of feeling, emotion, or affect.

3. Much the same is true of the organizational level (*Administrative Science Quarterly*, 1983; Ott, 1989; Schein, 1985). Leaders create organizational culture via symbolic acts. For example, if employees are not laid off in times of economic crisis, then this symbolic act says a great deal about a company's commitment to individual employees. Leaders who seek advice from subordinates and implement their ideas are also sending powerful symbolic messages. This is one of the chief characteristics distinguishing the large Japanese firms, which are so competitive internationally (Vogel, 1979). Again, the principle is the same. It is important to be consistent in word and in deed, and that consistency must permeate body language as a crucial media for symbolic communication.

4. A key interactionist question revolves around negotiation processes in role development, as explored in the work of Anselm Strauss (e.g., Strauss, Schatzman, Bucher, Ehrlich, & Sabshin, 1964) and other recent literature (e.g., Birenbaum, 1984;

Powers, 1981a; R. Turner, 1990; Zurcher, 1983). This is in contrast to the functional treatment of roles, as best exemplified in the work of Linton (1936), Nadel (1956), Merton (1968), and Gross, Mason, and McEachern (1958), which specified a great deal of prescription in roles, especially taking form in codification as a consequence of the process of rationalization. Sets of expectations were thought to remain more or less stable over time, which made anticipatory socialization feasible (Burr, 1976). But routinization processes are now being replaced by the process of complexification described in Chapter 2.

5

ROLE REDEFINITION
The Pivotal Micro Process

This book began with a discussion of the widespread breakdown of social roles and institutions. Each chapter, in its own way, deals with role redefinition as the inescapable social reality of PI life. Our intent in this chapter is to directly address the contemporary importance and the operating dynamics of role redefinition. We suggest that role failure is occurring because massive changes, broadly labeled as the transformation to post-industrial society, require people to redefine roles far more than ever before; but only those individuals with complex selves, creative minds, and well-developed two-channel communication skills can keep up with the pace of redefinition and take it in stride.

These changes require the development of a theoretical framework appropriate to the conditions of the postmodern epoch (Denzin, 1991). Unfortunately, past discussions of role making are quite static, as Ralph Turner (1990) points out. There has been surprisingly little research on changes in the definition of occupational roles (Miner, 1987, is one exception) and not much more on redefinition of family roles. So the question we pose for Chapter 5 is: When and how are roles and role relationships redefined (based on work begun by Powers, 1981a)?

Our imagery is that roles must be reconstructed or remade periodically. This does not mean that they are in constant flux. Indeed, we believe that an image of continual change has deflected people from perceiving either the need for periodic role redefinition or the necessity of having negotiations every so often. We prefer the terms *redefinition* and *remaking* to emphasize this and to stress the missing links among technology, role, and symbolic communication.

Our first task, then, is to convince the reader that role redefinition is one of the truly ubiquitous features of contemporary social life. Our second task is to not only explore the dynamics of role and self redefinition but also try to specify the conditions under which people are most likely to reshape their social attachments.

Role Redefinition: The True Locus of Social Creativity

Role redefinition has always been ubiquitous because movement through the life cycle makes it necessary for people to reconfigure their relationships as children grow and adults gray (R. Turner, 1990). This goes almost without saying, which is why we maintain that role redefinition justly deserves attention as one of the few truly generic and ubiquitous processes at work in the social world—ranking in importance with socialization and stratification (Powers, 1990).

What is needed is a theory of human agency that specifies the conditions under which people are likely to redefine their relationships with others. We see many signs that traditional role designs are not working well and need to be renegotiated. The widespread pattern of contemporary role failure indicates that traditional roles are somehow ill-suited to the changing circumstances in which many people must live out their lives.

Literature on roles has paid little attention to innovative role redefinition as a pervasive adaptive strategy (Powers, 1981a, and R. Turner, 1990, are exceptions). Family literature, for example, tends to emphasize how little change there has been in gender roles (e.g.,

Brayfield, 1990; Mason, Czajka, & Arber, 1976). And the innovation literature, which primarily resides in organizations (e.g., Aiken & Hage, 1971; Daft, 1989; Daft & Becker, 1978; Hage, 1980; Zaltman, Duncan, & Holbek, 1973), has ignored this analytical micro level, although Barley (1990) is an exception. As a consequence, we have been largely ignoring one of the most fundamental dynamics at work in the social world.

Creativity in the reconstruction of social roles cannot be taken for granted. We would note, for example, that the most striking observation to be made about the husband-wife and father-mother roles in recent decades is that so many people have chosen to abandon relationships in trouble rather than redesign them. Divorce is frequently the way out of relationships that no longer meet people's needs. The fact that one quarter of all the children in the United States are being raised by single parents is striking evidence that large numbers of men and women have been unable to make their husband-wife or father-mother roles work. We wonder why so many people have been unable to redesign their marriages to meet their changing needs. And we ask how people who have redefined their relationships have managed to do so.

There is a great deal of completely individual creativity involved in role redefinition; that is, individuals invent solutions to the problems they face. But a great deal of borrowing also occurs as individuals learn about new strategies from their friends or the popular media, especially television. Some mixture of independent invention and borrowing is usually what occurs. They are difficult to disentangle (Rogers, 1983), and they are both very much part of the role redefinition process. Roles are, after all, very complex combinations of activities, especially in the family and at the workplace. Independent invention might be responsible for one activity, for example, the distinctive family ritual of spending long hours talking at the dinner table on Friday evenings. Some other activity might be borrowed, for instance, swimming on Saturday afternoons at the Y.M.C.A. because your friends do it and you have heard them say that "a family that plays together stays together." Independent invention and borrowing are both examples of creative innovation, and the latitude for both is growing ever wider as we enter the PI period.[1]

The concept of alternative designs for a given class of role relationships (e.g., husband-wife) is like the problem of isotopes in chemistry: Many stable configurations are possible. Interestingly, the number of family and work forms has increased rather dramatically in recent years. This is a recurrent theme in our analysis of PI society: greater complexity and greater variety are possible. Successful role redefinitions are usually constructed by joint design and are therefore examples of group problem solving, a point missed in most approaches to human agency where the emphasis is on the single individual's experiences (e.g., Giddens, 1984). In the case of two-career couples, for instance, we would expect both members to be involved in negotiating spousal roles, and to agree on expectations and patterns of behavior tailored to their particular relationship.

This suggests one reason why so many marriages may be in trouble. Marriages used to stay together because the outside pressures against leaving the nuclear family were too great to ignore. But outside pressures—legal, economic, social—have now largely subsided, so there is a greater tendency for marriages to be blown apart by centrifugal force, unless the reduction of unifying pressure from outside the relationship is compensated for by greater internal adhesion based on interpersonal commitment. Such commitment can only be sustained if people creatively redesign their roles in light of shifting conditions, sometimes by borrowing ideas from others and sometimes by independently inventing change. It is hard to stay committed to a relationship when you feel the role demands you are being held to are inappropriate or impractical, given your own changing circumstances.

Role redefinition involves at least four different dimensions of social creativity: problem recognition, thinking up strategies for change, implementation of solutions, and conflict resolution. Each is more difficult than it sounds. Recognizing that something is wrong in a role relationship may not seem like a creative act, but it is usually the most difficult step in the role redefinition process. Many marriages falter because one or both members fail to recognize that something is wrong until it is too late; that is, until resentments have accumulated and hurts have built up so much that redefinition is no longer possible, and the marriage ends up being dissolved so that the partners can try their luck elsewhere (Clough, 1986). And the same often happens in business, with managers failing to recognize either the source or the magnitude of employee discontent until labor-management relations become unalterably adversarial.

It is critical that we learn to monitor changes in ourselves and in role partners. **Far too often, problems in role relationships go undetected because personal change builds continually, but is easy to ignore until a crisis point is reached.** In the space of a few years, a great deal of stress can build up but may not be perceived until some threshold is passed, when, as we have already observed, it may be too late. Signals of growing problems are observable in nonverbal communication, but are recognizable only to people who perceive second-channel communication fairly well (Chapter 4). If it sounds like we are describing an earth tremor, the analogy might not be too farfetched. Pressure builds quietly beneath the surface until, if it is not relieved by periodic role redefinition, it gives the relationship a real jolt. Relationships in which people read second-channel communication have internal seismographs; others do not.

Unfortunately, partners in role relationships—marriage being only one example—usually bring the concept of stable role expectations into the relationship. Signing marriage contracts is but one manifestation of this assumption. Whether formally or informally understood, agreements of this kind—ones that fix the expectations attached to role partners—should stipulate that annual renegotiation is necessary. Although partners may carefully negotiate a division of labor at the time of the contract, we doubt that any single arrangement can be permanent, especially in a contemporary marriage.

Reliance on traditional role scripts as a substitute for redefinition is a bad idea, for it puts people in the position of having to meet old expectations plus new demands that may be inescapable in the face of present socioeconomic conditions, such as the necessity of having two incomes to provide the same standard of living one income would have provided 25 years ago. When conditions change, old role designs often become untenable (R. Turner, 1990). It is impossible for a woman to be superwoman, maintaining unmodified the role behaviors traditionally associated with being a wife and mother while at the same time meeting all the demands of full-time employment.

The role of superwoman is a prescription for role disaster because it puts too much stress on the woman. The role of superman is the same. One person cannot be the attentive husband and father, always present and focused on the needs of family members, and at the same time completely absorbed with his work. Trying to do both presents a clear case of role strain because there is not enough time to do both (Chapter 6). And too often those strains are perceived as originating from a partner who is unrealistic and uncompromising, which changes the emotional tone of the relationship. This is not a formula for marital happiness, a fact to which a good many people can attest from experience.

Potential Solutions to Problems in Role Redefinition

The potential solutions are many. In the two-career family, for example, a husband can assume responsibility for concrete activities that were traditionally a part of the wife/mother role—shopping, doing the dishes, cleaning the house, doing laundry, or whatever. Unfortunately, recent research (Brayfield, 1990) indicates that only in child care, which is a nonroutine activity offering emotional rewards, is there much sharing. The routine and boring activities in the household are largely performed by women. We are asking for more from superwomen than supermen, but the risks are still the same: role burnout, conflict, and divorce.

Clearly the prescription is for more role redefinition; the right prescription is, in a sense, for less prescription. Tasks can be reallocated to create many new definitions of gender roles, spouse roles, parent roles and, we might add, even children roles. Latch-key children embody one new role definition, although not one that we would recommend. Day-care centers are also defining new roles for children, sometimes good and sometimes bad. But regardless of what reallocation takes place, the solution has to be **negotiated**. And the negotiation may involve third parties, including therapists, teachers in school, aides in day-care centers, and so on. It is a group product requiring group creativity.

Even if a successful solution is adopted, ongoing improvisation is always necessary; one round of negotiations is unlikely to be enough. For instance, in the dual-career couple, partners may discover that the husband has to adopt a more equal share of the load of maintaining the household. But solutions are not likely to be static. Instead, there is a continual need to redefine what the expectations are for each of the partners; that is, a need to periodically redesign the roles of both partners.

A major theme in the first two chapters is that roles are growing more complex and more demanding. One way of measuring pressure on the individual is by contrasting the amount of time one spends on job-related pursuits with the number of hours one feels he or she should work each week. The gap is a measure of **role strain** or stress. And as the number of hours demanded by one role expands, people are likely to feel they are shortchanging other roles by denying them the time they deserve (Coser, 1969).[2]

Boredom is another interesting issue. One consequence of rapid technological change is that people grow accustomed to variety and change, a need that may not be met very well by one role partner. The increasing propensity to complain about boredom in relationships—about inadequate variety—suggests that this is becoming more of an issue as time progresses. Boredom is an important source of entropy, even in those relationships where there is a deep and abiding commitment between partners (Simmel, 1950). The solution is variety (Ashby, 1956). Seeking variety in new role partners is, of course, an option. But this tends to be only a temporary remedy for a chronic deficiency because, with the passage of time, a new partner is likely to seem just as boring as the first did. Perhaps that is why second marriages are as likely to end in divorce as first marriages. A different solution to boredom is to redefine existing relationships to include new activities. Leisure activities are a good place to start. This can be done without having to change partners, but calls for more creativity than many people are in the habit of bringing into a relationship—again, the problem of industrial selves dealing inadequately with PI life.

Like everything else, adding new and more varied activities to the design of a relationship requires negotiation. But adding new activities has much to recommend it. For one thing, this can lead to many new insights about the people we thought we understood completely.

New sides of people come out when different activities are performed, especially if those activities are performed jointly. The directions in which role relationships can evolve in the future seem
almost endless, because PI technology is opening up alternative
forms of leisure and new ways of transacting business.

Parent-child negotiations are another matter and have quite an
interesting history. The period we call adolescence has lengthened
steadily (Shorter, 1975). The teenage years start earlier, in part because
of a drop in the age of puberty (Bullough, 1981). At the other end,
young people stay in school longer and start work later (Friday &
Hage, 1981). Educational and occupational changes thus work to keep
young people dependent on their parents longer (e.g., R. Collins,
1979) and delay entry into adulthood. This has created a contemporary crisis. College graduates who still live at home have a compelling need for rather drastic redefinition of the relationships with their
parents. Divorced children who return to live at home, even in their
30s, find themselves in much the same situation, embroiled in role
conflicts that require renegotiation of expectations.

Even more dramatic are those families who take care of their elderly
parent(s) or grandparent(s). This requires a whole series of role redefinitions as people grow more frail and become progressively less
capable of caring for themselves. It entails a clear reversal of roles
as the older generation loses power, and the authority to make the
most personal kinds of decisions gravitates into the hands of their
children. This marks a difficult transition for everyone. Roles need
to be thoroughly redefined, often in the face of stiff resistance and
understandable resentment. And we have not broached the question of changing relationships between grandparents and grandchildren, or between parents and children when a grandparent needing
attention has been introduced into the family. Complex families
must develop collective solutions if they are to stay together.

Role reversal has increased dramatically in recent years. Prior to
1970, most older people were able to care for themselves until some
debilitating illness set in, and death followed shortly thereafter, typically in a matter of months. The knowledge explosion has resulted
in a significant increase in life expectancy; and people are staying
healthy somewhat longer. But the real extension of survival rates in

later life has been in keeping people alive after debilitating illnesses have permanently reduced physical abilities and vitality. As a result of the knowledge explosion, it is not uncommon for life to continue for years or even decades after the capacity for independent living has been lost. In this situation radical role redefinition is inescapable.

People who want to facilitate role redefinition have to think about the best ways of implementing change. They have to help one another play new parts in the micro drama of the relationship. Among other things, this means finding situations where change is the easiest for the people involved. It means recognizing that one sometimes has to start with small steps in the right direction before large steps can be taken. Hence, for the husband who agrees to do the shopping, it may mean having the shopping done only once a week because that is easiest for him. It may mean relying more on frozen foods rather than fresh foods, since these last longer in the refrigerator.

Our analysis is one of hope. Relationships can be redefined, so relationships in trouble can be transformed rather than discarded, assuming both people are able to "listen" on an emotional level, have flexible self-concepts, and can entertain innovative ideas. And we are convinced that people start to develop these qualities when they live in a post-industrial milieu.

Failure to Successfully Redefine Roles

In the short span of a decade or two our society has moved out of the industrial era and into the PI era (Chapter 1), and **complexification has reduced the utility of role scripts** (Chapter 2). Unfortunately, individuals were not adequately trained or properly socialized for the enormous task and heavy responsibility of defining their own rules of conduct (Chapter 3). Here we find a kind of cultural lag, including the failure to change patterns of socialization to prepare people to read symbolic communication (Chapter 4). This has been especially true for men: one reason why male managers and husbands have not altered their behavior very much.[3] Our point is that the average person with an industrial mind-set does not have the interaction **skills** necessary to accommodate constant role change and maintain coherent interpersonal relationships at a time of rapid change, which is why roles are failing and social institutions are breaking down. Mead failed to foresee how important the ability to read emotions on the nonverbal level would become when industrial rationalization gave way to post-industrial complexification (Chapter 4).

Many in the transitional generation have suffered. Face it, the recent record of human happiness has not been all that great. Creativity becomes steadily more critical in PI society precisely as standard role scripts lose their utility, allowing people more freedom to co-determine the configurations of activities defining their role relationships. But this means being able to resolve role conflicts about the ways in which interdependent roles should have their duties and responsibilities reallocated.

The '60s people were largely correct in their claim that we could live without **societal** restrictions, but they were incorrect if they felt that anarchy could survive. **What is needed to replace societal ritual is customized ritual adapted to the unique personalities of role occupants in a given relationship**. The reason why the ritual has to be customized is that individuals have different tastes, which spring from professional specialization, cultural diversity, and the increasingly important leisure self (Dubin, 1979). As the office party is eliminated, one must discover what those in the office would prefer to do. This varies, of course, with each individual.[4]

Seldom in history have people had to live through such dramatic change with so little appreciation of the stress which that change has put individuals through. The only reasonable parallel is the first industrial revolution, which had devastating effects on the family and other social institutions. In fact, the damage caused by the first industrial revolution gave rise to sociology as a field of inquiry. A number of sociological classics that are still read today were born of that upheaval. The post-industrial epoch has similarly generated a whole series of new fields and subfields—network analysis, the sociology of the emotions, and the new cognitive psychology are examples, even if we still await the classics of this period.

Let us now shift to the micro level and think about what is needed. How can we construct role relationships that can endure? How can we design role relationships that simultaneously maximize human happiness and empower human agency? In essence, we are searching for the procedural link, the micro methods people use to construct and maintain social order (Hilbert, 1990). People need to improve in problem recognition, thinking up strategies for change, implementation of solutions, and conflict resolution.

Symbolic communication is the way in which we learn about the potential for role conflict. In close relationships we are likely to say "yes" to doing something when, in fact, we mean "no." The half-hearted tone is a signal that there is not much interest. The more each role partner is attuned to the nonverbal level, the quicker there can be the honest, open communication that good relationships need and that Habermas advocates for changing society. One of the paradoxes about role failure is that many people feel that something is wrong before they can verbalize. By the time the problem can be articulated, enough resentment has built up to produce an emotional explosion. The more that individuals block their feeling via impression management, the longer the delay before they recognize that something is wrong, and the more violent the explosion will be. Rage has its origins in previously incomplete presentations of self.

Toward a Theory of Role Redefinition

Each of our earlier chapters suggests that role change is the very essence of social life in PI society. Consequently, the dynamics of role change must occupy a central place in any theory having utility for this new epoch (Powers, 1981a, 1990). Ralph Turner pioneered the study of role making (1968, 1990) and inspired our unfaltering interest in role change. Each of the chapters in this book poses and answers a question. Our question for Chapter 5 is: When and how are role relationships and interpersonal attachments redefined?

Symbolic interactionism offers the clearest link between established sociological theory and the theme of role redefinition. For Mead (1964), the most fundamental tenets of symbolic interactionism are that people exchange gestures, role-take, imaginatively rehearse, self-evaluate, and adjust their responses as they interact with others. That is, whenever we communicate with others, we reach conclusions about their intentions. By reading nonverbal communication we can infer the commitment levels of others to particular activities and to the relationship in general. We can feel the amount of confidence and enthusiasm they have (R. Collins, 1981). Our own self-concepts then influence our thinking as we consider alternative lines of conduct and select behavioral options that we believe will lead to some satisfactory end (Heise, 1979).

Actors are, to a degree, able to replace culturally prescribed obligations with role relationships that are in some sense customized. Even where behavior would appear to be cast into preprogrammed roles, patterns of action are sometimes subject to far-reaching renegotiation (Powers, 1981a; R. Turner, 1990). In fact, most people prove themselves to be quite innovative in occasionally restructuring their relationships with others. The issue we raise has to do with frequency. Post-industrial attachments seem to us to be redefined far more frequently and more thoroughly than would have been the case in any earlier era; and that is, we argue, the best way to overcome future shock. Role renegotiation and redefinition are mechanisms for responding to change and easing the transition to PI life. Indeed, ease with role redefinition will be required of people hoping to function normally in a future characterized by an accelerated rate of change.

The balance of this chapter is an attempt to explain the underlying dynamics of role redefinition. Sometimes the correct analytical frame from which to approach this issue is at the role level and sometimes it is at the self level. We move beyond the present literature by crystallizing this distinction and drawing it into focus, which in turn will enable us to comment on differences in role systems observed from one society to another. What results is a micro sociological theory, which integrates the principles of symbolic interaction with role theory in what we feel is an important new synthesis.

Interactionist Skills for Successful Role and Self Redefinition

As discussed in Chapters 3 and 4, George Herbert Mead's primary goal was to explain the articulation between individuals and society to account for the fact that a plethora of seemingly unrelated individuals with different goals can interact in meaningful and coherent ways. His answer is that society becomes part of the individual during the socialization process (e.g. Mead, 1964, pp. 152-164). Children must move through a series of developmental stages in order to acquire the requisite social skills to function adequately in human society. On the developmental road to becoming adults, children learn conventional gestures (in forced interaction as infants), acquire role-taking skills (in unstructured "play"), and learn how to imaginatively rehearse with a multiplicity of other role occupants simultaneously (in relatively structured "games"). The acquisition of these skills allows actors to enjoy indeterminacy, that is, to redefine situations and relationships without destroying the fabric of social life.

Built into Mead's analysis is an important supposition: For prolonged interaction to be both fluid (indeterminate) and coherent (orderly), actors must have, and be able to use, skills for role-taking and imaginative rehearsal. This leads us to posit that:

The basic capacity for redefinition is a positive function of the (1) frequency, (2) duration, (3) intensity, and (4) concentration with which actors are able to utilize learned capacities for (a) reading both cognitive and emotive gestures, (b) role-taking on both cognitive and emotive levels, (c) imaginative rehearsal, and (d) adjusted response.

While our discussion is couched in terms of role redefinition, the same preconditions apply to self-redefinition. As we tried to emphasize in the Chapter 3, the self emerges and is transformed through interaction with significant others. Encounters characterized by affect-laden communication are the ones that cause people to stop and reconsider their conceptions of self, and to subsequently consider alternative images of the self as an object: "moments of truth."

The Interaction Network and Conditions Inhibiting Successful Redefinition of Role or Self

Just as symbolic exchange facilitates role redefinition, inhibiting factors are also at work. As a result, many role incumbents who do

engage in regular, intense symbolic communication are nevertheless discouraged from deviating from culturally prescribed forms of
action. This is perhaps nowhere more clear than with family roles
in traditional societies. Conjugal interaction is certainly intense in
many family-oriented cultures, yet sex roles and gender-based division of labor are highly resistant to change. Although most obvious
in the Third World, one sign of this in the United States is resistance
to women reporters in male locker rooms. The debate about females
in combat roles is another.

Why should there be resistance to role definition? Three interrelated sources of resistance might be posited: anticipatory socialization, routinizing, and validation. Sociologists have long recognized
that anticipatory socialization discourages improvisation by defining the range of behavior deemed applicable for a particular role
(Merton, 1968). Burr makes this point most clearly in his classic (1976)
article on transition between roles. Anticipatory socialization not only
makes the transition to a new role easier but also makes the transition away from culturally defined scripts more difficult. As it happens, the roles for which people tend to receive the greatest amount
of anticipatory socialization (family, school, and work) are the very
roles in which people generally enjoy their richest symbolic exchanges.
Hence, the inhibiting power of anticipatory socialization is most
strong precisely where forces facilitating role redefinition—intense
interaction with people one knows well—are most clearly present.
Factors stimulating and retarding role redefinition can cancel themselves out.

Role scripts also inhibit role negotiation and improvisation. People have a tendency to produce and perpetuate a sense that things
are familiar in order to secure themselves against a fundamental fear
that our extended system of social relations may unravel. This is
accomplished by creating routine that makes the world more familiar and more predictable (Moscovici, 1981). Routine then becomes
a powerful inhibitor to change; people cleave to it because it reassures
them that their social world is intact and stable. It therefore tends to
reaffirm the status quo. There are many examples of this in the business
world, where past practice all too often inhibits future change: the
groupthink phenomenon, for instance.

Validation, the degree of approval expressed for a person's current role performance, can also act to inhibit change. The inhibiting effects of validation have been briefly noted by Zurcher (1983) and Birenbaum (1984). One of the authors first became aware of the awesome power of validation while working on a crisis intervention/ suicide prevention hotline. People seek affirmation and encouragement, and the search for affirming feedback can become quite overt and active when validation is not provided automatically by others. If absence of validation is prolonged, people eventually seek to design a role change. The new role design then needs validation and encouragement if it is to be acted upon. In contrast, the presence of validation for old patterns of behavior operates to inhibit change by encouraging similar role performance into the future.

Validation for role performance also encourages people to ignore the appearance of other problems. For years, American managers concentrated on profits as a sign that they were doing well, despite steady loss of market share to foreign competition. And too many American husbands take pride in their material accomplishments and fail to either see their kids taking drugs or notice that their superwoman wives are about to crack. Reactive rather than proactive management, both at home and in the workplace, reflects failure that is born of insufficient role redefinition: too little too late. Much of the problem stems from people's craving for validation, itself a peculiarly industrial addiction. Thus, we can begin to understand how social structural factors, as well as interaction dynamics, influence the actual propensity for social relations to evolve in a fluid and creative way (Powers, 1990). Combining these ideas leads us to posit:

> The degree to which people are inhibited from utilizing their capacities for redefinition is a positive function of (1) anticipatory socialization to role scripts and impression management, (2) routinizing of behavior and of feelings intendant in role scripts, and (3) need for validation from others.

And again, the same observations can be extended beyond roles to the self. For identities tend to be highly stable when old images are acknowledged and validated by others, but highly unstable when the self goes without validation for prolonged periods.

Recognizing that validation for past performance inhibits change in social relationships has important and far-reaching theoretical implications. It offers a challenge to any presumption of structural primacy by calling attention to the fact that something active must happen in order for the status quo to be maintained in present form. **Structural patterns only retain their stability as long as they are periodically reaffirmed by people engaged in symbolic interaction**. Structure must be actively maintained through symbolic interaction. Otherwise, it decays over time and eventually evaporates. This is another reminder that Blumer (1969) was right when he wrote that "society is symbolic interaction."

Characteristics of Roles and
Prospects for Role Redefinition

There are four major properties of roles themselves that seem to either facilitate or impede role redefinition. These are: (a) the scope of activities (e.g., job complexity), (b) rank in power or status, (c) degree of codification or formalization, and (d) the number of role relationships, or the size of the role-set.

Some roles, such as those on the assembly line, have only a few prescribed tasks (Blauner, 1964). There is little interaction among role occupants in such positions, except to ask for supplies. They have little control over the pace of work, and jobs tend to be low in power and status. Obviously, individuals on an assembly line have little opportunity to redefine their roles. In fact, this is part of the classic Marxian analysis of alienation, which views people as slaves to machines, controlled rather than in control. Workers can try to increase their collective influence by banding together in a union, but their personal status or power remains about the same, and their ability to redesign their jobs rarely increases.

At the other extreme are such roles as that of the president of a small corporation. This position is left largely unprescribed, with enormous latitude for the self to find expression. Much of the enactment time in the role is spent interacting with others. High rank makes it easier to redefine roles. The scope of activities is enormous as well. And different managers frequently choose to emphasize some of these over others, for example, advertising or sales or production or transportation or whatever, which gives special character to their management. Yet, there are clear limits as to how far the role can be redefined unless the entire organization is restructured (Wright, 1980).

Another important attribute is the size of the role-set, that is, the number of role relationships attached to a particular position (see Chapter 7). As the role-set increases in size, which tends to happen with the PI transformation, so does pressure to redesign roles by individualizing reciprocal patterns of rights and obligations. This latter point has not been recognized in the organizational literature. Extensive role-sets provide greater structural opportunities to redefine the nature of rights and obligations linking different positions. The opportunity occurs via role conflict, that is, the demand for change in the definition of the role relationship. Paradoxically, many of the problems of the role-set tend to disappear as role-sets expand and opportunities for role redefinition increase, provided that role conflicts are acknowledged. Finally, when the person-set is small, there is more pressure and more opportunity to individualize the role relationship. Combining these ideas together, we posit:

> Roles can more easily be redefined when their scope of activities is greater, when they are higher in autonomy and power, when activities are less prescribed, when there are many role relationships in the role-set, and when person-sets are small.

This proposition leads to some interesting conclusions when it is juxtaposed against the chief defining characteristic of PI society—an emphasis on research. Research leads to growth in role knowledge and the scope of activities attached to roles (see Chapter 2). Activity overload sets in motion pressures for the creation of new positions—in other words, structural differentiation—but it also sets in motion pressures for the redefinition of existing roles by reassigning activities and/or customizing the way in which activities are performed. The PI case is especially pertinent because professional and managerial occupations are expanding while unskilled and semiskilled occupations are contracting. High-autonomy roles are growing in number while low-autonomy roles are becoming a smaller proportion of the total labor force, fast-food chains notwithstanding. Consequently, role occupants are allowed ever-increasing amounts of latitude in orchestrating their ties with others.

Redefinition of Selves

It may strike readers as curious to ask which kind of selves are most comfortable with redefinition. But just as the characteristics of roles can either stimulate or retard change, so can characteristics of selves. Psychological stage theories call attention to variable qualities of the human psyche that can nourish self during the life course and therefore the need for change, a theme echoed in Ralph Turner (1990). We suggest that PI men and women will discover that the complexity of self grows as more roles can be co-determined and a greater variety of role definitions are tolerated.

But which selves are more likely to grow in complexity? Certainly not all do. Just as roles have properties, so do selves. The symbolic interactionists (Stryker, 1990) have observed that selves vary in the number of identities they combine, their ego strength and self-esteem, and in rigidity. We would add to this list the number of interpersonal relationships a self maintains.

Ego strength—which is not the same as a needy ego, or one who demands a lot of attention—also has implications for the redefinition of self. As ego strength increases, we are more inclined to make our needs known and we are less willing to remain in a dependent position. In this sense, growth in ego strength can be considered a form of maturation. A good measure of it is tolerance of cognitive inconsistency and acceptance of differences. The variety of friends of different perspectives a person has, and the ability to verbalize his or her own opinions with them, are thus good indicators of ego strength.

Symbolic interactionists have not talked much about the size of the person-set, but it is important for understanding how the redefinition of self takes place. As the size of a person-set decreases, it becomes more difficult for the self to be defined narrowly, in terms of either one role or a few personality attributes. One problem with juvenile delinquents is that they typically have few significant others (Friday & Hage, 1981), whether at work, in the family, or at school. As a consequence, their definition of self is determined by interaction with a very small group of others, and they are typically powerless to effect a renegotiation. Whyte demonstrates this in *Street Corner Society* (1981). In contrast, PI networks bring people into contact with a large number of diverse others, which not only makes it easier for people to envision alternatives but also increases the range of confederates who can help foster the difficult task of self-redefinition. Combining these ideas, we posit that:

> Selves can be more easily redefined when the scope of identities is greater, when ego strength and self-esteem are elevated, when there is less rigidity, and when there are more interpersonal relationships.

As interpersonal relationships increase, there is the possibility that these relationships can become more superficial. But if they do, we would suggest that these interpersonal relationships are by definition no longer interpersonal. In our opinion, a true interpersonal relationship requires that individuals confront individuals qua individuals; that is, engage their personalities, understand their identities, and comprehend their nonverbal communication.

For individuals the rapid technological change associated with the arrival of the PI era means frequent moves from one social role to the next, accompanied by periodic redefinition of continuing roles. This implies the acquisition of a large number of identities, with a corresponding increase in the complexity of the self. And as our selves grow in complexity, we increase our capacity to redefine what we see ourselves as: how we view ourselves as objects. In PI society people have increasingly more complex selves, which in turn means much more room for renegotiation and redefinition of self as well as social roles and role relationships.

Interplay Between Redefinition of Role and Redefinition of Self

We have been considering two different streams of redefinition: role and self. Macro societal change impacts directly on the definition of roles; then the self must change. In a sense the self must grow up to the role. But at the same time, the personal growth associated with changes in the self produces further critical reassessment and redesign of roles. We think of this as endogenous micro change. Successfully coping with new situations leads to a stronger self, which in turn is more likely to make new demands and be more comfortable with further change.

We started this chapter by saying that our main concern is with changes in social roles, but we have also maintained our interest in complex selves. A highly dramatic source of change, especially in the transitional period between industrial and PI society, is a misfit between characteristics of a person's roles and the self occupying these roles (Turner, 1990). Complex selves with strong egos tend to crave complex roles—and many of them. On the other hand, selves with only a few identities and little self-esteem tend to prefer simple roles—and few of them, preferably with little responsibility. Disequilibrium occurs when the roles a person occupies are poorly matched with that individual's self. This type of disequilibrium allows us to predict the likely direction of role change, and is therefore worth explicating.

One mismatch comes when we have highly complex roles where little is prescribed, with high rank and extensive role-sets, occupied by individuals who have few identities, weak ego strength, low self-esteem, rigid personalities, and few significant others. These selves are likely to play power games, for people with weak egos will compensate by using power to bolster their own self-esteem. Their game is "you must agree with the boss." A person with a strong ego would welcome and even encourage disagreement, but not so the individual with a shaky ego. Processes by which dissent is discouraged are amply described in Wright's (1980) description of Donnor in General Motors. When we keep the distinction between self and role in focus, it is easier to appreciate how major corporations can go wrong.

Family examples are harder to come by, yet any clinical psychologist knows of parents who lack complex selves and whose weak egos create problems for their children. Industrial fathers are very competitive and must win in competition with their sons. People are surprised to find middle- and upper-class parents capable of physical and sexual abuse. The surprise reflects a mistaken presumption about the fit between self and role. Knowing something about that fit allows us to make some predictions about the direction any role redefinition might take. When we focus on the fit between the nature of the self and the nature of social roles and psychological identities, we are again suggesting a functional argument that is built upon the assumption of consistency. Our predictions are as follows:

1. Selves with little ego complexity, low ego strength, and low self-esteem, in complex roles with high rank in power and status, tend to redefine those roles in the direction of more routine, greater ritual in interpersonal relationships, and more power games.
2. Selves with high ego complexity, high ego strength, and high self-esteem, in roles that lack complexity and have low rank, tend to redefine those roles in the direction of less routine, less ritual in interpersonal relationships, and fewer power games.

Symbolic interactionists appear to assume that most people want greater latitude for deciding how they will perform their roles; but this is not necessarily true. Just as some women want traditional roles (Gerson, 1985), some people feel more comfortable with codified scripts and impression management. Our first disequilibrium hypothesis accounts for this with what might be called the escape from freedom thesis. In this and the hypothesis that follows it, we have specified two sets of circumstances when role redefinition is likely to occur due to a mismatch between the characteristics of a role and the self occupying that role, a scenario that is particularly common during periods of great social transition, like the one we are in now. Furthermore, we have done a most un-Meadian thing: We have used his ideas to explain how capacity to read gestures, take the role of the other, imaginatively rehearse, and adjust responses

Table 5.1 Principles of Role and Self Redefinition

1. The basic capacity for redefinition is a positive function of the (1) frequency, (2) duration, (3) intensity, and (4) concentration with which actors are able to utilize learned capacities for (a) reading both cognitive and emotive gestures, (b) role-taking on both cognitive and emotive levels, (c) imaginative rehearsal, and (d) adjusted response.

2. The degree to which people are inhibited from utilizing their capacities for redefinition is a positive function of (1) anticipatory socialization to role scripts and impression management, (2) routinizing of behavior and of feelings through role scripts, and (3) need for validation from others.

3. Roles can more easily be redefined when their scope of activities is greater, when they are higher in autonomy and power, when activities are less prescribed, when there are many role relationships in the role-set, and when person-sets are small.

4. Selves can be more easily redefined when the scope of identities is greater, when ego strength and self-esteem are elevated, when there is less rigidity, and when there are more interpersonal relationships.

5. Selves with little ego complexity, low ego strength, and low self-esteem, in complex roles with high rank in power and status, tend to redefine those roles in the direction of more routine, greater ritual in interpersonal relationships, and more power games.

6. Selves with high ego complexity, high ego strength, and high self-esteem, in roles that lack complexity and have low rank, tend to redefine those roles in the direction of less routine, less ritual in interpersonal relationships, and fewer power games.

can be used both to make roles more script-like and to ritualize role relationships. Taken together, the principles presented in this chapter offer a powerful propositional inventory capturing important micro-dynamics of contemporary society.

Post-industrial society is providing many more opportunities to engage in renegotiation; but not all selves are capable of coping with this openness. One wonders if the growing category of never-married people reflects our lack of will or incapability to cope not only with changing jobs but also with changing family roles. If so, then future shock manifests itself in rigidification in some roles and in withdrawal from other roles because renegotiation, role redefinition born out of periodic adjustment to others, proves to be too much to handle. The current divorce rate does not argue well for people's skills at successfully accomplishing the high degree of renegotiation required in PI life. Similarly, one wonders if many of the people who opt for life-style rather than career are really opting out of having to confront role change in the PI workplace, particularly demands for problem solving in the face of uncertainty.

Keeping these many qualifications in mind, we can still say that the long-term thrust is for movement toward more complex selves and symbolic roles. At the same time mismatches between self and roles do occur, with the consequence of both much more rigidification at the top of the status hierarchy and many more attempts to break the mold at the bottom of the status hierarchy. Put another way, the arrival of the PI era is producing a lot of role conflict (Merton, 1968) in the classical sense of the term (Chapter 6). This is a pervasive problem, because society's basic social institutions are being restructured. The resulting mismatches between selves and roles produce conflicting expectations, and these trends will continue to magnify until either society nourishes creative minds with complex selves and teaches individuals how to read symbolic communication, or individuals learn this on their own. How these themes play themselves out will be explored in the chapters that follow.

Conclusions

Our intent is to carefully link macro societal change with micro consequences in the way social roles are defined. Turner (1990) notes that widespread societal change tends to be associated with role change on the individual level. We make a definitive connection around the theme of technological change. The current pattern of technological change is resulting in complexification of social roles and of selves. As a consequence, the definitions of behavior, of duties, and of obligations in roles are becoming more open, more subject to the effects of human agency, then ever before. This is quite liberating, but can also be destabilizing. For being able to redesign and reconstruct our relationships requires well-developed interaction skills, constant effort, the will to sustain a certain amount of emotional oscillation, and a great deal of cooperation from role partners. In our estimation, recent signs of widespread role failure reflect the failure of society to adequately train people to meet the demands for social creativity attendant in life in PI society. Right now we have what is rapidly becoming a PI society peopled principally by individuals who were raised in and shaped by an industrial milieu. As we nurture better interaction skills and help people be more comfortable with ambiguity, however, the promise of a socially satisfying life will be realized for more people.

The symbolic interactionist framework allows us to understand how role change and self change can occur, but does not tell us the direction change is likely to take. Nor does it provide a clear explanation of probable outcomes in the case of a misfit between role demands and qualities of self. As we indicate, the direction of change can be either toward choice or away from choice, depending upon the particular kind of mismatch found between self and significant roles. Thus, weak selves handle the movement toward indeterminacy by trying to routinize their social life or by retreating from roles altogether.

In the next two chapters, we develop the theme that role-sets are growing larger as more and more role relationships are added to the social configuration of each person's life. At the same time each reciprocating role is occupied by fewer and fewer people. Hence, there is much more opportunity for personality differences to exert themselves. In the old days, as functional role theorists correctly noted, ritual reduced individual differences and smoothed over personality conflicts. But now that the social prescriptions carefully designating the content of roles have been swept aside, and be assured that they have been swept aside, people must confront more of the naked beast of personality.

Any new theoretical synthesis should see role change as a source of self change, and vice-versa. And symbolic interactionism could be strengthened by placing more stress on larger societal changes that are increasing role indeterminacy: the focus of Chapters 6 and 7. Symbolic interactionists have also tended to downplay role conflict, a deficiency that role theory can help alleviate. That is the theme we consider in Chapter 6.

Notes

1. Once a need for role definition is recognized, it is common for a great deal of information search to follow. The emergence of magazines for female executives is

a form of this. Equally common are various self-help groups organized around particular role failure problems. Alcoholics Anonymous and drug rehabilitation centers are good examples. The government in some areas has also moved in with crisis centers and hotlines for people with various kinds of difficulties—suicide prevention lines and senior information and referral lines are now found in most urban areas.

2. In previous generations women had more children than they desired. Now they are having **fewer**. In other words, if given an opportunity, many childless women would have children, and many mothers would have larger families. A good many men feel the same way. This tells us something about the role strain people are now under.

3. One reason for the failure to adapt to PI society is the lack of socialization of men to read cues, especially nonverbal ones. This shift toward symbolic communication may be especially hard for males, since societally defined roles for men in the United States were historically based on the suppression of their own feelings and on relative insensitivity to the feelings of others, while societally defined roles for women have historically placed more emphasis on flexible response to individual personalities and unique situations (Ruddick, 1977).

4. Dramatic role failures are not necessarily the most common ones. More typically, role relationships "die" with a whimper via benign neglect, rather than flaming out with a bang, especially when miscommunication turns people off from one another—when we fail to read the symbolic signals. This happens to friendships all the time. Yearly change in Christmas card lists would make an interesting subject for studying social attachment and detachment.

6

ANALYTICAL TOOLS FOR UNDERSTANDING ROLE STRUCTURES

It is not enough to describe role redefinition as a micro process. We want to place role redefinition within a broader structural context. We are able to do that by drawing from two seminal works from the 1950s. Prominent among the central pillars of modern social theory is the conceptualization of role systems advanced in different contexts by Robert King Merton and Siegfried Frederick Nadel. Merton, in sociology, and Nadel, in anthropology, sought nothing short of explaining how the many roles occupied by a plethora of people are organized into the systems of relations that give society its structural form and organizational coherence. Both Merton and Nadel focused on ways in which roles might be integrated, but Merton was more concerned with the face-to-face aspects of role conflict and its resolution, while Nadel envisaged a broader problem of the patterning of relationships in the larger society. The two operative concepts that we want to draw from their work are **role-sets** and **role matrices**.

These can be seen as the forerunners of much of the current work in social network analysis (Boje & Whetten, 1981; Burt, 1977, 1980; Marsden & Lin, 1982).

The advances made by both Merton and Nadel are stunning for their parsimony. Merton's insights are alluded to throughout his book **Social Theory and Social Structure** (1968), and were developed in pointed form in his brilliant article on role-sets published in the *British Journal of Sociology* (1957), while Nadel's theories (1956) are presented in a compilation of brief papers published as a thin but provocative monograph, which was in press at the time of his death. The brevity of these works does not detract from their conceptual clarity, penetrating insight, and theoretical importance. We believe that, taken together, these works represent one of the great social scientific advances of the twentieth century. They establish that interpersonal relationships must be viewed as much more than a product of interaction among individual actors with different biographies, as Mead or Blumer would have done. Merton and Nadel offer us a meaningful way of understanding the social order as institutionalized arrangements of role-sets linked in social networks. But we believe that both men placed too much stress on scripts, and consequently failed to appreciate how dynamic role relationships really are.

Social Interaction From the Bottom Looking Up: Robert King Merton

The works of Robert King Merton need no introduction. Perhaps more than anyone else, he is responsible for the wave of structural-functional thinking that overtook American sociology during the 1940s, 1950s, and early 1960s, for it was Merton who introduced American sociologists to the British anthropological functionalism of Bronislaw Malinowski and A. R. Radcliffe-Brown, which had in turn been inspired by the earlier efforts of Emile Durkheim (see, for example, J. Turner & Maryanski, 1979). This was a fascinating period in American intellectual history.

Merton was one of the most inspiring advocates of structural-functional thinking, rejecting Parsons' rigidly predefined system of typological categories (e.g., presented nicely in the Appendix of Parsons & Platt, 1973) in favor of more open-ended analysis (e.g., Merton, 1968) and in his plea for middle-range theory in his presidential address to the American Sociological Association.

The Mertonian perspective advocates treating roles as different packages of socially recognized rights and obligations associated with a given social position or status, each package (father and husband, for example) representing a different role for the occupant of that position. It is his view of a social status having a set of roles attached to it, that we find useful for analyzing the changing face of PI society.

Basic Concepts: Status-Sets, Role-Sets, and Person-Sets

True to his understanding of middle-range theory, Merton suggests what seems like a simple and straightforward reconceptualization, but one that has far-reaching implications. Merton posits that each occupant of a status position interacts with not just one role but a set of roles, hence the term *role-set* (Merton, 1968). So a medical student who interns at a teaching hospital occupies the roles of student (with respect to faculty), doctor (with respect to patients), colleague (with respect to fellow students), and a rather ambiguous supervisory role relative to nurses.

To avoid possible misunderstanding, we should note that Merton uses the term *role-set* in two ways. In Merton's terminology a role-set is the agglomeration of roles a person maintains by virtue of occupying a particular position. But the term is also used by Merton to connote the people occupying the complementary roles with which one comes into contact. We prefer to call this latter concept a *person-set* (a term Merton used in some of his lectures but never developed) to avoid confusion (see Table I.2). These complexities have never really been dealt with in the role literature (Biddle, 1987), yet they allow us to build bridges between role theory, network theory, and Nadel's concept of role matrices.

We are emphasizing this analytical distinction because, as we shall suggest in the next chapter, as the number of **distinct counterpart roles** in a role-set increases, the size of each person-set paradoxically decreases. As this occurs there are more opportunities for the identities or the personalities of role partners to find expression. Consequently, interaction in role-sets is becoming more particularistic (Parsons, 1951). Person-sets vary a great deal in size. For example, a typical college professor will have hundreds of students and dozens of colleagues but only one dean and one department chair at a time. With fewer individuals connected to us in a given role relationship, we are more likely to engage in informal conversations that in turn allow for all the dimensions of the complex self to be expressed, and we become much more conscious of role style: energy level, personality traits, abilities, and so on.

At the time, Merton's formulation was a departure from conventional thinking. There had been discussion of the multiple roles people occupy, such as being a subordinate worker at the factory and coming home to the superordinate position of parent (Lenski, 1954). **But the concept of role-set is entirely different, because it accentuates the extent to which continued performance in a particular setting necessitates our simultaneously being involved in a host of different roles, which structure and coordinate our activities with the other people present in that same social environment.** Merton's focus is on relationships within a particular institutional sphere of activity: family roles, work roles, leisure roles, and the like.

It is thus that Merton suggests a role theory approach to the problem of order. For Merton, an inner tension rests in the fact that the people in role-sets must balance many different bundles of obligations that compete for time, even if they are not mutually incompatible on the face of it (also see Goode, 1960). Furthermore, each of us is constantly interacting with people who typically occupy different positions and are therefore likely to have expectations, viewpoints, and interests that differ from our own. Consequently, the potential for conflict and disruption is ever present. The perception that social systems need to maximize continuity thus motivated Merton's explorations in role theory. Of course, our own motivation is almost a polar opposite, although nonetheless still tacitly functionalist. We believe PI social systems must better prepare people for discontinuity. But before developing our own ideas, there are some very valuable insights to be gleaned from Merton's analysis of role conflict.

Basic Concepts: Role Conflict Over Expectations

Role conflict provides Merton with the central question he tries to address in the 1957 paper. How is order possible if tension is inherent in the very way in which humans organize their lives around role-sets?

> [M]embers of a role-set to some degree, [are] apt to hold social positions differing from that of the occupant of the status in question. To the extent that they are diversely located in the social structure, they are apt to have interests and sentiments, values and moral expectations differing from those of the status-occupant himself . . . this, then, is the basic structural basis for potential disturbance of a role-set. And it gives rise, in turn, to a double question: which social mechanisms, if any, operate to counteract such instability of role-sets and, correctively, under which circumstances do those social mechanisms fail to operate, with resulting confusion and conflict. (pp. 112-113)

Several of the implied ideas in this paragraph have gone undeveloped. But what they suggest to us is the possibility of integrating a wide number of major areas of scholarly inquiry.

Merton makes six observations about conflict and order in role-sets: First, some social roles are more important than others. When occupying statuses that are highly important to our sense of self, typically family and job roles, we are unlikely to compromise our judgment or alter our behavior in order to meet demands of the other social roles we occupy (Stryker, 1980).

Second, in most person-sets some individuals have more power than others, and there is some tendency for less influential people to bow to the wishes of more influential people. However, this is frequently less noticeable than one might expect because the influence of powerful personalities can be partially offset by coalitions among less-central or less-powerful people (Caplow, 1968).

Third, people are often protected by what Merton called "insulation from observability": It is frequently the case that not everyone involved in a person's role-set is present at the same time, so the person concerned can do some things without everyone knowing about it (Coser, 1961). For example, teachers feel free to say things to colleagues that they would be reluctant to say in front of students, and they may feel free to say things to students that they would say only reluctantly to colleagues.

Fourth, one interesting feature of social structure is that some positions are afforded far more "insulation from observability" than others (Crozier, 1964). Merton (1957, p. 116) argues that "there is an optimum zone of observability, difficult to identify in precise terms and doubtless varying for different social settings, which will simultaneously make both for accountability and for substantial autonomy, rather than for a frightened acquiescence with the distribution of power . . ."

Fifth, it is normal to find some degree of social support among people who occupy similar positions in the role-set. Sometimes the support is local; sometimes it comes from distant contacts, such as members of national professional associations. At root, this is something like what Marx had in mind when discussing class consciousness (Marx & Engels, 1967).

And sixth, some situations allow for replacing people if role conflict becomes pronounced. For example, many firms have a trial employment period during which they can relieve workers who seem, for whatever reasons, to be incompatible, and relieve them without any special justification.

This last mechanism is actually a logical error in Merton's own formulation. Replacing a person does not deal with a structural cause of role conflict. Structural change would involve the addition, subtraction, or redefinition of roles for the purpose of resolving or minimizing conflict. Analytical separation between the structural level of the role-set and the personal level is hard to maintain, but it is very important for understanding the structural basis of conflict, as opposed to interpersonal grounds for conflict.

Merton's role theory work had substantial impact. In particular, it paved the way for an entire body of literature on role conflict. Role conflict emerges when people are expected to live up to expectations that are incompatible (e.g., Gross, Mason, & McEachern, 1958). For instance, line foremen in factories find themselves in a difficult position, juxtaposed between the rank and file and management (Crozier, 1964). Noncommissioned officers in the military occupy positions similarly subject to role conflict. In addition, people sometimes face a combination of demands, which, taken together, are overwhelming, even when they are not technically incompatible or mutually exclusive. Goode (1960) referred to this as role strain.

Some very good work has been done on role conflict (see Gross, Mason, & McEachern, 1957; Kahn, Wolfe, Quinn, Snoeck, & Rosenthal, 1964) in the workplace (see Lawrence & Lorsch, 1967; Walton, Dutton, & Cafferty, 1969) and the classroom (Corwin, 1969, 1970; and for a recent review, Biddle, 1987). We feel that the concept of role conflict is even more relevant for sociology today than it was in the past because many of Merton's mechanisms of insulation are breaking down, as we shall indicate in Chapter 7.

We want to maintain a clear distinction between role conflict, status conflict, role or status stress and strain, and burnout. **Role conflict** refers to disagreements over what is expected from the occupants of various roles. Role conflict occurs, for example, when faculty expect students to study the night before an examination, and peers want their friends to drink beer until the wee hours of the morning. In contrast, **role strain** is the discrepancy between the amount of time we spend in one role and the amount of time we feel we should spend. **Status strain** is the discrepancy between the amount of time we spend on all the roles associated with a particular position or status, and the amount we feel we should spend. And **burnout** occurs with the sustained expenditure of more emotion in a particular role or position than the person thinks he or she should have to expend. **Status conflict** occurs when people in one role-set complain about commitments to other statuses as, for example, when a spouse complains that his or her partner spends too much time at work and too little at home. Status strain has come to be more common than role strain because it directly taps one of the most critical problems of PI men and women: integrating the demands of the different social roles that are given equal saliency. Burnout reflects an emotional component, a component that has usually been ignored in the role literature. Risk of burnout is becoming the norm in PI society, which is one reason people need more complex selves and fluid relationships to survive. It is also a reason recreation and leisure are gaining importance.

Table 6.1 The Problems Inherent in Status-Sets, Role-Sets, and Person-Sets

Role conflict =	differences in expectations governing what role occupants expect of one another.
Status conflict =	personal dissatisfaction or the dissatisfaction of people related to us in one role-set or status with the nature of our commitment to or our performance in another role-set or status.
Role strain =	the amount of **time** spent in a social role relative to the amount of time ego feels he or she should spend.
Status strain =	the amount of **time** spent in the salient social roles attached to a position, relative to what ego feels he or she should spend (the set of role strains).
Burnout =	the sustained expenditure of more **emotion** in a role or position than one feels he or she should expend.

Running through these various concepts are the following ideas. Role and status conflict resides in what others tell us to do, while role and status stress/strain and burnout reflect how we handle it. Strain reflects dissatisfaction with the way we spend our time and has become more prevalent precisely because the self is now more complex, and the compartmentalization of social life has been broken down. Concretely, as we add more and more complex roles and integrate work and family, status strain has become quite common and its manifestations are everywhere. Similarly, as emotions and feelings are expressed more in person-sets and we interact more with the whole personality and complex self, the emotional demands made upon us cause burnout to also become more typical. In general, strain and burnout are not being handled well, as evidenced by high rates of role failure.

Criticisms

One reason for the lack of development of middle-range theory is that neither Merton nor anyone interested in role theory ever identified properties of role-sets that are empirically measurable as well as theoretically interesting. Some are relatively simple; others are more complex. The dimension of complexity, we believe, is very important for understanding what is happening to role-sets in PI society and is a major theme in our analysis. Complexity of the self, role-sets, and role relationships are concepts that will allow us to explicate the impact of social change on the individual.

Beyond this, the relative emphasis on scripts has prevented the integration of role-set theory with the more radical forms of symbolic interaction (Chapter 5). As the formalization of rules declines, and role partners are given more choice to choose when, where, and with whom they interact, the independence of role relationships and role-sets increases and there is more room for human agency. But there is also more role ambiguity, which leads to more role conflict, status strain, and burnout. Blumer's (1969) ideal of creative, spontaneous people happily constructing their lives (see Furstenberg, 1990; Ihinger-Tallman, 1988) leaves out the downside (see Adler, Adler, & Fontana, 1987).

It is the instability of role-sets in post-industrial society that impresses us the most; or perhaps on a more positive note, it is their fluidity, to say nothing about the role redefinition we have already discussed. The fluidity of role-sets is manifested in a number of ways, including the addition of new positions and the subtraction of others. Unfortunately, the idea that a role-set is itself an analytical unit, like a group, was never pursued. We need to identify measurable dimensions, allowing us to describe role-sets and their implied networks and how they change across time, so that we can develop theories about role-sets and test them in rigorous ways.

Even the role conflict issue—Merton's basic question of social order —was never satisfactorily developed. Merton's interest in functional thinking led him to restrict his focus to those dynamics which maintain equilibrium and promote order, thus downplaying role conflict. We believe that there is much more conflict in role relationships and roles-sets than Merton appreciated and that role conflict will increase for a clear set of structural reasons.

Merton's work suggests a view of society as a complex configuration of role-sets and status-sets. The roles-sets we are allocated, or in some cases we choose, determine what persons we will come into contact with, what demands we will confront, and how our interaction with others will be structured. Role-sets provide a linkage between the individual and society.

This notion of role-set seems to us to be the best way of conceptualizing the social universe as it appears from the perspective of the individual. But what is missing from Merton's approach is an analysis of the way large numbers of roles-sets are concatenated into extended social systems, and how dynamic changes in the society at large articulate with and produce change in the role-set configuration of the average person. Merton looks up from individual experience to the level of role-sets. What is needed to complement this vision is a view downward, from the societal level to the level of the role-set. For this downward view we turn to S. F. Nadel.

Social Interaction From the Top Down:
Siegfried Frederick Nadel

Siegfried Frederick Nadel was Austrian by birth. He was a scholar of wide-ranging interests and earned a doctorate in psychology from the University of Vienna, in addition to a doctorate in anthropology from the London School of Economics. Nadel was a multidimensional man. Prior to attending the London School of Economics, he produced radio and music programs in Central Europe and toured for a time with his own opera company. Nadel's ear for sounds was very important to his career as an anthropologist, for he proved to be exceptionally quick to learn indigenous languages when he did fieldwork, and he appears to have been extraordinarily sensitive to linguistic nuances and distinctions. It was natural, then, for Nadel to be intrigued by the subtle distinctions in social relationships that find expression in terminology and other dimensions of language use. This drew him to the study of role systems as the topic for what proved to be his final book. Unfortunately, Nadel died unexpectedly at the age of 52, just before publication of *The Theory of Social Structure* in 1956. His death was a great loss to social science.

Among anthropologists, Nadel is best known for his earlier publications. He did his first anthropological fieldwork among the Nupe in Nigeria. What he and his wife discovered was a complex social order with a well-developed economy and a sophisticated legal system. They returned to the Nupe at the end of 1935, this time capitalizing more directly on his previous psychological training by focusing on the relationship between culture and personality. His study of the Nupe, *A Black Byzantium*, published in 1942, attracted great attention in the anthropological community and was long considered a classic. His later work took him to other parts of Africa and eventually to Australia.

Nadel visited Britain in 1955 to give a series of lectures on his theory of society, which were published in monograph form just after his untimely death on January 14, 1956. It is this series of lectures in which we are most interested, for it is here that Nadel provides readers with a highly useful analytical picture of social structure, looking down from the vantage point of the society as a whole to the level of the role-set. By doing so Nadel makes full use of the concept of social structure, too often neglected in favor of "culture" by anthropologists of his time, and gives that concept more definitive meaning than it receives in most sociological treatments. Nadel sought, and we follow him in this, more insightful treatment of the ways in which social roles are connected into social networks, and how these networks in turn are organized into the role matrices that make up the fabric of society.

Rather than focus on conflict as Merton had, Nadel is concerned with control as it takes place in the social roles associated with social positions or statuses (although he does not use those terms). It is important to recognize that Nadel conceptualized things much the same as Merton had. A single location or position in the social structure can implicate the individual in several distinctly different, though integrally related roles: Merton's role-set.

Basic Concepts: Control Through the Coherence of Roles

Nadel views roles as the locus of control in society. Hence, there is an important difference between saying that someone is a bad father and saying that someone deserted his children. In the first case the individual is viewed as failing to conform very well to the rights and obligations normally associated with that role. But the person is still subject to social pressure, with an eye to "improving" (in this case, making more conventional) role performance. Indeed, the use of evaluative terms suggests either: (a) that pressure is currently being applied in an attempt to better control behavior, or (b) that the role performance is presently used as a model for others (here as a negative model of what one should not do), or both. However, the deserter is in an entirely different position. To the degree that the deserter can be said to enact a role at all, that role is defined by its exclusion from the role-set and extended network, rather than by (poor) quality of performance. In the case of desertion there is no father, as the situation is socially defined. Vacant roles enter what Nadel refers to as a "zone of indeterminacy" (pp. 49-50).

Social control is largely exercised through exchange among roles in the same set (pp. 51-52). For example, Nadel notes that, at least in horticultural and industrial societies, people find it harder to dismiss what others say about immediately relevant role performance (such as co-worker reactions to job behavior) than comments about performance in some distant domain (such as co-workers' reactions to one's family behavior). For role guidance, correction, sanctions, and the like to be effective, people must feel as though the person offering advice or comment has a legitimate right to do so and/or the power to do so (Nadel, 1956, pp. 54-55).

Nadel created a rather elaborate inventory of roles among the Nupe. But he recognized that the overall structure of the role system varies from society to society. For Nadel, it is the nature and configuration of the role system that gives the society its tangible structure. And herein lies the heart of his theoretical analysis of society:

> In the discussion that follows I propose to concern myself further with the mutual implications of roles, the system they constitute, and the limits set to its coherence. Now all this can be expressed in different terms. Since the mutual implication of roles means that the behavior incumbent upon the actor in any one role always bears a reference to the behavior of other actors in their roles, it also means that the respective actors stand in definable relationships to one another. And inasmuch as the roles existing in any society combine to form a system, in virtue of the actor relationships, they also build up that ordered, overall arrangement which we have decided to call a social structure. Here, then, the present discussion links up with the earlier stages of our inquiry. Everything that we shall now have to say about the way roles implicate one another (or fail to do so) will serve to demonstrate

the kind of social structure we can hope to extract from or define for concrete societies. (p. 60)

In comparatively undifferentiated societies, all the various role-sets in which an individual is involved keep binding him or her to the same person-set. So kinsmen can be co-workers, co-workers are fellow religious believers, fellow religious believers are neighbors, and neighbors are participants in the same leisure circles. It often happens, moreover, that allocation to one role automatically determines which other roles one will be allocated (Nadel, 1956, pp. 66-67). For instance, birth into a particular family, when combined with gender, may determine where an individual will work, what job that he or she will perform, with whom he or she will associate, and what he or she will do during leisure time.

We may thus speak of the society being institutionally undifferentiated (Lenski & Lenski, 1974), if by "institution" we mean a package of roles that: (a) are found together again and again in the society (e.g., mother, father, son, daughter, and other kinship roles); (b) are commonly associated with a particular space and time (e.g., religious observance in holy places); (c) help people meet basic needs (e.g., acquisition of technical skills via education); and (d) involve most members of the society at some time during the life cycle (J. Turner, 1972). In institutionally undifferentiated societies all these various need-related tasks are subsumed with the same set of roles, technically speaking, within one undifferentiated institution. But most societies are institutionally differentiated, and exactly how different institutions are interrelated is a matter of considerable theoretical importance for social systems theorists (Bott, 1957).

The idea that structural differentiation poses a threat to the very existence of society has been one of the central themes in sociology since Durkheim. This is why integration and the problem of order have preoccupied so many theorists (Powers, 1981b; Teune, 1984; and also in organizations, see Hage, 1974, 1980; Lawrence & Lorsch, 1967; March & Simon, 1958; Mintzberg, 1979). Parsons (e.g., 1951, p. 36 ff) was one of the first sociologists to examine integration in terms of linkages between institutional role-sets, as Nadel was to do a few years later in *The Theory of Social Structure*. But as with so much of Parsons' work, his treatment of this issue ends up presuming order rather than accounting for it as a problematic or unexpected outcome. For Parsons, every role is part of a broader configuration of roles, with each role placing demands on every other. This interconnected webbing provides structural unity for the overall system of roles, and leaves very little room for change (Powers, 1981a).

Nadel sees system integration as truly more problematic. Once there is more than one institution, which is the case in almost all societies, it becomes necessary to establish a system of social networks interconnecting the different collective entities in one institutional sphere (e.g., individual families), with the collective entities making up other institutional spheres (e.g., churches, commodities markets, schools, and so on), because all the institutional spheres perform vital functions, and none is closed, autonomous, or self-sufficient. In essence, the multiplication of institutions means that each must procure services from and provide services to every other institutional sphere. But Nadel recognizes that simply taking this for granted, as Parsons was inclined to do, does little to advance our understanding of societal dynamics.

Nadel grapples with system integration by suggesting that **institutional role-sets, like the family, are attached through social networks acting as bridges to other institutions**. Role relationships within an institution tend to be what Nadel calls "relational" roles, while relationships making up networks that bridge institutions are very often what he terms "non-relational." By "relational" Nadel means roles that are defined in terms of their connection to a counterpart role occupied by known people (there can, for instance, be no mother role without a child role) and allow little substitutability (the existence of a patron-client relationship, for instance, presumes specific people acting in reciprocity).

Nadel argues that things change substantially with industrialization because of the homogenization of roles that takes place. For example, the roles of customer and clerk are essentially the same, regardless of whether customer A is at counter 3 or customer B is at counter 1. Many of the roles are, furthermore, quite similar in grocery stores, clothing stores, banks, offices, and hot dog stands. This makes substitution of personnel very easy, one of the characteristics of non-relational roles, but also diminishes interpersonal commitment and, consequently, motivation (Bradley, 1987; J. Turner, 1987).

Nadel implies that industrial societies risk losing their integrative coherence as more social roles lose their relational character. He feels that non-relational roles tend to lack commitment and might therefore easily evaporate, so that social life would become more entropic. Our thesis in the next chapter is the exact opposite, but Nadel is calling our attention to some critical properties of social roles—their links to other roles, the amount of time spent in interaction, and the integration of person-sets across our role-sets.

Basic Concepts: Complex Matrices

At the center of Nadel's approach is the concept of network. This marks an important difference between his analysis and that common in sociology at the time he was writing. "Networks" are structures identified by interconnections, whereas sociological definitions of that period often portrayed "structures" in terms of distributions of recurrent behavior (e.g., Parsons, 1951). The idea of network shifts the discussion from behavior to interaction and furnishes a starting point for the study of integration by focusing on the linkages tying interrelated parts in extended systems of relations.

> I do not merely wish to indicate the links between persons; this is adequately done by the word relationship. Rather, I wish to indicate the further linkage of the links themselves and the important consequence that, what happens so-to-speak between one pair of knots, must affect what happens between adjacent ones. It is in order to illustrate this interrelatedness or interlocking of the relationships (each link between two knots), that we require an additional term, and network seems the most appropriate. (Nadel, 1956, pp. 16-17)

It is this theoretical component that gives the network approach its real value, and this is clearly implied in the work of Harrison White and his associates (White, 1970, 1981; White, Boorman, & Breiger, 1976). To do justice to Nadel's theory, we need a method that will enable us to map out a person's many relationships, to see how those relationships are indirectly linked with others to form concatenated chains, and to examine the ways in which institutionally bounded role-sets interpenetrate (e.g., Bradley, 1987). Our emphasis on the complex self represents one way in which the separateness of institutional spheres is breaking down.

As we map the ways in which role-sets and networks are interwoven to make up the role matrices constituting the fabric of society, we may complete the work begun by Nadel (1956). His fear was that interpersonal commitment would be lost as more and more of our roles fell into the category of network linkages that cross-cut institutional boundaries. A concrete example is when a family member has responsibility for household maintenance and calls a plumber. When most people need to call a plumber, any plumber will do. Such relationships connote neither deep commitment nor lasting attachment. One role occupant is easily disposed of and substituted for another. Relationships of this sort are easily disrupted. Thus, Nadel feared that the social fabric as a whole would become more tenuous, less coherent, less well integrated; that the various role-sets around which social life are organized would become decoupled internally because individuals in the various person-sets are no longer all interconnected. However, Nadel did not foresee the pattern of PI change. The fact that commitment—as distinct from social exchange —is inverse to the size of the person-set, to use Merton's term, is very important in allowing us to address Nadel's thesis.

Criticisms

A central problem in Nadel's work is that he perceives social control to occur effectively only through institutional rules and prescriptions. He does not appreciate the control that occurs via multiple weak social ties (Granovetter, 1983). His imagery is too much affected by the importance of ritual in horticultural societies employing fairly rudimentary technology. As a result, he stresses the integrative consequences of having social roles with large amounts of interaction and overlapping person-sets.

We agree with much of Nadel's analysis, as far as he carried it. As society becomes more technologically advanced, institutionally bounded role-sets, such as the family, implicate members in an increasing number of role relationships with outsiders. In industrial societies those relationships tend to be emotionally flat and without much commitment. Lacking commitment, they tend not to be very meaningful or to last very long, and the wider networks formed by those relationships are consequently unstable (e.g., Cook, Emerson, Gillmore, & Yamagishi, 1983). Hence, Nadel's conclusion that industrial society lacks integrative coherence has some empirical grounding.

But we suggest that there is a remedy for this problem: Get rid of the role scripts that get in the way of emotional expression. In fact, this is precisely what seems to us to be happening with the transformation to PI society. Role scripts are becoming less constraining (Chapter 2), making it socially acceptable for people to express unprecedented levels of emotion (Chapter 4). This facilitates the development of a sense of interpersonal commitment and the redefinition of roles over time (Chapter 5). If people have the capacity to express emotions, they will perceive the relationship—even if it does not endure very long—as more meaningful. Furthermore, if people from different spheres of life are integrated, then the control comes not from role prescriptions but from the web of group affiliations, as Simmel (1955) long ago appreciated. This suggests that we must focus on how much person integration there is.

Another problem with Nadel's work is that network patterns were not perceived by him as fluid. This is perhaps understandable, given his research on the kinship structures of traditional societies. But while borrowing his concept of role matrices, we do not want to include preconceived notions about permanent patterns in the linkages connecting institutions.

However rich Nadel's ideas are about social roles connecting different institutional sectors, there remain the same general difficulties that we observed in Merton's (1957) work. Without developing variables for measuring the properties of role matrices, it is difficult to describe and analyze the changes in them across time. There is a great deal of intellectual interest in networks (Boje & Whetten, 1981; Burt, 1977, 1980; Marsden & Lin, 1982), but much of this work examines either information networks, as in *The Inner Circle* (Useem, 1986), or resource networks, as in the analyses of PACs (Clawson,

Neustadtl, & Bearden, 1986; Mizaruchi & Koenig, 1986; Neustadtl & Clawson, 1988). Other forms of interaction and joint activity are much less analyzed because social scientists lack a framework for describing and analyzing role networks.

What Is Needed: A Vocabulary for Role Networks

While Merton (1968) developed a list of group properties, these were never assigned and are not applicable to role-sets or status-sets. Nor does Merton's strategy of middle-range theory lead one naturally to a consideration of the interconnections between different role-sets. In this sense, Nadel's attempt at a broader and more coherent theory of social structure built on role matrices points in the right direction. But to pursue this line of work, we need to differentiate and connect the concepts of networks, role-sets, and role matrices.

Networks Link Role-Sets

Our focus has been on role relationships, that is, the interconnections between social roles. Merton focused on sets of role relationships that revolved around a single role occupant and were internal to an institutional setting, such as school, ignoring those role relationships that cut across institutional boundaries. In contrast, Nadel focused considerable attention on connections between institutional spheres. The boundary spanner literature on organizations (Aldrich, 1979) and the growing literature on systemic networks (Alter & Hage, forthcoming) are contemporary illustrations.

Role-sets and role matrices are not isomorphic with social networks. Most of the social network analysis has examined connections between people, positions, or social collectives established by the transmission of information and resources (for reviews, see Alter & Hage, forthcoming; Morrissey, Tausig, & Lindsey, 1985). Social networks are defined by linkage among positions, rather than any characteristics of the social roles in isolation. They are built around role relationships that come to be linked, that is, that implicate one another. Each relationship is analogous to an individual link in a chain, while social networks are the chains.

Social networks, unlike role-sets, include the indirect links between various positions, bounded in some way, which is precisely what Nadel used the term *network* to connote. A role-set views the world from a single focal position and, therefore, is only concerned with the number of direct links. This is an important conceptual distinction. As we shall argue in the next chapter, people increasingly admit more and more latitude in replacing partners or activities in role-sets through the process of role redefinition. Social networks increasingly admit more and more fluidity, not only in partners, but also in patterns of interlinkage.

A Typology of Variables for Role Relationships, Role-Sets, and Role Matrices

The many distinctions advanced above—role-sets, role matrices, and social networks—are not very useful without a concrete set of easily measurable variables, allowing us to develop testable hypotheses about change in the social fabric as we move from industrial to post-industrial society. Much of the problem of measurement is solved if we recognize that role relationships are the basic building blocks of role-sets, social networks, and role matrices. If we look at what role partners do together and ask ourselves the famous journalistic questions—who, what, when, where and why—we can construct a vocabulary for analyzing role networks.

What are some dimensions for describing the links between positions, whether in role-sets or as social networks bridging role-sets? Here we build upon the work of Hage and Marwell (1969) and Marwell and Hage (1970). The first dimension is scope. This can be measured in a variety of ways: the number of activities involved, the number of places in which action takes place, and the number of times roles are enacted. But consistent with Nadel's concerns about the number of people in a role relationship, we suggest that scope is, as a general rule, inversely related to the size of a particular person-set. The variety of joint activities, as distinct from the frequency of interaction, is the single most critical component of a broad-scope role relationship. As the variety of activities increases, so do the locations, times, and circumstances of interaction. We have suggested that as we do different things with people, different aspects of our personality emerge, and even the nature of what we discuss changes. In broad-scope role relationships, we can more easily learn to read both levels of communication (Chapter 4) and the more likely role partners are to expose their complex selves (Chapter 3). This emerges not only because there are few role partners, but also because of the variety of activities.

Our second dimension taps the intensity or involvement of people in the relationship or network (see Table 6.2). Again, this can be measured by examining a variety of indicators, including how much emotional involvement there is, concentration of activity, compactness of space, and the average duration of each interaction. Intensity and scope are closely connected; however, intensity does add a certain qualitative dimension that allows us to understand the depth of a role-relationship. For example, the longer the average duration of interaction, even with the same frequency of interaction, the more committed role partners tend to be. Families that eat a meal together for 2 or 3 hours, rather than in 5 or 10 minutes, tend to share a tighter bond by virtue of that fact. A particularly striking example is the police team, which interacts together for 8 hours a day.

Nadel (1956) felt that, other than with scripts, there was only one sure way of integrating relationships. Nadel's alternative to clear role scripts was the relational role, or overlap in person-sets. This is our third dimension for describing role relationships, namely, the integration of our work, family, cultural, and leisure-time role-sets so that all or many role partners know each other. Activity integration is a powerful mechanism of control. Among other things, it makes poor performance in one sphere visible to many people.

In past discussions about action versus order (e.g., Alexander, 1980-1983), the relative independence or autonomy of relationships has been lost to view. This is our fourth dimension. It is a very important feature of roles, especially of many contemporary relationships. Incumbents in most modern relationships can choose their partners as well as the activities that define the relationship, and the times and places in which the relationships play themselves out. The romantic love complex developed when people could choose their spouses (Aron & Aron, 1986). One of our major observations is that flexibility in role relationships, role-sets, and social networks is increasing and as it does, there is more and more room for human agency.

The fifth and more dynamic dimension is the stability or fluidity of the relationship or network over time. Many sociologists assume that integration means stability or the lack of change. But constant change in relationships common today necessitates that we tap this dynamic dimension of the social fabric in some way. As before, our indicators reflect changes in people, activities, places, and times. One can choose to eat breakfast at 7 a.m. on the patio, rather than 6:30 in the kitchen. Mixing locations and times for standard activities adds a needed dimension of variety. Flex-time in organizations is another example. The less stability and/or the more independence of a relationship or a network, the more critical are symbolic communication and the capacity to take the role of the other.

These skills facilitate the initial definition and subsequent redefinition of roles. As we shift focus from positions and role-sets to role relationships and networks, the natural interface between role theory (scripts) and symbolic interaction (freedom to choose) becomes clearer and clearer. Furthermore, these two dimensions are themselves interrelated. Independence allows us to make our role relationships more fluid, building in the variety that we suggest is a requirement. Conversely, fluid relationships necessitate more independence, so that the necessary adjustments can be made.

We can now provide a solution to Nadel's problem or concerns about industrial society. In post-industrial society commitment to role relationships increases as: (a) scope expands, (b) intensity enlarges, (c) integration occurs, and (d) independence increases. Role partners tend to be committed to each other and integrated into society to the degree that role relationships have these properties. But the very same variables that increase commitment also heighten problems that Merton recognized: conflict and inadequate social control. High scope, high intensity, and especially high fluidity of role relationships produce considerable role conflict and reduce compulsion in the traditional sense. Hence, the very high rates of role failure that we have documented, and the need for better interaction

Table 6.2 Variables Describing Role Relations and Social Networks[a]

| Role Relationships and Social Networks | | | | | |
Dimensions	Occupants	Activities	Places	Times	Links
Scope	Inverse of the number of people[b]	Diversity of behaviors	Number of locations	Frequency of interaction	Number
Intensity	Self-involve-ment[c]	Activity concen-tration	Compactness	Duration of interaction	Strength of bond
Integration	Overlap in person-set	Activity flow	Public meeting places	Public meeting times	Connect-edness
Indepen-dence	Choice of partners	Choice of behavior	Choice of locations	Choice of timing	Random-ness of pattern
Fluidity	Change in people	Redefini-tion of behavior	Change in setting	Change in timing	Change in pattern

[a] An adaptation of Hage and Marwell (1969).
[b] We are more likely to see a relationship as broad-scope when only a few people are involved as role partners.
[c] Self here refers to the impulsive self or set of personality characteristics and not the affective, work, or leisure selves. However, it is the variable that explains access to these other selves.

skills and role redefinition abilities to help people compensate for the diminution of traditional control, become apparent as old role prescriptions weaken.

Implications for Role Matrices

Nadel used the imagery of knots and patterns or what today might be called "network analysis." Consistent with this imagery, we want to emphasize that the dimensions of scope, intensity, integration, independence, and fluidity translate into ways of describing whole role matrices, whether internal to an organization/ family/market or connecting it to other institutional arrangements in other sectors.

The links in a role matrix can be constituted from either simple and single interactions or complex and lengthy ones. Just as we have been concerned with the intensity of a role relationship, we want to measure the magnitude or "thickness" or strength of the links connecting the various social roles in our matrix. This can be done in a variety of ways by using one or more of the various components of scope and intensity of role relationships. A simple measure is the amount of time spent in a role relationship, which is equal to frequency of interaction multiplied by average duration. This can in turn be weighted by the variety of activities and their average effort.

Nadel recognized that this decoupling at the level of role relationships is one of the most important features of social change. Nor does Nadel stand alone in his concern with decoupling. Luhmann (1986) posits that the institutional role relationships are becoming increasingly disconnected from one another in our society. To cite only one example: With the rise of romantic love, people are allowed almost complete independence in the selection of a spouse. On a more meso level, Weick (1969) argues that organizations are internally becoming decoupled. But neither Luhmann nor Weick pointedly asks how much human agency will be tolerated in societies with decoupled institutions, nor does either tell us when human agency is most likely to be exercised.

As role relationships grow in scope and intensity, role incumbents must be given more freedom to redefine their roles precisely because of the difficulties of handling many activities that demand effort. Furthermore, as these negotiated role relationships are integrated with others in highly connected role matrices, pressure mounts to allow role partners the freedom to alter their relationships because of the problems of matrix coordination and integration. Role relationships in highly fluid networks cannot be easily defined by prescriptive codification; thus choice devolves to the role partners to co-determine what they expect of each other.

Conclusions

That Robert King Merton and Siegfried Frederick Nadel were towering figures in their own disciplines cannot be denied. But what has been overlooked is the degree of conjunction between their respective treatments of social structure. For each, society is organized around networks of positions (or statuses) that come with bundles of roles (or role-sets). Merton (1968) provides us with the conceptual tools for describing how this structure appears in concrete and tangible daily experience. Nadel (1956) provides us with mapping conventions for understanding how institutional sets of role components are linked and interwoven to make up the social fabric.

But Merton underestimated the importance of role conflict and how this would grow over time, while Nadel failed to see the potential of fluid networks for providing a new kind of control. And both missed the evolutionary changes occurring, in part because they did not develop a vocabulary for describing the properties of role relationships, role-sets, social networks, and role matrices.

In the next chapter, we will take a detailed look at the forces of technological change moving organizations away from codification of role scripts toward independence in the definition of social roles. Here we merely observe the thesis of Chapter 2 about declining routinization of role scripts and its implication for greater human agency. As role-sets increase and person-sets decrease in size, role conflict increases and relationships become more personal in character. Both factors call for the kind of role redefinition described in Chapter 5.

7

THE METAMORPHOSIS OF ROLES
INTO INTERPERSONAL
RELATIONSHIPS

In earlier chapters we developed the thesis that growth in knowledge and rapidity of technological change are transforming the micro
level of social roles via the process of complexification. In this chapter
we ask how the society itself is being reconfigured. Our answer is
that society is being refabricated from the ground up. Role-sets are
increasing and person-sets are decreasing in size. As a result, most
social bonds are losing some of their role properties and gaining
more of the properties of interpersonal relationships.[1]

Although the dynamic character of relationships has always been
taken as an article of faith among symbolic interactionists (Adler,
Adler, & Fontana, 1987; Blumer, 1969; Blumstein & Kollock, 1988),
the hypothesis that society is evolving from close to distant attachments, in Toennies' (1963) terms from gemeinschaft to gesellschaft,
is still largely accepted. Toennies' analysis was quite appropriate for
the industrial epoch but not the PI era. Organizational ecology is

changing (Carroll, 1988; Hannan & Freeman, 1989), evolving new forms (Aldrich & Mueller, 1982) that foster the growth of affective bonds. Understanding this change requires that we seriously consider findings from the organizational literature, which interactionists (e.g., Stryker, 1990) have tended to ignore. By doing so, we can identify interrelational configurations in which feelings are more easily expressed and the dynamics of role redefinition are more easily utilized. Thus, we are adding a new meso level of analysis to the micro-macro link (Alexander, Gresen, Munch, & Smelser, 1987).

The Rise of Interpersonal Relationships and the Expression of Sentiment

Why do some social roles have stronger relationships than others? This question was originally posed by Homans (1950). We approach Homans' question by considering the ways in which configuration of social structure influences the number of roles a person occupies and the number of others with whom a person interacts while performing each role.[2] In Chapter 2, we suggested that the long-term trend in post-industrial society is for the process of complexification to diminish the routine activities associated with social roles. This inevitably increases the number of role relationships people maintain and the variety of activities engaged in for each of those role relationships, while simultaneously reducing the number of role partners in any given relationship and increasing the effort required because mental labor, especially creative work, requires a lot of attention. Expansion in the size of role-sets and reduction in the size of the person-sets corresponding to each individual role means that role relationships are increasingly perceived as interpersonal ones; role scripts are losing their content and role style is of growing importance, and the locus of social control is consequently moving from conformity to interpersonal commitment.

To simplify our discussion of how properties of role relationships impinge on the expression of feelings or emotions, we will group variables into major categories: occupant and activity characteristics on the one hand and location and time characteristics on the other. Growth in knowledge has impacted on the first set, while increased variety of leisure activities has impacted upon the second.

Occupants and Activities

Perhaps more than any other variable, the variety of activities role occupants engage in with one another stands out as important. The major way in which people build bridges, thereby cementing a more enduring relationship, is by doing different things together. Interpersonal relationships are first fused and later transformed through the sharing of diverse experiences. Interestingly, having long conversations that involve personal topics may not be the best way of achieving an intimate bond. Instead, having multifaceted contact (e.g., taking walks, seeing movies, and attending concerts) is how relationships really blossom and mature. We come to know others through their actions and reactions, which are ultimately more revealing than opinions people verbalize. For the more things people do together, the more aspects of self that are likely to be disclosed.

In PI society relationships are growing steadily more complex, that is, they are gaining many more activities than they previously had. The important consequence of these changes is that role scripts lose their importance and the interpersonal character of relationships gains in importance.

Equally striking is a shift in the number of role partners people typically have. For as the size of people's role-sets increases, there is a corresponding decline in the size of person-sets; we deal with a greater number of other positions, but fewer people in each of those different positions. The fewer partners one has in a particular type of role relationship, the more likely one is to view the role partner as a unique personality (Blumstein & Kollock, 1988).[3]

Also of importance is the intensity of effort required in whatever activities define a relationship. The critical point here is that problem solving in the face of uncertainty, the defining characteristic of PI interaction, is high-intensity work, creating a need for even more socio-emotional interaction to reaffirm bonding and provide for tension release (following from Shibutani, 1978; Strauss, Schatzman,

Bucher, Ehrlich, & Sabshin, 1964).[4] What Parsons (1951) called "role distance" is on the decline.

Another theme in the analysis of personal relationships is how each partner will be affected by what the other does. Affect grows stronger with integration of activities (Kelley & Thibault, 1978; Thibault & Kelley, 1959) and task interdependence (Hickson, Henning, Lee, Schoeck, & Pennings, 1971). The integration of role occupants across a number of role relationships also has an enormous impact on the knowledge that we have about other people and the extent to which they engage in impression management. When there is high occupant overlap, other members can provide needed pieces of information that allow us to understand and recognize symbolic gestures, to read the nonverbal level of communication, and to discover the true self.

The impact of these variables on sentiment is diagrammed in Figure 7.1. Variety, intensity, and interdependence increase the frequency of interaction, enabling role partners to learn how to more accurately interpret symbolic communications at the interpersonal level.

Of course, the hypothesized associations are to a certain degree two-directional, which is very much in keeping with Homans' analysis. When occupants in a role relationship interact more frequently, especially as they have warm feelings, they are also likely to engage in a wider variety of activities together. For example, as a couple moves toward becoming engaged, we would expect them to want to do different things together. In some measure this may be because of simple probabilities: the more time spent together the greater the chance for trying new things. And yet, the proverbial couch potato family illustrates that time spent and range of activities engaged in do not automatically correlate.

Time and Location

There has been a series of major changes in PI society that impact on the locations and times in which role relationships articulate. Technology has an enormous influence on the opportunities for social interaction. Telephones, fax machines, computer networks,

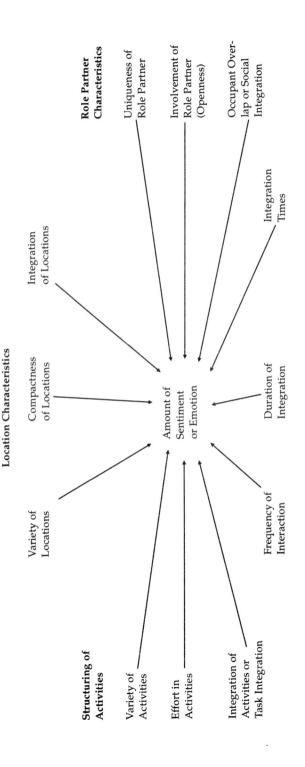

Figure 7.1. The Strength of the Social Bond in a Role Relationship

and the like allow us to interact frequently with people all over the world. Distance no longer has a meaning. We can instantaneously start a conversation if the role partner is within range of some known telephone number. The point is obvious but not typically discussed in the role literature.

Similarly, the cost of airplane, bus, train, and car transportation has steadily declined, allowing us to gather friends, convene business meetings, or reunite far-flung members of the family more frequently than ever before. Not only does the telephone allow us to "touch someone," but the car allows us to do so in a different place.

Quick and cheap transportation has also allowed for the enormous increase in the variety of leisure-time activities. Cars in particular make amusement parks, marinas, mountain ski resorts, beaches, hiking trails, national parks, museums, and so on much more accessible. And the variety of activities people can engage in is strongly influenced by the variety of locations in which these activities can be performed. There is not a one-to-one correspondence, however. Previously one activity would be found in only a few locations. But now convenience has overtaken efficiency as a preferred utility.

The key theoretical idea is that as more opportunities are provided for role incumbents to interact, the more affect-laden the role relationships is likely to be. Some firms (Peters & Waterman, 1982) establish special rooms where people can discuss ideas on a spontaneous basis. Academic departments are much more likely to be productive when they have a lounge where people can have coffee and interact.

One ignored aspect of the study of ecology is the association between the compactness of the space and the duration of interaction, or what we might call the intensity of the ecological arrangements. Some activities, such as sports, concerts, plays and the like, provide the context for a number of role relationships to be played out simultaneously in small spaces for relatively long periods. The expression of sentiment tends to be a function of how confined the space is and how long the interactions are. And, as we are physically closer, we experience the role relationship differently.

Choice and Fluidity

Most of the above discussion assumes the development of positive feelings, but there can be negative ones as well, and we can suggest circumstances when negative feelings are likely to be aroused, or when positive feelings decay across time. In a fluid world with rapid technological change, role incumbents lacking independence to redefine their relationships will tend to engage in impression management, which emotionally isolates people from one another. Instead of responding to role failure by changing the character of activities the relationship revolves around, there is a tendency on the part of many people to try to recapture the old role by switching role partners. In other words, people get divorced, change jobs, find new friends, or join a different church. Patterns of negative sentiment are diagrammed in Table 7.1. Low independence and high fluidity produce the managed heart phenomenon found in salesclerks or prostitutes. There is total impression management. These role styles are possible as long as the relationship is of some limited duration; but if the relationship continues, it becomes more and more difficult to maintain impression management.

Strong negative feelings are most likely to develop when there is little choice of role partners or activities. Under these circumstances, strong negative emotions are generated. In prisons and in other totalitarian institutions where people lack choice, emotions run high. Violence is one expression of emotional intensity.

Quite different forms of disequilibrium are produced when integration and fluidity are at different levels. High integration with low fluidity can produce feelings of fatalism or a sense of despair or emotional burnout expressing itself, for example, in that special hatred that can develop in seemingly normal families. As Simmel (1955) recognized in his analysis of conflict, hatred is not only an emotion, but also a very special bond.

The opposite situation is low integration and high fluidity. In these role relationships, anomic feelings are generated. A blasé attitude develops and people feel detached. Other possibilities also exist. But the ones presented here indicate how patterns of disequilibrium can occur during the process of change discussed in Chapter 2.

Table 7.1 Patterns Likely to Produce Negative Sentiments or the Decay in Feelings

Disequilibrium	Kind of Sentiments
High independence Low fluidity	decay of feelings across time produces change in role partner (e.g., divorce)
Low independence High fluidity	absence of any feelings, total impression management
High integration Low fluidity	fatalistic feelings, sense of despair, burnout
Low integration High fluidity	anomic feelings, blasé attitude, detachment

Evolution in Role-Sets and Role Matrices

Within the past few years investigators have begun to raise the question of how organizations evolve, focusing primarily on the organizational forms that survive (Aldrich & Auster, 1986; Aldrich & Mueller, 1982; Carroll, 1988; Hage et al., 1991; Hannan & Freeman, 1989). We ask a slightly different question How have role matrices changed in organizations across time? As we observed in the previous chapter, this was Nadel's question, but it has not received the attention it deserves.

To understand how complexification and routinization (Chapter 2) have impacted on role matrices in organizations, we took typologies that have been suggested in the management literature (Hage, 1980; Mintzberg, 1979; Perrow, 1967) and synthesized them with a sizable economics literature by focusing on the sophistication of technology and the economics of scale/scope. Essentially, the process of complexification impacts on roles by eliminating manual labor and expanding activities in remaining roles. But how do these changes transform the systems of roles that give organizations their definitive character?

An evolutionary sequence of change seems to have occurred in the business world. Enterprises tended to be craft-oriented when complexification was low and economies of scale were small, prior to the first stage of the industrial revolution. Mechanical-bureaucratic organizations emerged with the first stage of the industrial revolution, when rationalization was clearly more prominent than complexification, and economies of scale increased. Mixed mechanical-organic organizations emerged during the second stage of the industrial revolution, when complexification and rationalization were both prominent (Woodward, 1965). And organic-professional organizations are taking form as we enter the PI era. Each of these forms of organization will be described below. In the process we give historical perspective to our analysis of contemporary role change, the sweeping and even revolutionary character of contemporary social change at the meso level, where the reformulation of the social fabric works via expansion of role-sets and the development of networks of roles crossing institutional boundaries. Whole organizations become networks of working teams in PI society. In turn, every organization is a member of a network made up of the other organizations that are its suppliers, customers, regulators, and financial backers. Organizations are being deconstructed, and their parts are being refabricated in systems of network relations (Carnevale, 1991, pp. 57-58).

Although no one has addressed the issue in quite this way, there are several existing empirical studies on role-sets and role matrices in complex organizations, especially those organizations we might loosely categorize as government agencies, for-profit corporations, and nonprofit volunteer associations (e.g., Blauner, 1964; Hage, 1974; Weiss, 1956). These studies allow us to test our ideas about whether the role structure of complex organizations is changing. We also address the issue of members reconstructing organizations from the bottom up. Typical management texts focus on the theme of the great leader or strategy/structure and not on the design of the organization by its members, but the latter is gaining in importance.

Internal Role Matrices in Traditional Craft Organizations

In his book, *Alienation and Freedom* (1964), Robert Blauner describes the role of printers in small printing firms, which were fairly typical craft organizations at the time. The printers Blauner describes are self-motivated craftsmen who have a great deal of job autonomy. This

Table 7.2 A Typology of Organizational Forms

Process of Complexification	Process of Rationalization	
(Level of Education,[a] Sophistication of Technology,[b] Research Emphasis[c])	(Personnel Size/Economies of Scale[d])	
	Small	Large[e]
Low	Traditional-craft, Type One	Mechanical-bureaucratic, Type Two
High	Organic-professional, Type Four	Mixed mechanical-organic, Type Three

[a] Years of education required to hold the position.
[b] Sophistication of technology, as measured by the Amber scale.
[c] Research emphasis varies from none to more than 10% of sales or of budget in the public sector.
[d] Large personnel size in a business unit or public department of 500 or more, where economies of scale are possible. The focus is on profit centers or divisions that have some autonomy and are distinguishable by the nature of their task, technology, product-group, and market (Hage, 1980).
[e] Strangely enough, little attention has been paid to the large size of public bureaucracies as the equivalent of economies of scale in industry; for example, custodial mental hospitals, prisons, and the military.

means that they are free to roam around the shop floor, rather than always being tied down to one machine. In fact, printers will frequently perform a variety of job tasks and operate several different kinds of machines. There is a fair amount of variety in the work because most jobs are done in small batches, rather than large runs. Having variety, job autonomy, and the ability to control the pace of work means that the craftsperson is generally quite happy with his or her work and tends to have high job satisfaction.

Many small businesses that cater to individual or local tastes are based on craft or artisan knowledge. Gourmet restaurants, health food stores, hardware stores, home construction firms, independent book stores, independent automobile garages, boutiques, and many of the other stores that we will still find on "Main Street" are good examples. Hence, traditional craft **organizations** are still very much a part of the American landscape, even if what we tend to think of as the "traditional crafts" are not.[5]

There are actually many professions that utilize traditional craft-type organization, even if they are not commonly thought of that way. The work of a primary school teacher is a good example. Again, there is considerable job autonomy and variety. Teachers are largely unsupervised and prepare different lesson plans across a range of disciplines (reading, math, and so on), interact a great deal with students and tailor their activities to meet their needs. Such jobs are anything but routine (Aiken & Hage, 1968) but at least until recently (i.e., prior to the PI transformation), tended to be characterized by simple role-sets in which the occupants of one position interacted with occupants of a few other positions. The role occupants may have interacted with many **people**; however, those people were usually occupants of only one or two positions: students, clients, customers, or the like—a small role-set with a large person-set.

Since there are few status differences, workers feel free to ask questions of people higher in the chain of command, whether they are in the same department or are in other departments. Semiprofessional organizations typically have few levels in the hierarchy and few departments. What is distinctive about this role matrix is that most of the communication is upward, both within the chain of command and across departments. This reflects the informal nature of work and the relative autonomy of workers, whether these be fire fighters, teachers, social workers, or construction workers. They feel quite free to ask anyone for advice because there are few status impediments to communication.

Work is not exactly teamwork in the technical sense of the term, although one finds cooperative behavior and interpersonal dependency in the craft firms and professional agencies of industrial society, especially at the worker level. Organizations tend to work via informal connections or role relationships (Kidder, 1985). Individuals in craft and semiprofessional organizations develop friendships on the job and use lunch hours and evenings to interact socially. Lipset, Trow, and Coleman's (1956) study of the printers' union made this very clear. Expressive communication is essential for releasing tension as well as for professional socialization and the maintenance of an occupational ethic (Bales, 1950; Parsons, Bales, & Shils, 1953). These friendships translate into occupant overlap and also ensure that the roles in the matrix are interconnected.

Internal Role Matrices
in Mechanical-Bureaucratic Organizations

The first stage of the industrial revolution saw the emergence of large, highly rational organizations (Chandler, 1977), and here we have the example of the kind of disconnected role matrix that concerned Nadel. Textile mills were first to develop, followed by railroads, the post office, department stores, steel companies, cement and glass manufacturing firms, and so forth (Chandler, 1977). Mechanical-bureaucratic organizations also include those agencies that provide highly standardized services to a large public, such as state departments of motor vehicles or county welfare agencies.

Assembly lines best illustrate how role relationships are structured in mechanical-bureaucratic organizations. Each job or position is reduced to a few tasks that are endlessly repeated throughout the day (Taylor, 1967). The assembly-line mode of organization gradually spread to industries throughout the economy, which took a heavy toll on craft employment. Once the work of a craftsman is broken up into many roles via a process of task specialization, each new role can be carefully defined and codified in terms of a short series of simple motions that can be performed with only the most rudimentary of skills: "deskilling" (Braverman, 1974). Even managers and clerical workers follow bureaucratic procedures and role scripts. Simplification of roles to their most rudimentary form does not mean an absence of social interaction, but it does mean that most task-relevant interaction is highly scripted. Most role-sets are reduced in size to their absolute minimum in mechanical-bureaucratic organizations, especially on the assembly line. Similarly, task interaction is reduced to the lowest possible amount. Most task-oriented communication is vertical, with operating instructions coming down from the top. This applies to social service bureaucracies as well as manufacturing firms (Hage, 1974). Social workers in large old-style bureaucracies seldom communicate across departments. Even the top administrators have little communication with those in other departments, and there are few committees or equivalent structures to coordinate and integrate the organization. This results in a role matrix that is quite loosely interconnected.

Role matrices are constructed from the top down via all the mechanisms described by Weber (see Table I.1). Therefore, these organizations are the exact antithesis of those where people, especially people at the bottom of the hierarchy, are involved in the construction and redefinition of role-relationships. Indeed, the system actively militates against role redefinition.

Role Matrices in Mixed Mechanical-Organic Organizations

In a study of the impact of technology on society in Western Europe, Landes (1969) observed that the second industrial revolution led to the creation of firms in which technology took on new importance. The rise of chemical, electrical, and telephone technologies witnessed the creation of a new form of organization: the mixed mechanical-organic firm, composed of mechanically bureaucratic production units interfaced with organically structured units devoted to product design and development. One of the most distinctive characteristics of this new kind of organization was the establishment of large and well-funded research laboratories, which turned out a constant stream of new products for the corporation (Freeman, 1982). Research budgets and research staffs are quite large in such firms, and projects typically continue for long periods of time. On the public sector side, the health care industry and universities offer the best examples of comparable organizations.

The importance of research and development cannot be stressed enough. In R&D departments there is a great deal of construction of roles and relationships. In other words, those parts of the organization most responsible for creativity also offer the greatest opportunities for innovative role redefinition. But equally important, as Perrow (1967) has noted, is that decentralized research and development units with an organic structure operate alongside mechanically organized corporate divisions specializing in mass production. The roles and role-sets in the different divisions of these organizations vary accordingly. Although the roles of factory workers change as research and development creates new products, it is still the case that there is considerable standardization of role performance at mass-production points within these firms. A public sector example is the Veterans Administration branch of the U.S. Public Health Service. There is considerable emphasis on research and development in one part of veterans hospitals, yet people recognize the necessity of having some organizational units that are quite codified and bureaucratic. As a consequence, one finds both routine and nonroutine roles in the same organization, that is, both roles with scripts and roles in which negotiation is constantly occurring, where role redefinition (Chapter 5) is, in effect, part of the regular routine.

Workers in these industries control the pace of work, rather than the reverse. They are given a great deal of responsibility. If something goes wrong in the manufacturing process, they have the power to stop production (Lawrence & Lorsch, 1967). New integrative mechanisms, such as committees, become important. Most of the interpersonal relationships that exist are constructed and built up at the bottom of the power and status hierarchies. It is the nature of the production systems that necessitates and encourages contact across departmental lines.

Mixed mechanical-organic organizations have many more divisions of distinct product groups, smaller divisions and plants, and fewer hierarchical levels than do mechanic-bureaucratic organizations. The volume of communication is therefore higher in mixed mechanical-organic organizations than in craft or mechanical-bureaucratic organizations. Furthermore, the links are quite different, horizontal between departments rather than vertical. Horizontal linkages proliferate in committees at the top of the pyramid and within networks at the bottom.

Organic Organizations

As we move into the PI era, we find relationships organized around problem-solving task groups, which avoid paperwork as much as possible and disband when their task is done. Thus, they are the antithesis of the bureaucratic model as described by Weber (1946). Instead of clear lines of hierarchical authority, specialized division of labor, assignment based on formal training, decisions made according to prescribed rules, and detailed written records kept as organizational property, one finds hierarchical distinctions are ignored; task differentiation is blurred; people are selected on the basis of creativity and the ability to contribute to good working chemistry in a team; decisions are made collectively, with an eye toward innovation rather than adherence to convention; and with the group process left largely unmonitored in order to stimulate an open expression of ideas, the development of new approaches, and the progressive transformation of groupthink. Thus, there are few scripted roles in the organic work teams. Instead, such groups are free-wheeling. Status differences based on job position are leveled as much as possible to stimulate higher rates of interaction and encourage exchange that is circular rather than vertical, and to involve the generation and transformation of ideas rather than the mere transmission of instructions. The work these groups do can best be described as teamwork. Role relationships are high in intensity, but do not necessarily last beyond the life of the task force. Here we see the kind of construction of even whole organizations that Blumer (1969) felt was true everywhere. Thus, experimentation is encouraged in organic PI organizations.

Because products come and go and do not have long lives, production workers are also constantly being retrained for different kinds of work. This introduces the paradox that one worker may occupy many different roles in the course of employment in the same company. **Role** mobility replaces job mobility, in the traditional sense of changing companies. This is especially true in firms that try to provide job security as one way of maintaining high productivity and a positive climate in the workplace.

A caveat is in order. Traditional craft organizations (epitomized by guilds) were the archetypical organizational forms of pre-industrial society; yet they remain important today. This demonstrates that the transformation from one epoch to another, although rapid, is never instantaneous or complete. Hence, the present always contains telltale hints of the future as well as a continuity with the past. All four forms of organizations are to be found in PI society, even though there is decided movement in the direction of organic organization.

Post-Industrial Role Matrices

Karl Marx and Friedrich Engels (e.g., 1967) were important because they recognized that a new epoch (industrial capitalism) was at hand and they provided a coherent framework for analyzing it. Moreover, they recognized that the changes taking place were by no means limited to the economy. Indeed, their analysis went far beyond changes in the workplace, for Marx and Engels recognized that a truly revolutionary transformation was under way. Changes in the workplace were to reverberate into every sphere of life, modifying the very fabric of family relations, changing the meaning of friendship, altering the bonds of community, transforming religion, and ushering in new standards and strategies of government.

Marx and Engels developed a portrait of capitalism that was not always correct, but was certainly thought provoking and, in most cases, superior to the scholarship that had preceded them. And they did so based on their understanding of a few new textile mills and other cutting edge firms operating in a very small geographic enclave, surrounded by what was essentially a pre-capitalist and certainly a pre-industrial world. We also look along a cutting edge, and see earth-shaking changes in the making.

Rather than large-scale mechanical-bureaucratic organizations displacing smaller and more organic units, small organic organizations are presently displacing larger mechanical ones. Instead of a process of deskilling, highly trained professionals and technical personnel represent a growing share of the work force. Rather than an emphasis on competition, the new focus is on cooperation. And it is the process of complexification rather than routinization that will define roles in the future (Chapter 2). Roles in organic organizations are generally left rather open and ambiguous so that they can be periodically redefined to fit the task at hand (Chapter 5). Everyone works as part of a team or a group. Leadership in the group is not fixed but changes, depending upon who has expertise and creative ideas in a particular area. All this makes for a great deal of negotiation, and there is a constant reshuffling of the boundaries defining operative work units. Occupational specializations even lose much of their meaning, for these organizations are on the frontiers of research and development, and frontiers are not easily bounded by labels. Relationships also tend to be more random and unpredictable, affected by team building needs (Allen, 1978; Shinn, 1982).

Although the image of PI society is caught by the phrase "small high-tech," there are a number of other changes occurring that, while not quite the same as small high-tech, reflect a parallel in the structural conditions leading to more affective role relationships and role-sets with stronger bonds. These are:

1. Upgrading of many semiprofessional organizations, such as schools, local government services, police departments, and the like into more professional or knowledge-intensive organizations;
2. The conversion of some mechanical-bureaucratic organizations, such as General Motors and AT&T, into more mixed mechanical-organic structures;
3. The splitting up of many mixed mechanical-organic organizations into relatively small profit centers;
4. The creation of many new small joint venture companies;
5. The establishment of many new small high-tech companies.

Running through all of these changes are an increase in complexity and a reduction in personnel size, which in turn have consequences for the nature of social interaction and the integration of role matrices (Mintzberg, 1979). They tend to be organically organized. Roles are flexible and the composition of work teams is fluid. In these kinds of organizations problem solving is an important part of the daily work flow and is usually accomplished in teams. Whether in provision of services or in the manufacturing of products, a growing emphasis is placed on customization to meet each customer or client's unique combination of needs.

Work in organic firms revolves around the development of creative solutions to problems; and the opportunities for creativity are endless. These organizations are therefore **human capital intensive**, as indicated by the proportion of staff with advanced degrees. Thus, the "worker" is usually a scientist or a professional, a person with a substantial amount of advanced education. As we have suggested, the creative mind finds many opportunities to realize its potential in an organic organization. Thus, the last stage on Maslow's (1954)

hierarchy of needs may finally be reached for the average citizen as
we move into the post-industrial era.

Reading *The Soul of the New Machine* (Kidder, 1979), one can gain
some insight into the real nature of roles in such organizations.
Kidder reports on a group of computer researchers who develop a
new computer, all the while working without authorization. Their
jobs are not well defined. The young engineers work as a close-knit
team with very high task interdependence and they experience high
levels of task and expressive communication. These engineers were
attracted by the opportunity to work on the frontiers of computer
design. Many worked long into the night and on the weekends
(Schael & Fassel, 1988). No one felt that he or she could let down his
or her fellow workers, which again demonstrates the importance of
team spirit, and the exact opposite of what Homans (1950) described
in his analysis of norms against rate-busting in the Hawthorne
studies, where workers conspired to keep production down to a
relatively low level so that work would proceed at a slow and comfortable pace. In contrast to manufacturing at the Hawthorne Western Electric plant, **workers in PI firms are implicitly driving each
other to produce more—often at great cost to their personal lives
and sometimes without any clear promise of economic reward**. The
motivation, as Burns and Stalker (1961) observed, originates in the
desire to produce innovative solutions for problems—to make progress. The drive is nonmaterial, and will necessarily be so when the
basis of self-esteem and self-actualization moves from completion
of tasks to mastery of problems (Chapter 3).

Two networks of communication develop when task complexity
is high (Hage, 1974). Under these conditions, workers generally experience horizontal as well as vertical communication, and everyone
feels free to consult with and seek advice from everyone else in the
organization, and frequently from people outside the organization
as well. More important, executives confer with and seek advice from
workers at lower levels of the organization. And generally speaking,
organic organizations have a large number of committees. This makes
them very different from the traditional craft organizations described

earlier in this chapter. A heavy volume of communication is required in organic organizations because complex tasks cannot be designed, planned, or coordinated by rigid rules, manuals, or job descriptions (see Hage, 1974, for a development of this thesis). Therefore, coordination must occur via human interaction rather than prescribed role scripts.

On average, individuals have the largest role-sets in the organic organizations. This comes from teamwork, task interdependence, and high communication rates, all of which result from the need to coordinate complex tasks. It is also a function of the relatively small size of the organizations. Moreover, person-sets are small and role relationships are continually being redefined in organic firms. Not even occupational or professional boundaries are fixed in organic organizations. There is more than just a flexible structure; structural fluidity would be a more appropriate description. This is a new phenomenon and calls for innovative management strategies (Hall, 1977; Hollingsworth & Lindberg, 1989; Van de Ven, Delbecq, & Koenig, 1976).

Fabricating, sustaining, and directing fluid structures requires constant negotiation and a highly developed capacity for taking the role of the other. This means a new kind of mind and self (Chapter 3), with finely tuned social skills (Chapter 4) to redefine roles in accordance with changing organizational needs (Chapter 5). Critical interpersonal skills include the ability to judge how appropriate the behavior is and to cope with undesirable behavior, stress, and ambiguity (Carnevale, 1991, p. 104). In sum, organic organization represents the wave of the future (Boyett & Conn, 1991). It is composed of role relationships and role-sets that are quite different from the organizational forms that characterized earlier epochs. Roles in organic organizations are far removed from scripts in the imagery of 1950s role theory. Inside organic organizations, boundaries are not well defined and job content remains rather ambiguous and is continually being redefined. Even occupational or professional boundaries lose much of their meaning. Role-sets are quite large, that is, each position is attached to many other positions, but person-sets are small, so that every relationship develops unique character.

Table 7.3 The Typology of Organizations and the Expression of Emotion

Characteristics of Role Relationships, Role-Set	Type of Organization			
	I	II	III	IV
Number of Activities	some	very few	some	many
Effort	moderate	task special-ization low	moderate	high
Integration of Activities	low	high	moderate	high
Occupant Uniqueness	moderate	very low	moderate	high
Involvement of Role Partners	moderate	low	moderate	high
Size of Role-Sets	moderate	very small	small	large
Fluid Network	no	no	somewhat	a great deal
Emotion	moderate	low	moderate	high

The Determinants of Emotion in Work Organizations

Homans' basic question regarding the social roots of sentiment or emotion has been answered in several ways. **First,** we indicated how properties of activities and occupants can have a positive multiplier effect on the amount of feeling expressed, provided that there is choice of activities and role partners (see Table 7.3). This analysis indicates that there is some truth in Naisbitt's (1982) characterization of the trend toward high tech and high feel, although he never specified the causal dynamics involved.

Second, properties of the role matrix vary considerably, depending upon the type of organization. In mechanical-bureaucratic organizations role-sets are small, person-sets are large, role scripts abound, and there is little communication and thus little emotion. **In organic-professional organizations role-sets are large, person-sets are small, scripts lose their power, and relationships are personalized.**

Third, we have integrated the theory of organizations with the work on emotions and with Nadel's analysis of role matrices by suggesting that role matrices became disconnected in the first stage of the industrial revolution but are now much better interconnected, at least in PI organizations. Again, it is worth emphasizing that this is not true everywhere but primarily in the kinds of organizational units that are of growing importance, small organizations that use large numbers of professional and technical personnel who perceive technical progress as their main objective. Nadel's (1956) concerns are correct when applied to certain old-style organizations, but not when we examine new organizational forms born out of the knowledge explosion, sophisticated new technologies, and a more educated labor force.

In this chapter, we have linked the micro and macro level by arguing that as educational levels and technological sophistication increase, and economies of scale and personnel size decline, role relationships take on many more activities, more occupant uniqueness, more task effort and greater organic integration, and usually more openness of occupants as well. Role-sets also expand in size while person-sets decline in size. These are observable ways in which **the structure of society is being reshaped at the meso level**.

Society can afford to allow role scripts to disappear precisely because people are plugged into complex role-sets that are large, where role partners negotiate over appropriate activities. Furthermore, with high levels of communication and large role-sets, there is high visibility of poor performance and relatively quick feedback about it. PI society is in some ways more controlling, even if it does not control directly via role scripts but instead allows the role partners in complex and large role-sets to do the regulating via individualized role redefinition and creative solutions to problems.

The Reconstruction of Society

Our analysis has important implications for the study of social networks, for it is our assessment that as society undergoes the metamorphosis to post-industrialism, **markets and hierarchies are being largely supplanted by network structures**. In short, the organization of society is changing (e.g., Florida & Kenney, 1991).[6]

Early capitalist economies were organized largely on the basis of market principles. Entrepreneurs orchestrated value-adding processes by locating suppliers, subcontractors, and consumers in an open marketplace. The cottage textile industry provided the archetype, with entrepreneurs delivering raw materials to the doors of country weavers and seamstresses, and returning later for finished products. The market ruled.

By the end of the nineteenth century, with the widespread introduction of steam power, economies of scale could be achieved by centralizing all the manufacturing activities associated with one product under a single roof, and by the vertical integration of suppliers, manufacturers, and distributors under a single corporate banner (Marcus & Segal, 1989). This marked the rise of "big business," and firms such as Standard Oil, British Petroleum, Royal Dutch Shell, U.S. Steel, and Singer Sewing Machine made their appearance. This was the age of hierarchy, when successful firms tried to acquire subordinate units capable of performing each of the essential aspects of one's business (Chandler, 1962).

By the 1960s a growing number of people began to appreciate the limits of hierarchy, since some things are more expensive to provide internally than to procure in the marketplace (Tyebjee, 1991, pp. 36-54). "Markets versus hierarchies" (Williamson, 1975) was one of the important business questions of the seventies, as firms repositioned themselves by moving away from the strategy of wholly self-contained, autonomous self-sufficiency. After all, why maintain a rather expensive rubber gasket factory when rubber gaskets are abundant and we can buy them more cheaply on the open market than we can produce them ourselves?

By the 1980s firms began moving even more rapidly away from the hierarchy strategy, this time because of the speed of technological change and the need to accelerate the rate of product and service innovation. Rapid technological change means that capital equipment depreciates very quickly. So capital investments that serve the needs of one firm exclusively make sense for only the largest producers. The response of growing numbers of firms has been to contractually establish long-term strategic alliances among otherwise independent concerns. These strategic partnerships have found their way into all kinds of commercial enterprises.[7] The key to understanding this new phenomenon is recognition that **strategic partnerships are not hierarchies, nor are they markets. They are networks.** And networks are rapidly becoming the most important organizational form in post-industrial society (Ghoshl & Bartlett, 1990).

For example, Corning Glass Works now calls itself a "global network." It maintains partnerships or joint ventures with 15 companies in 13 countries. Among other things, these strategic alliances allow Corning to increase its command over expertise and to expand into new markets (Alter & Hage, forthcoming), which not only gives Corning far more flexibility than it would have on its own, but also makes it a more formidable competitor. This is consistent with Campbell, Hollingsworth, and Lindberg's (1991) argument that European and Japanese firms have been able to outmaneuver and outcompete against Americans in the global marketplace precisely because they have rejected the strategy of vertical integration, which has been so popular in American business circles. An increasing number of American firms are now following suit, giving up on hierarchy but turning to network structures as an organizational form: partnerships with suppliers and customers as well as providers of complementing products and services.

One of the most dramatic and visible signs of the reconstruction of society is the creation of joint ventures. There were only a few at the beginning of the 1980s and now there are thousands. In some cases, these combinations are between competitors. The Toyota-General Motors joint venture in Fremont, California, is a highly visible example. In other cases they are between firms with complementary facilities: national and local carriers in the airline industry, for instance.

Similar developments are occurring in the nonprofit sector. Agencies that once duplicated activities and offered fragmented services recognize that they can better respond to client needs, and at less cost, by plugging people into a networked array of care providers from different agencies and groups. These networks have the capacity to be more flexible, faster moving, and more responsive than any single agency could, thus allowing people to choose from a wide range of customized interventions for problems that are best addressed with reference to their uniquely individual features. Effectiveness seems most assured when most of the work flows through one or more central points in the network, with those points monitoring progress and serving as clearinghouses. Whether the task is R&D or serving clients with multiple problems, networks increase the probability of creative outcomes by expanding the range (backgrounds, experiential base, occupational training, worldview) of those who are in the pool of potential members for an intervention team (Alter & Hage, forthcoming).

This is even more obvious when we consider research and development, and production and service innovation. Innovation is essentially a human capital enterprise, and the only way for firms to stay on the leading edge in tomorrow's economy will be to produce a steady stream of innovations (Chapter 1). However, so many things are in flux that the in-house human capital of any firm is certain to be inadequate to meet the challenges for innovation the future will bring. But this problem does have a solution, one which increasing numbers of corporate firms and government agencies are discovering. Network to keep the human capital of employees up to date. Network to build joint ventures where independent success is unlikely. And network to bring in supplementary human capital (e.g., consultants) on an as-needed basis when new projects are launched. Again, the solution to PI problems is being found, not in markets or in hierarchies, but in networks. Families do the same thing, as parents increasingly look outward for advice in child-rearing and assistance in child care.

We have already argued that people's minds are being reshaped for life in PI. But the point of this chapter is that changes are not limited to individuals or their interaction styles. Society itself is being reorganized. The web of interconnections constituting the warp and woof of the social world is no longer to be found in either markets or hierarchies, but is located instead within the domain of social networks, which have extended across and permeated through society as the PI transformation has progressed. Networks are forming the connection between individuals and organizations at a time when the hierarchical links predicated on legal and traditional authority are being decoupled (Alter & Hage, forthcoming).

Rebuilding Organizational Structures

One of the standard insights of organizational theorists (for reviews, see Hall, 1987; Scott, 1987) for many years has been the importance of structure as a way of integrating and coordinating activities (also see Hage, 1980; Hull & Hage, 1982; Mintzberg, 1979; Mintzberg & McHugh, 1985). We argue that designs for interrelating roles that give organizations their structure are changing fundamentally. Hage, in a pilot study of bio-tech funded by the National Science Foundation, found that the crux of the organization was a series of process committees consisting of individuals involved in research, quality control, marketing, and product development. Powers has found the same in his work with MBA students who are employed in Silicon Valley. There is a team for each product or problem so that individuals are involved in multiple team meetings (each week) in which problem solving is the main activity. In teams that unite functional departments, we see the beginnings of the establishment of the organic model suggested by Burns and Stalker (1961) but never, to our knowledge, adequately researched. The most distinctive aspect of these internal role networks is their high fluidity.

As individuals participate in more process teams, the organizing devices discussed in every management text, such as occupation, department, and level, all lose their meaning. Interestingly enough, this is exactly what Japanese managers ("The rise," 1989) excel at: moving from task to task, working in teams, and not being bound by the structural arrangements so popular with American managers and in most MBA programs (see Daft, 1989; Tosi & Carroll, 1982). Occupation (skills), department (function), and level (authority), are deconstructed because of the short lives of products/services and the rapid pace of technological change.

Internally, the power structure of organizations, especially business organizations, is going through very interesting changes. Rather than the usual rule of thumb that one can serve only one master, more work teams report to multiple bosses (Galbraith & Kazanjian, 1986). This is especially true in global corporations, and falls under the rubric of matrix management in the business literature. Research is beginning to look at organizations that have two or more presidents and even asking if it is possible that small high-tech companies need this kind of arrangement to be successful. The decomposition of power structures within organizations (Weick, 1976) as a consequence of the growth in knowledge and technological change (for a preliminary analysis, see Hage, 1988) moves us away from traditional hierarchical forms of organization into much more decentralized systems (Siljak, 1991), where fluid action networks are taking hold.

This has had another consequence as well: the creation of external role networks linking together different parts of society in ways that Nadel could never have imagined. Boundaries of organizations are being pierced, and role matrices are being constructed between organizations.[8]

The necessity of going outside the organization to acquire the information needed to stay competitive in the age of innovation is not the only way in which organizational walls are being pierced. Equally important is the construction of joint ventures to bring together expertise from different countries and industrial sectors. Agencies of comparable size (Aiken & Hage, 1968) and companies located in different industries but involved in considerable trade are most likely to form joint ventures (Pfeffer & Nowak, 1976). Common research endeavors also increase the likelihood of joint venture activity. There are now an estimated 12,000 joint ventures in the United States ("Business without borders," 1988). Similarly, the products developed in the research laboratories compel firms to move in quite different ways, necessitating new strategic alliances. All these trends require a radical reconstructing of the traditional view of hierarchy and of power in bureaucratic organizations.

External Networks as Role Matrices
and Governance Mechanisms

Nadel's imagery of role matrix—essentially mapping how roles in society are connected together in one way or another—is especially useful for PI society because of the sudden appearance of a large number of inter-organizational relationships that transcend economic sectors and institutional spheres. However, Nadel did not move beyond his concept of **role matrices to think about their poten-**

tial as governance mechanisms, which seems to us to be **one of the keys to understanding the emergent organizational structure of post-industrial society**, for it is here that we find the real social architecture of a new era.

As long as we recognize that there are different kinds of social networks, the concept of social networks can be used loosely to include linkages inside bounded social units, like organizations or families, and also inter-unit linkages that span across collectives and institutional spheres. There is a big conceptual difference between intra-organizational and inter-organizational networks because inter-organizational networks are less likely to be coordinated by a hierarchy of authority. The problems of coordination and control become much more difficult and theoretically more interesting when systemic networks bridge organizations or families, because conflicts cannot be resolved by someone higher in the chain of command and there are few rewards or punishments that can be deployed to coerce people into conformity.

In PI society inter-organizational networks are proliferating and are increasingly replacing hierarchies of authority as the dominant institutional mechanism of coordination and control. This involves an increase in the complexity of governance and necessitates complex selves having considerable negotiating skills to handle the many boundary disputes and role conflicts that arise. Although social network analysis (for some reviews, see Marsden & Lin, 1982; Morrissey et al., 1985) has become an important part of sociology and other disciplines as well, there has been little theoretical work on the central question of networks as a governance mechanism, which is one of the pillars of our analysis of the post-industrial transformation.

To date, the literature in network analysis has tended to concentrate on information networks (Boje & Whetten, 1981) and resource exchanges (Burt, 1980) or networks such as the analysis of PACs (Clawson et al., 1986; Mizaruchi & Koenig, 1986; Neustadtl & Clawson, 1988). Much less attention has been paid to the creation of networks designed to provide complex services, or where organizations band together and share in decision making. Figure 7.2 suggests how networks are evolving with the PI transformation. What

Embryonic ◀ ▶ Developed

	Exchange Networks	Action Networks	Systemic Networks
Interorganizational Activities	Almost None / Ad Hoc	Tangential	Essential / Enduring
Emergent Properties	Boundary Spanners	Pooling of Resources	Division of Labor
Goals	Individual Member Needs	Superordinate Problems of Members	Superordinate Problems in Society
Examples	Patterned Resource Exchanges and Client Referrals	Federations / Trade Associations / Coalitions / Joint Ventures and Programs	Service Delivery Systems / Research Consortia

Figure 7.2. Model of Network Development

differentiates prototype systemic networks from earlier information or resource-sharing networks is that newly evolved systemic networks have a division of labor and are working together to achieve some superordinate goal (Morrissey, et al., 1985). A detailed study of 15 of these networks plus a large number of references to the growing literature on network analysis are available in Alter and Hage (forthcoming). Here our concern is with their prevalence.

Consistent with our predictions, the elaboration of inter-organizational networks is greatest in those sectors of society where the investment in research and development is most substantial, where professional and technical occupations are most concentrated, and where product and service innovation is most critical. For instance, the National Science Foundation recently embarked on a policy of trying to create some 150 national centers of research, which will be funded partly by the federal government and partly by private businesses. One example is the artificial robotics center at Rutgers. Equally important, the choice of research projects and decisions about which companies will market what products will be made collectively by formally organized boards that are really inter-organizational oversight networks concerned with coordination and control. The objective of the National Science Foundation is to create inter-organizational systemic networks to solve complex problems that are beyond the reach of any single firm, and to do so much more quickly than has been the case in the past. These developments indicate how fast America as a society is moving away from both markets and hierarchies. We see similar movement on other fronts as well. More and more customers are also becoming involved in the design of the products—the steady movement toward customization (McQuarrie, 1991). Again, this means establishing a kind of action network of joint decision making, a far cry from Henry Ford's famous pronouncement that customers "can have any color they want, as long as it's black" (Harris, 1984, p. 78).

But perhaps the most dramatic example of this movement toward role matrices among organizations is to be found in the relationship of parts suppliers to automobile manufactures in Japan (Womack et al., 1990). Unlike the American automobile industry, which has exploited suppliers, the Japanese realize that product quality and

manufacturing flexibility can best be achieved in a climate of cooperation. Networked organizations solve problems together, and the
automobile companies insure that suppliers make a good profit. The
age of customization is arriving in Japan, where networks of organizations are used to respond to the preferences of individual
purchasers.

Conclusions

**One of the most striking analytical features of the transforma-
tion to post-industrial society is that role-sets are increasing and
person-sets are decreasing in size.** This personalizes all relationships and forces a replacement of traditional patterns of hierarchical
authority with fluid network structures.

The creation of systemic networks, where there is shared decision
making and some division of labor, marks a reconstruction of society. Brand new nonhierarchical co-determined role relationships are
being created: relationships with no traditional past of expectations,
where all meaning must be constructed from the beginning. From
Nadel's vantage point, this means society is constituting role matrices where none previously existed. And these new organizational
forms need a governance mechanism if society is to maintain its
coherence (Nadel, 1956), the ubiquitous problem of integration in
sociological theory (Powers, 1981b; Teune, 1984).[9] As organizational
and occupational specialization increases in post-industrial societies, new mechanisms of social integration are necessary. The concepts of complex role matrices and inter-organizational systemic networks are ways of describing the emergence of these new ways of
achieving social integration, for role networks seem to be replacing
both markets and hierarchies as the locus of organizational coherence in contemporary society. The most interesting (and promising)
examples of the new order are to be found in the banding together
of organizations to create complex research networks that include
not only companies that are normally competitors, but also universities and various government agencies when relevant. This reflects
the crossing of institutional spheres. And interestingly enough, it

also reflects the end of the university as an ivory tower. Society is thus being woven together in new ways at the meso level and perhaps even at the macro level as well. The best known example of this kind of research network is to be found in the semiconductor industry, where IBM and Apple have concluded that cooperation is their common path for the future. As the negative trade balance of the United States continues year after year with no end in sight, the pressure will mount for more and more collaborative efforts, particularly as one more industrial sector after another fails in this country as a consequence of foreign competition.

But if society's role matrices are becoming tightly connected, and thus social networks are connecting people into endless chains of social interaction, it is also true that these role matrices reflect a growing amount of conflict precisely because there is neither a central authority nor even any history of rules or expectations. Thus while the concerns of Nadel about the connectedness of society are being resolved, the concerns of Merton (1957) about role conflict are being aroused anew. This means that people operating in a post-industrial environment characterized by rapid technological change need to be free to use their interaction skills to constantly reshape their role relationships at the meso level of social organization.

Notes

1. Nisbet (1970) actually uses the term *social bond* to cover all the various concepts employed in sociology. We prefer to limit the meaning to the affection felt toward a role partner.

2. Connections to larger structural processes are completely missed by Homans (1950). Even when Homans described the wirebank room in the Hawthorne studies, he focused on a small group of interpersonal relationships rather than the role-relationships linking people to broader structural configurations within the organization. Indeed, Homans reached the misguided position that one can describe the larger society on the basis of micro behaviors (1974). Our whole intent here is to indicate how major structural processes involved in the growth in knowledge are restructuring the micro level of human interaction and to explore the consequences this has for the larger society, as well as the reverse process.

3. In Simmel's (1950, Chapter 1) formal sociology, a major theme is the way in which numbers qualitatively alter the nature of relationships, for example, Simmel's

discussion of the shift from a dyad to a triad. Our analysis of the uniqueness of the
role partner is inspired by this aspect of Simmel's work.

4. Will Rogers commented that he had never met a man he didn't like. We
interpret this to mean that where the entire person is involved in a role relationship,
and all aspects of selves are revealed, then we are much more likely to understand
people, including their foibles and even their nasty side. When symbolic interaction
is not blocked by impression management, the emotional messages sent back and
forth between role occupants are powerful reinforcers (Cook & Emerson, 1978).

5. It is surprising, but with automation, craft occupations frequently become less
rather than more routine. The construction trades are an interesting case in point.
Building homes is more complicated now than it used to be, despite the introduction
of labor-saving materials and the growing importance of prefabrication. A wide
variety of newly developed construction materials is now in use, and workers must
know the performance characteristics and application procedures associated with
all of them in order to be versatile (Kidder, 1985).

6. Table 7.3 actually understates the paucity of role relationships because
mechanical-bureaucratic organizations have many levels and many departments.
The only communication is within the chain of command and therefore is vertical.
Furthermore, the person-sets associated with role relationships interacting within
themselves are quite large and account for half of the relationships in the role matrix.
Needless to say, most are quite impersonal except for the co-worker or co-supervisor
or co-department role relationships. Formal committees are used, but only at the top.
A good case study of how these operate, or at least did in the past, is to be found in
On a Clear Day You Can See General Motors (Wright, 1980). Eventually the committees
are dominated by the CEO and there is little genuine discussion. The level of
communication or frequency of interaction is low except at the top, where groupthink takes over.

7. Big appliance assemblers often purchase major internal components, such as
compressors for refrigerator freezers, on a contract basis from other producers.
Custom producers like boutique wineries frequently share production equipment
(Delacroix & Solt, 1987). And many major airlines share landing facilities and
passengers with ostensibly independent regional commuter lines.

8. Innovation necessitates new skills and new sources of information. As a
consequence, teams must be reconfigured as projects move through different stages.
Teams reflect available expertise within the company. Frequently, however, necessary expertise is not contained within the organization, so corporate firms and
government agencies are discovering that they must pierce the walls of the organization and seek out experts wherever they may be. They use information networks
to tap into new sources of information in a variety of ways. Some companies, such
as IBM and General Electric, systematically contribute to research centers so that they
are involved in dense networks. Other tactics of businesses, especially in the biological area, are for companies to form particularistic relationships with specific universities, whether Harvard, Columbia, or MIT, that are in effect joint research programs.
Again, the intent here is to speed up the diffusion of information process. Finally,
small high-tech companies may offer internships to engineering or graduate stu-

dents in the physical sciences from specific universities as a mechanism of being "plugged-in" to the latest research advances.

9. The concepts of role matrices and external social networks may appear to be a simple repetition of Durkheim's famous organic solidarity. But Durkheim never made clear exactly what he meant by organic solidarity, except to suggest that in a society with a division of labor, there was considerable interdependence. And Durkheim's argument that the specialized rules of the professions would replace the universalistic rules of society is an inaccurate description of what is happening.

EPILOGUE
Sociology for the Post-Industrial Era

We live in a time of rapid social change. Yet, most people are only aware of the crisis dimensions of change, such as high crime and divorce rates, government deficits, dismal SAT scores, and poor balance of payments performance. Lost to view are the more subtle, more rudimentary, more fundamental changes now under way. Society is being transformed at the level of social roles, and with that transformation of roles and relationships comes a reconfiguration of family groupings, work units, and other forms of social organization that give society its structure. These changes suggest a sociological research agenda for the future, a need for a new approach to sociological theory if we are to make sense of contemporary events or make any progress in our efforts to develop a science of society (Powers, 1990).

Changes in the Way People Live

We have self-consciously grounded our analysis in the real matters people confront in their daily lives. Rapid change has been the

inescapable truth of the late twentieth century. Not only have there
been dramatic political upheavals, but the rudimentary ways in which
people relate to one another are also being transformed. This book
suggests the essence of that transformation in social roles, interpersonal interaction, and social networks. Taken together, the transfor-
mations of these three domains constitute nothing less than the total
reconstruction of society as we have known it.

Social Roles Transformed

Role relationships are the most basic building blocks of social
order, and they are changing fundamentally in three ways: (a) They
are becoming less routine; (b) they are becoming more personalized;
and (c) they are becoming more conflict-ridden, meaning that there
is an increase in role conflict, or disagreements over what is expected
of the occupants of roles. All three types of change translate into less
reliance on traditional role scripts and more customization and redefinition of roles over time.

The first major way in which roles are being transformed is through
the reduction of routine. This comes about primarily because of the
knowledge explosion and improvements in technology. To begin
with, knowledge growth has increased our ability to measure all
sorts of phenomena and has simultaneously increased our awareness of the ways in which different phenomena interact with one
another. Every problem is therefore seen as more complex and calls
for more individualized investigation, diagnosis, and treatment. And
at the same time that new levels of complexity enter into the way in
which we approach problems, the routine tasks that once dominated our attention are being taken over by machines. Thus, as automation reduces the amount of time people spend performing routine tasks, our growing awareness of complexity results in an
increase in the amount of time people spend on nonroutine tasks. Information search followed by creative problem solving, rather than
routine performance of well-scripted roles, dominate PI life. As sociologists our research agenda for the future should include exploration of contemporary adjustment problems (stress and burnout) as
well as the ways in which changes in roles are shaping how people

map out and make sense of events on a deep structural level (creative minds and complex selves).

The second way in which roles are changing is that they are becoming more personalized. Role-sets, the collections of companion roles a position comes into contact with, are increasing in size. To be a mother, or a fire fighter, or a teacher, or an insurance agent implies having to deal with a wider range of other social positions now than it did 20 years ago. For example, most of the calls fire fighters now respond to are injury or resuscitation calls rather than fighting fires per se, which means fire fighters have to cooperate with and obtain training and information from a wide array of health care professionals. The first aid dimension of the job also exposes fire fighters to new risks, including exposure to blood-borne diseases such as AIDS and hepatitis. Even when fire fighters are fighting fires, a larger proportion of those fires are industrial and/or involve exposure to toxic fumes. In preparation and response, the set of other roles with which fire fighters come into contact has greatly increased. And this is just one job. The same pattern is being repeated almost everywhere. Part of sociology's future research agenda should be to investigate how people handle the growing complexity of role-sets and the information overload that can result from it.

At the same time that role-sets are increasing in size, the number of people in each of those other positions, what we call person-sets, is diminishing. Taken together, these two factors tend to make every role relationship more personal. For although we are coming into contact with a greater number of different positions, those positions are generally occupied by fewer people at any given time, so that our relationships develop more personal orientation. This trend is particularly noticeable in the workplace. Over time role occupants come to be seen less as role automatons and more as unique people. PI relationships are personalized by virtue of this structural tendency in the direction of large role-sets and small person-sets. But we need to know how people maintain a sense of structural order as roles come to be more individualized and personalized.

The third change in the nature of role relationships is a manifestation of the first two. Role conflict, disagreement about what is expected of people in a relationship, is on the increase. This is a structural given. For as roles become less routine, traditional role scripts are less tenable. And as relationships become more personalized, our willingness to adjust to the needs of others increases, as does our expectation that others will adjust to our individual needs. But by how much is role conflict really increasing? And how much role change does a given increase in role conflict actually imply? What kinds of people are capable of making the requisite changes and what kinds are not? All these questions require exploration if sociology is to remain abreast of and relevant to the times.

Decline of routine activity and greater personalization of relationships, complicated by growth in role conflict, have the effect of calling traditional role scripts into question. Roles are becoming less script-like. **Role redefinition has become a part of everyday life. It is this change that is at the heart, from a conceptual and analytical point of view, of the transformation to PI society**. So the process of role redefinition should be central to the future research agenda in sociology (Powers, 1981a, 1990; R. Turner, 1990). In post-industrial societies people periodically redefine roles in creative ways in order to be more adaptive to circumstantial conditions and more responsive to the needs of others. We need more case studies leading to improved generalizations about the process of role redefinition.

The conclusion to be reached from all this is that human agency is on the increase (Touraine, 1988).[1] That is, people have more choice in structuring their lives. The choice to stay in or depart from a particular position was never uncommon, but now people go further, reshaping the role relationships by redefining their obligations to others. Reliance on agency is built into the nature of PI organization (Hage & Powers, 1990). A conceptual analysis focusing on roles helps us to understand that agency is a functional requisite in post-industrial society, and also helps us to explain why human agency has been expanding across time. For as roles become less routine, more personalized, and more conflict-laden, the need for adjustment increases. The ways in which different patterns of social structure variously effect human agency call out for more investigation.

Some people assume that predictability is impossible where human agency is involved. That is, people like Blumer (1969) seem to imply human agency translates into "anything goes." But this is far from the case. In post-industrial role relationships characterized by agency, the partners **co-determine** what will happen. This allows for a great deal of variability, but obligations still structure the activities of the person in that role, and the characteristics of those obligations are reached in accord with others. The implication is that the locus of social control has moved closer to the individual. Tradition and authority have less to do with shaping people's lives; they exert less control now than ever before. But anarchy has not resulted, because a new form of social control is taking the place of tradition. This new social control is to be found in interpersonal understanding and commitment (Bradley, 1987). That is why we must consider the ways in which role relationships, and also interaction, are being transformed as we enter the post-industrial era. The decomposition and replacement of traditional social control mechanisms need to be studied.

Interaction Transformed

The transformation of roles from script-like relationships into personalized, customized relationships has far-reaching implications for symbolic interaction. It means, in essence, that role relationships no longer gain their stability from the force of conformity to traditional norms or stereotypic models. If a role relationship is to be lasting in post-industrial society, it must gain its stability from within. If they are unable to rely on standardized role models as surefire guides for behavior, the people in a working relationship need to have a sense of trust between, a sense of confidence that the relationship as it is presently defined is workable for all concerned, and a sense that the people involved are sufficiently in touch with one another that they will recognize when further change is necessary and will be able to redefine the relationship as called for.

Since relationships have grown more personal, commitment comes to be predicated on a sense of mutual understanding and acceptance. But these do not develop automatically. They develop over time, through shared activities, and above all through communication that extends beyond a cognitive level to an emotive level of awareness.

We have added emotion to the role theories of both Nadel (1956) and Merton (1968), as well as the symbolic interactionisms of Mead

(1964) and Blumer (1969), by defining symbolic communication as having two interconnected levels: verbal and nonverbal, or cognitive and emotional levels (Chapter 3). Four distinct messages are communicated in the nonverbal emotive channel: (a) the relative importance of what is being said; (b) whether the role partner believes in what he or she is saying; (c) emotional directionality, including intensity (e.g., happiness versus anger); and (d) the degree of salience of the audience to the speaker. Using the nonverbal emotive channel of communication allows us to interpret the symbolic meaning of what is being said by placing the cognitive or verbal level of communication in an evaluative context, for the verbal level does not have much meaning unless the nonverbal or emotive level is added.

Each of these four nonverbal emotive messages is important. Nonverbal signals about the importance of the message to the speaker focus on the old problem of motivation. The more others seem to believe in what they are saying, the more convinced and more motivated we listeners become. This does not mean that we necessarily accept everything they say, only that motivation to act together is in part fed by the speakers' own feelings as expressed in a variety of nonverbal signs.

This leads naturally into the next signal or message that is sent: Does the speaker believe in what is being said and done? A basic problem in Habermas' (1984) scheme, and also in J. Turner's (1987) analysis, is the issue of trust that lies at the heart of motivation. Habermas leaves as unanswered how we develop a sense of trust or how are we able to pierce through the various presentations of self that manipulate impressions. Our insight is that people find it much more difficult to manage feelings than words. Nonverbal expressions of feeling help us ascertain whether people are sincere. Obviously we need to know a person fairly well before we can successfully decode the nonverbal level, and increased experience with a role partner provides more occasions when impression management breaks down and true convictions are revealed—moments of truth. Trust develops when we learn to tell whether a person is being truthful with us. With emotional slips, the masks people project through impression management fall away and a great deal is revealed in a short period. This can change the feeling tone of a role relationship overnight. PI life implicates people in more complex, less routine relationships, and therefore provides them with more opportunities to learn to read one another's feeling tones.

The third message is critical for two reasons. The expression of emotions is important for the affirmation of the self. Scheff (1979) has argued that it is vital for people to express rather than block their feelings. As we have suggested, one price of impression management is that it is likely to block genuine feelings until people are no longer in touch with themselves, what they really want, or what would actually make them happy. When this happens, unexpressed emotions eventually creep out in a variety of unpleasant ways that have a deadening effect on relationships. Furthermore, individuals who engage in impression management are less likely to receive the feedback that would allow them to find their true selves. The recognition that impression management cuts off others and reduces our own sensitivity to feedback helps explain why organizational leaders can be so slow to change, even when experiencing failure.

Just as the expression of feelings validates the self, how we feel about our role partners validates their participation in the relationship. It is not just the verbal communication that is important; the nonverbal level is essential for validating membership in groups. Again, the price of impression management is to reduce the capacity for the speaker to validate role partners, which weakens the relationship because, as we argued in Chapter 5, relationships that are not validated suffer entropy. Thus, aspects of nonverbal communication speak to fundamental issues involving the affirmation of self and of others. They speak to the ways in which trust and motivation are built.

Lasting bonds, especially for people who are not very verbal, are likely to be created and sustained by doing things together rather than by talking. At the same time, if we do not enjoy the person we are with, this will be communicated as well, which is why forced efforts to revive affection sometimes accentuate problems rather than relieve them. Both parties have to have the right directionality of emotion. Trying to either get closer to someone who isn't ready to be close or rekindle closeness only repels them.

One intriguing implication of our ideas is the prediction that emotional bonds are deepening as we move toward role relationships characterized by variety of activities, uniqueness of the role partner, activity integration, and so on. The post-industrial transformation is creating a society predicated upon gemeinschaft, even more than was the case in pre-industrial times, when emotional bonds were generally based on blood relationships and therefore involved little choice. With more leisure time and much more choice of what can be done with it, with better communications systems and more opportunities to interact, even kinship relations can develop stronger emotional bonds. The growing recognition of the importance of emotions as a topic for sociological study reflects the new reality of more intimate social relationships in post-industrial society.

Emotions also play an unheralded role in the post-industrial workplace. Intuition and insight are more likely to emerge when individuals are in contact with their feelings. Emotions are also critical for creativity and problem solving because they allow us to more easily detect the ideas and suggestions of others. If we are in better contact with our own feelings, we more readily observe those of others; that is, we become better listeners and interpreters of symbolic communication. Frequently, when ideas are being exchanged, their importance may not be well expressed on the verbal level—new ideas are by definition usually not well thought out and therefore are usually not expressed well with words. Their significance will be expressed first and more accurately on the nonverbal level. Joint efforts at successfully building innovative ideas into something useful is a distinct kind of work requiring this second-channel communication; for in groups confronting uncertainty, objections are seldom clearly stated. **But if group members are "listening" to the feeling tones, they will understand when they must take the time to explore vaguely formulated ideas or unspecified objections**.

Studying the way in which feelings allow for the choice of correct or creative solutions will be a particularly fruitful line of inquiry because it touches upon so many contemporary issues. For example, some ideas are not heard and others are. Coming to understand how group members "hear" a new idea and build upon it would be an extremely important and immensely practical contribution to research on innovation. This speaks directly to the heart of the idea-building process. Furthermore, in creative problem-solving groups there is probably a special set of roles, with some people suggesting ideas, others evaluating them, and still others providing the necessary technical information relative to those ideas, and so forth. We believe the emergence of new and specialized roles in creative groups will be a particularly useful avenue of research for those concerned with the management of innovation.

One final dimension of this phenomena has to do with the growing importance of telecommunications. Accurately gauging the importance of a message requires great astuteness if the message arrives via electronic mail. This raises a series of practical research questions about the best sociological strategies for effectively promoting the meaningful interaction needed for team creativity in an age of telecommuting and telecontacting.

Social Networks Transformed

Changes in the character of social roles and interaction lend new importance to networks. As role-sets increase in size, and as demand for flexible response or creative solutions to complex problems increases, people must be able to reach out for help and ideas to an ever more diverse and constantly changing array of others with unique talents, training, and insights. This need cannot be satisfied under the umbrella of a formal organization with fixed personnel, for a fixed organization cannot maintain a large enough talent pool to meet every possible array of contingencies that might arise on a case-by-case basis. Nor can this need be met in an open market, for effective solution of complex problems requires a depth of communication that can only come from sustained interaction. Fluid networks seem to offer a solution, helping people meet needs that were once met in markets or hierarchies. But the degree to which this has happened, the process through which it occurs, and the precise forms it takes need to be systematically explored. And issues of coordination and control need to be studied, especially multi-organizational coordination where different units are linked together by semifluid networks.

We predict that the fluid network will be the defining form of social organization in the PI era. Formal organizations will continue to exist, but interorganizational networks, which span organizational boundaries and provide for the interpenetration of functional activities, will grow in importance. Joint ventures are an example. This raises several important research questions. How permeable will the fluid networks of the future be? How will resources, rewards, or revenues be allocated within those networks? What structures of coordination will develop? How will the growing importance of interorganizational networks transform the organizations being linked? In what ways will markets be either supplanted or disrupted by the growing importance of fluid networks?

The elaboration of roles-sets, which occurs largely through the extension of social networks, provides an analytical tool for understanding how the institutions of society are being reshaped. It is no accident that network analysis has become an important aspect of sociological theory in recent years. The corporations and families of today are being reconstituted by the linkage of group members to outside experts via relatively personal yet fluid networks, and sometimes those units are even reconstituted into multiple organizations and families. Blended families created by divorce and remarriage are an example. Institutions are being reshaped in the process. In the corporate world the standard benchmarks of organizational design— occupation, level, and department—are being deconstructed into process committees in profit centers, joint ventures, and other emergent social forms. Here is another quite promising avenue of research, especially for those interested in the future of organizations.

And as network structures grow in size and fluidity, people find that interpenetration of the various institutional aspects of our lives grows. We devote more work time to family role obligations: bringing our children to work, getting on the office phone to locate support services for aging parents, and so on. Nor is this a one-way street. We also tell our children to go watch videos while we finish the work we feel an inner compulsion to bring home, and we take more work with us on family vacations. Sociology needs solid research on how much interpenetration of various role-related activities actually occurs in different settings. And we need to study successful strategies for formalizing and orchestrating the interpenetration of activity, such as Apple Computer's on-site day care for children of employees, and IBM's information and referral system for employees who are responsible for young children and/or aging parents with special problems.

The Deconstruction and Reconstruction of Society

The new post-industrial agenda is reconstruction of the society from the bottom up. This starts with redefinition of family and work roles and assumes another important form in networks that break through old organizational boundaries. But novel network arrangements can work only after relationships have been redefined, a point that may be obscured somewhat by Figure E.1, which directs attention to the fact that institutional changes necessitate new kinds of minds and selves.

Social roles, the obligations that attach people to one another, are being redefined as traditional scripts give way to co-determined, customized sets of obligations that fit people's changing needs. The ways in which people interact with one another are changing as we abandon impression management and seek more genuine, honest, and open communication. And the interlinkages that tie people in the society together are changing, as fluid networks replace hierarchical organizations and supplant reliance on open markets. The social force of knowledge, as manifested in technology, rising levels of education, and increased R&D, has resulted in rapid deconstruction of industrial organizations and traditional families. But from the standpoint of this book, the most critical changes are the deconstruction of social roles and role-sets (see Tables E.1 and E.2).

These changes are not easy. They generate an astounding amount of role conflict, placing individuals at risk of burnout or information overload and producing high rates of role failure. But we are adjusting to new conditions over time. Society is literally being reconstructed in ways people would never have imagined 20 years ago. If we have helped readers understand the shape of the new social order, then we have achieved our primary objective.

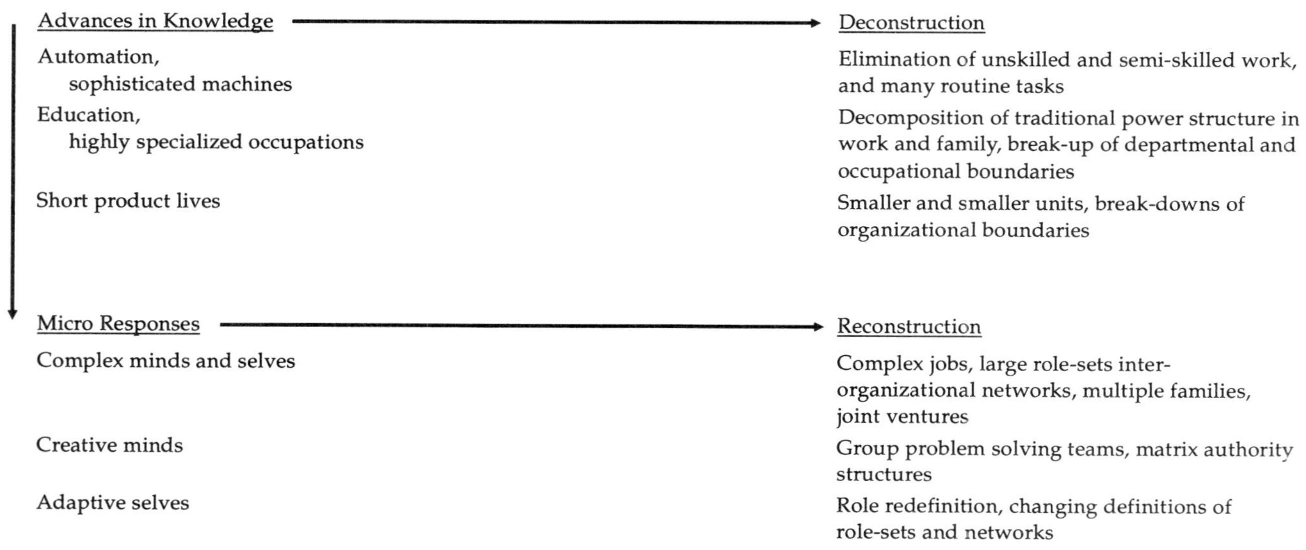

Advances in Knowledge

Automation,
  sophisticated machines

Education,
  highly specialized occupations

Short product lives

Deconstruction

Elimination of unskilled and semi-skilled work,
and many routine tasks

Decomposition of traditional power structure in
work and family, break-up of departmental and
occupational boundaries

Smaller and smaller units, break-downs of
organizational boundaries

Micro Responses

Complex minds and selves

Creative minds

Adaptive selves

Reconstruction

Complex jobs, large role-sets inter-
organizational networks, multiple families,
joint ventures

Group problem solving teams, matrix authority
structures

Role redefinition, changing definitions of
role-sets and networks

Figure E.1. The Twin Processes of Deconstruction and Reconstruction

Table E.1 The Reconstruction of Society

Post-Industrial Selves	Behavioral Outcomes	Institutional Requirements
Creative minds	Quality of group problem solving	Product innovation, technological innovation
Flexible selves in problem-solving groups	Quality of role redefinition	Rapidity of technological and product change
Complex minds	Sophistication of creative solutions	Matrix authority structures
Complex selves in problem-solving groups	Capacity to handle complex solutions	Network governance structures
Complex roles	Amount of renegotiation	Deconstruction of occupations, hierarchical and organizational boundaries
Complex role relationships and role-sets	Amount of role conflict	

Table E.2 The Reasons for the Growth in the Independence of Role Relationships or Human Agency

Dimensions of Role Relationships	Essential Argument
Scope	Difficulty of programming a variety of activities in different places and at different times
Intensity	The above difficulty is compounded by long-duration activities that require great effort
Integration	Coordination of many role relationships cannot be programmed because of the complexity of the problem
Fluidity	Rapid changes prevent programming of role relationships

Sociological Theory Transformed

Our primary objective was to describe fundamental changes in the ways in which people are connected to one another. But we also hope this book contributes in important ways to the reorientation of sociological theory. For if our analysis is correct, sociological theorists need to change the way in which they think about society on an analytical level. We need to focus on different issues, getting past our myopic preoccupation with wealth and power so that we can focus on knowledge growth as the engine of social change. We need to understand sociological phenomena in a new light, recognizing that agency is itself a communal rather than an individual enterprise, and that range of choice is a variable property reflecting the nature of social structural conditions. And most important, we need to construct different types of theory, combining useful insights from different theoretical schools to produce a viable analytical scheme for studying the meso level of social organization, where individuals are influenced by and in turn influence the character of a social order that extends beyond themselves.

Knowledge Growth: The Engine of Social Change

If society is being transformed in fundamental ways, we need to ask ourselves where that change comes from and what kind of internal logic the new order will have. Earlier sociological theorists tended to approach the question of change while preoccupied with power (e.g., Marx, 1967; Pareto, 1984). This preoccupation diverts attention away from the true underlying logic and real engine of change in PI society. That is knowledge growth. The logic of the industrial order revolved around the mobilization of power and the concentration of wealth, but the logic of the post-industrial order revolves around knowledge growth. Knowledge growth makes roles more complex, implicates people in less standardized interaction, and prompts people to enter more complex networks bridging bounded social units. At the same time, the objectives of activity are changing. Whereas power and wealth are the final objectives and ultimate pursuits of life in industrial societies, the greater knowledge and better understanding in the interests of mastery over difficult problems and uncertain conditions are the ultimate objectives of life in PI society. They are the things people pursue as tests of self-worth and personal meaning.

This marks a profound change in orientation, but one that sociologists seem reluctant to embrace. The history of our discipline has revolved around the study of inequality for too long. We have always looked at society in terms of who gets what, and how, and what the consequences of a given distribution of wealth tend to be. But if we are to understand the workings and inner logic of post-industrial society, we must now turn at least in part to the issue of knowledge growth, discover the structural conditions and interaction dynamics under which knowledge growth will proceed most quickly, examine the ways in which knowledge is expanded and used, and explore the impact of the knowledge explosion as the ripple effects from that explosion radiate through society.

This does not mean that the distributions of wealth and power are meaningless or irrelevant. Far from it. They are important precisely because they impact on knowledge growth and the application of knowledge for improved problem-solving. The mechanisms of exploitation, which have produced a great underclass and denied large segments of society a realistic opportunity to develop to their human capital potential, have simultaneously denied society the contributions those people are capable of making. A society that easily discards millions of people is unlikely to succeed in PI competition. That path is so obviously dysfunctional that ignoring the problems of the underclass seems incomprehensible.

The key to our argument is that knowledge shapes events in PI society even more than the distributions of wealth and power. One of our special contributions to the study of knowledge has been to pinpoint the connection between technology, education, and R&D. As knowledge grows through expanded R&D, we implant more knowledge in machines via automated technology, and in people via education. Only by looking at the three together can we begin to develop a real sense for the ways in which our society is changing. The current state of knowledge and rate of knowledge growth is such that more knowledge is being embedded in minds than in machines. As we have noted throughout the book, this has radical implications for the ways people are called on to live and work.

Agency by Co-Determination

The transformation of roles induced by knowledge growth has a tremendous impact on choice. The growing importance of fluid networks means we can choose who we want to interact with and in what capacities. And the growing prevalence of role redefinition means it is more acceptable for people to shape and design the nature of their relationships with others. At the same time, our capacity to do so is increased by the availability of cars, telephones, fax machines, and electronic mail, all of which expand our ability to activate relationships at will. Moreover, the development of new technologies, and their integration with old technologies, will further accelerate this process. For example, interfacing "virtual reality" with phone systems will make it literally possible, from a sensory point of view, to reach out and "touch" one another, and see one another, and smell one another, and feel one another. We will be able to really be there without really being there. Imagine the implications for enacting, sustaining, reviving, and altering social relationships along the concatenated networks that link people together in PI society!

In the past, agency has been viewed as the question of choice. Can individuals choose, or do they lack choice? Our analysis suggests that this conceptualization is inappropriate for the times. For where choice exists, it no longer tends to be individual choice. The choices PI people exercise most often are those requiring negotiation and co-determined agreement among people who must cooperate, but can no longer look to traditional scripts to guide behavior. Choices must be made, more than ever before. But these choices are increasingly made by people acting collectively, rather than by individuals acting unilaterally as if they were autonomous.

On the surface, our formulation sounds like that of Blumer (1969), who assumed that people construct society. But Blumer failed to show how that construction occurs or why it occurs some places more than others (Powers, 1981a). We demonstrate that knowledge growth, and more specifically the ways in which new knowledge is implanted in minds, in machines, and in patterns of social organization, determines the level of structural need for the exercise of agency as a functional prerequisite to flexible adaptation in the face of uncertain and changing conditions.

Knowledge explosion has made the world a different place. People want customized solutions to complex problems, which means that cooperation and flexibility are both necessary. People have to have the freedom (not as individuals, but as partners) to modify their roles and reconfigure the systems of relationships in which they work and live. Post-industrial society cannot function effectively unless people are able and willing to exercise that kind of agency. The severity of contemporary social problems is evidence that society has a good distance remaining to go in its reconstruction, and that we have a long way to go in preparing people for dealing with the demands of post-industrial life.

Sociological Theory on the Meso Level

Roles are becoming more relational; human agency is on the increase; and networks are gaining importance and growing more fluid, providing a substitute for markets and hierarchies in the interface between social units. In theoretical terms, we focus on the meso level of social analysis, which provides a link between the micro world of the individual and the macro world of the wider society (Collins, 1988, has a similar intent). In the process we offer a new synthesis of old theoretical perspectives, and a new solution for old theoretical problems in the discipline.

In PI society people are called on to constantly reconstruct their roles to allow responsiveness to the changing needs of others, while organizations are called on to produce creative solutions to complex problems and rapidly adapt to changing circumstances. Both sets of demands, micro individual and macro organizational, are satisfied on the meso level of role relationships and network interconnections, where people work collaboratively, pool human capital, and redesign relationships to maximize creativity and improve problem-solving potential. This assumes creative minds and complex selves working in an environment where impression management sub-sides and makes room for genuinely effective communication, and where social networks are fluid enough to allow people to change the mix of talents they can call upon at different times.

A recent American-German theory conference (Alexander et al., 1987) on the problem of micro and macro linkages highlighted re-newed interest among sociologists in how the individual and soci-ety are connected. Our theoretical contribution has been to combine a macro structural-functional analysis of society with micro sym-bolic interactionism. The new functional requisites of PI society are actually interactional characteristics. PI society produces rapid tech-nological change to which individuals must respond with flexibility, and it creates complex new social problems that people need to learn how to deal with creatively. People who are comfortable both with multiple identities and with expressing their feelings are more likely to be creative and flexible than individuals with one central or core identity to which all other identities are subordinated. Rapid tech-nological change makes role scripts functionally obsolete and re-quires the constant redefinition of role relationships and role-sets as well as reconstitution of social networks. The new functional imper-ative is for fluid structures that nourish constant innovation.

Role theorists and symbolic interactionists have had the right ideas in principle. But they have largely ignored the organizational settings where role redefinition and fluid networks are most obvi-ous, and have consequently failed to produce a body of theory that captures and explains the full richness of the real world. We try to correct this problem by fully integrating structural-functionalist and symbolic interactionist perspectives to develop a new, empirically grounded, and testable theory that is directly linked to an identifi-able research agenda.

Many have been critical of the structural-functionalist perspec-tive because of a perception that it places heavy emphasis on stabil-ity without change. Our functionalist approach is the very opposite. The essence of our theory is that constant change in the society—produced by growth in knowledge—implies functional requisites at the individual level. Rapid change is inescapable. But not all societies will be successful, or competitive, in a PI world. Societal success rests on having a populace composed in large part of individuals with complex selves and creative minds who are capable of performing in symbolic roles and fluid social networks. The best test of a mature functionalist perspective is precisely its ability to accommodate change, which our theory does. How is adaptive change possible? How does it occur? Our analytical framework provides answers to those questions.

One sign of the coming post-industrial society is the appearance and subsequent failure of many new social forms. Another sign is to be found in a widespread pattern of role failures. Failure is the best evidence that a functional perspective is indeed viable.

Similarly, the many experiments that are occurring are healthy signs of a society in which people are attempting to adapt social structural arrangements to changing conditions, another structural-functionalist tenet worth rescuing. But this should not be taken to suggest that all experiments will be equally successful. Quite the contrary. All the current evidence indicates that the United States and many other countries are having a great deal of difficulty in adapting to post-industrial social problems and to the new rules of global competition. Japan, by contrast, is a society in which people learn cooperative teamwork strategies from an early age, giving the Japanese what is, from a sociological point of view, a built-in competitive advantage when commercial success rests on coming up with integrated solutions to complex multidisciplinary problems— another issue that warrants sociological investigation. Societies have to adapt, especially in periods of wrenching socioeconomic change. Given the widespread pattern of adaptive failure in the United States, this is an appropriate time to redirect attention to the problem of societal adaptation.

Admittedly, many people rejected the structural-functional perspective because adaptation was made an article of faith, just as the inevitability of class conflict was in the Marxist perspective. But by calling attention to the importance of role conflict and institutional failures (e.g., Coser, 1956), adaptation is transformed from an a priori assumption into a research question and a pressing theoretical problem.[2]

Most of the discussions of micro and macro linkages in the German-American conference mentioned above avoided any analysis of the intervening links between the individual and society (for an exception, see Munch & Smelser, 1987). They were usually strong in either their sense of the individual or their sense of society, but not of both. In this book we have tried to provide equal time to the individual (Chapters 3, 4, and 5) and to society (Chapters 1, 2, and 7), as well as to role-sets as a bridge between the micro and macro order (Chapter 6). In each of those chapters we discuss and explore different dimensions of the linkage between individuals and society—between micro role relationships and macro institutions. As sophisticated technologies eliminate routinized activities, the tasks left for people to perform are those requiring ingenuity and problem solving, rather than execution of routine procedures. Role relationships expand in number, and social networks become both more extensive and inter-actionally intense. Role matrices gain importance in the orchestration and maintenance of intra- and interorganizational relations.

People are not only reconstructing society via the redefinition of roles and the construction of more complex role-sets and more fluid social networks, they are also creating new products and developing new services, inventing new techniques and therapies, and exploring new ways of sustaining interpersonal relationships (Forester, 1985). We thus offer a theoretical synthesis, which melds micro and macro approaches to sociology and has practical and applied as well as theoretical dimensions. By studying how roles in work organizations and families are being redefined, why they are changing, and how this impacts on the role relationships in them and the networks between them, we grasp much more effectively how the individual and society are intertwined.

Functional change is both increasing choice in role relationships and increasing variety in role-sets. Thus, part of the macro-micro linkage is a casting adrift of roles from societally defined role scripts, precisely so that they can become complex and flexible in the face of demands for more detailed information search and more innovative problem solving. The accent is on group creativity, co-determination of strategies, and interpersonal negotiation in an environment characterized by role conflict. The reconstruction of society has only begun. It necessitates symbolic communication where honest feelings, rather than impression management, are expressed. This is a problematic aspect of the "new world order."

Although Mead, Merton, and Nadel overlooked the importance of knowledge or technology in their various theories, we have found that other concepts they introduced are critical in building a satisfactory theory of post-industrial society. From Mead we take the basic question: What kinds of minds for what types of societies? Our answer is that knowledge growth and technological change in post-industrial society require creative minds and adaptive selves. From Merton we borrow the ideas of role-sets, role scripts, and role conflicts. We suggest that as role-sets become more complex, role scripts disappear and role conflict increases. From Nadel we borrow the ideas of networks and role matrices, and argue that the growth in knowledge is resulting in a movement toward more network integration of role matrices both within organizations and external to them.

As we have synthesized Mead, Merton, and Nadel, we have added to their cognitive theories a heavy dose of emotion as well as co-determination. In all these instances we have made predictions that would run counter to the expectations of Mead, Merton, Nadel and others, for our theory is a novel synthesis. This is as it should be. Synthesizing inevitably means borrowing some ideas, eliminating others, and developing new insights.

Looking to the Future

The knowledge explosion will not produce a trouble-free world. As we have stressed, the transformation to post-industrial society is causing enormous difficulties. In particular, there is a growing population of people who are disenfranchised because they lack the training and disposition to be problem solvers. This is a human capital problem. It presents an enormous challenge to society, a problem made all the more serious by lack of resolve on the part of political leaders to abandon programs and policies conceived in the industrial age. We must tailor a forward-looking agenda.

Nevertheless, society is being transformed from the ground up. Symbolic interaction gains importance in post-industrial society because of the constant role redefinition generated by technological change. Role redefinition is one of the truly ubiquitous features of social life and therefore one of the really fruitful areas for future sociological research (Powers, 1981a, 1990; R. Turner, 1990). A focus on role redefinition should not only shed a great deal of light on the specific techniques people use for maintaining relationships, but also enable us to address a wide range of practical questions. Analysis of role redefinition forces an awareness of the increasing number of role conflicts people find themselves having to deal with. These conflicts provide opportunities for studying symbolic communication and the place of emotions in the role redefinition process, for only by carefully reading the symbolic level of communication can role conflicts be successfully resolved. This is especially true for those close role relationships involving teamwork or invoking a great deal of affect.

On a wider plane, network structures are beginning to supplant markets and hierarchies as the structural bulwark of society. In the process, new forms of interunit combination are emerging, and society is being reconstructed.

It is our prediction that the real expansion in research and development, and all of its consequences for knowledge growth, has yet to occur, which makes this book timely. We have made a series of predictions about the direction in which post-industrial society is evolving, and these predictions can be tested as the future unfolds. One thing that our synthetic theory should do is reduce the sense of future shock or the fear of uncertainty by providing a satisfactory explanation for the way in which societal transformation will help people cope with change.

Notes

1. Agency has been an important theme in sociological theory from the beginning (e.g., Parsons, 1937) to the present (e.g., Cohen, 1989; Giddens, 1984) and was the focus of the 1990 German-American Sociological Theory Conference.

2. Perhaps the most controversial point we have made is that the high divorce rate is a sign of failure. Divorced readers might resent this and argue with us. But surely most would admit that if they could have avoided the pain that their divorce engendered, they would have. We suggested a number of reasons why divorce is more common today than it was in the past and—most debatable of all—we predict that the incidence of divorce will decline in the future. We feel the primary cause of divorce is the inability of one or both partners to redefine spousal roles as personalities and situations change over the course of the life cycle. This inability seems to us to be a common characteristic of industrial personalities and industrial times. But one of the truly distinctive traits of post-industrial people is the comparative ease and comfort with which they are able to redefine roles over time.

REFERENCES

Adler, P., Adler, P., & Fontana, A. (1987). Everyday life sociology. *Annual Review of Sociology, 13,* 217-235. Palo Alto, CA: Annual Reviews.

Administrative Science Quarterly. (1983). [Special issue on organizational culture], 28.

Aiken, M., & Hage, J. (1968, December). Organizational interdependence and intra-organizational properties. *American Sociological Review,* 912-931.

Aiken, M., & Hage, J. (1971, January). The organic organization and innovation. *Sociology, 5,* 63-82.

Alba, R. (1990). *Ethnic identity. The transformation of white America.* New Haven, CT: Yale University Press.

Aldrich, H. (1979). *Organizations and environments.* Englewood Cliffs, NJ: Prentice-Hall.

Aldrich, H., & Auster, E. (1986). Even dwarfs started small: Liabilities of age and size and their strategic implication. In B. Stow & L. L. Cummings (Eds.), *Research in organizational behavior* (pp. 165-198). Greenwich, CT: JAI.

Aldrich, H., & Mueller, S. (1982). The evolution of organizational forms. In B. Stow & L. L. Cummings (Eds.), *Research in Organizational Behavior* (pp. 33-87). Greenwich, CT: JAI.

Alexander, J. (1980-1983). *Theoretical logic in sociology* (4 vols.). Berkeley: University of California Press.

Alexander, J., Gresen, B., Munch, R., & Smelser, N. (1987). *The micro-macro link.* Berkeley: University of California Press.

Allen, S. (1978). Organizational choices and general management influence networks in divisionalized companies. *Academy of Management Journal,* 341-365.

219

Allison, P. (1985). *Event history analysis* (Quantitative applications in the social sciences: Vol. 46). Beverly Hills, CA: Sage.

Alter, C., & Hage, J. (forthcoming). *Systemic Interorganizational Networks.* Newbury Park, CA: Sage.

Ambry, M. (1988, December). At home in the office. *American Demographics, 10,* 30-33.

An unstoppable export machine. (1988, October 6). *The New York Times.*

Aron, A., & Aron, E. (1986). *Love and the expansion of self: Understanding attraction and satisfaction.* New York: Hemisphere.

Ashby, E. (1956). *Introduction to cybernetics.* New York: John Wiley.

Azumi, K., & Hull, F. (1986, February). Productivity improvement and socio-technical systems. In *Japanese versus American factors: Beyond quality circles report AJ-1.* Submitted to National Science Foundation.

Azumi, K., Hull, F., & Hage, J. (1983). Managing high technology. In an International Perspective: A Comparison between Japan and the United States, *The challenge of Japan's internationalism: Organization and culture* In H. Nennari & H. Befu (Eds.). Kwonsei Galian University: Kodensha International.

Bales, R. (1950). A set of categories for the analysis of small group interaction. *American Sociological Review, 15,* 257-263.

Bane, M. J., & Ellwood, D. (1989, September). One fifth of nation's children: Why are they poor? *Science,* 1047-1053.

Barley, S. (1990). The alignment of technology and structure through roles and networks. *Administrative Science Quarterly, 35,* 61-103.

Bateson, G. (1972). *Steps to an ecology of mind.* New York: Ballatine.

Bauman, Z. (1988). Is there a postmodern sociology? *Theory, Culture, and Society, 5*(2-3), 217-238.

Bell, D. (1973). *The coming of post-industrial society.* New York: Basic Books.

Bellah, R., Madsen, R., Sullivan, W., Swidler, A., & Tipton, S. (1985). *Habits of the heart: Individualism and commitment in American life.* New York: Harper & Row.

Biddle, B. (1979). *Role theory, expectations, identities, and behaviors.* New York: Academic Press.

Biddle, B. (1987). Recent developments in role theory. *Annual Review of Sociology, 12,* 67-92.

Biddle, B., & Thomas, E. (1966). *Role theory: Concepts and research.* New York: John Wiley.

Birenbaum, A. (1984). Toward a theory of role acquisition. *Sociological Theory, 2,* 315-328.

Blau, P., & Schoenherr, R. (1971). *The structure of organizations.* New York: Basic Books.

Blau, P., & Scott, R. (1962). *Formal organizations: A comparative approach.* San Francisco, CA: Chandler.

Blauner, R. (1964). *Alienation and freedom: The factory worker and his industry.* Chicago: University of Chicago Press.

Blumer, H. (1969). *Symbolic interactionism.* Englewood Cliffs, NJ: Prentice-Hall.

Blumstein, P., & Kollock, P. (1988). Personal relationships. *Annual Review of Sociology, 114,* 467-490.

Boje, D., & Whetten, D. (1981). Effects of organizational strategies and contextual constraints on centrality and attributions of influence in interorganizational networks. *Administrative Science Quarterly, 26*, 378-395.

Bott, E. (1957). *Family and social network.* London: Tavistock.

Boyett, J., & Conn, H. (1991). *Workplace 2000.* New York: Dutton.

Bradley, R. (1987). *Charisma and social structure.* New York: Paragon.

Braverman, H. (1974). *Labor and monopoly capital.* New York: Monthly Review Press.

Brayfield, A. (1990). *Gender, wage-labor characteristics, and the allocation of household tasks.* Unpublished doctoral dissertation, University of Maryland.

Bullough, V. (1981). Age at menarche. *Science, 213*, 365-366.

Burawoy, M. (1979). *Manufacturing consent.* Chicago: University of Chicago Press.

Burns, T., & Stalker, G. M. (1961). *The management of innovation.* London: Tavistock.

Burr, W. (1976). Role transition. *Journal of Marriage and Family, 72*, 407-416.

Burt, R. (1977, Winter). Power in a social typology. *Social Science Research, 6*, 1-83.

Burt, R. (1980). Cooptive corporate action networks. *Administrative Science Quarterly, 25*(4), 557-582.

Burton, L., Dittmer, J., & Loveless, C. (1986). *What's a smart woman like you doing at home?* Washington: Acropolis.

Business without borders. (1988, June 20). *U.S. News & World Report*, p. 48.

Busino, G. (1987). La sociologie, l'unite de la science et la pluralite des cultures [Sociology, the unity of science and the plurality of cultures]. *Revue Europeene des Sciences Sociales [European Review of the Social Sciences], 25*(74), 161-180.

Campbell, J., Hollingworth, J. R., & Lindberg, L. (1991). *The governance of the American economy.* Cambridge, UK: Cambridge University Press.

Camus, A. (1988). *The stranger* (M. Ward, Trans.). New York: Knopf.

Caplow, T. (1968). *Two against one: Coalitions in triads.* Englewood Cliffs, NJ: Prentice-Hall.

Caplow, T. (1982). Christmas gifts and kin networks. *American Sociological Review, 47*, 383-392.

Carnevale, A. (1991). *America and the new economy.* Washington, DC: American Society for Training and Development/U.S. Department of Labor.

Carroll, G. (1988). *Ecological models of organizations.* Cambridge, MA: Ballinger.

Chandler, A. (1962). *Strategy and structure: Chapters in the history of the American industrial enterprise.* Cambridge: MIT Press.

Chandler, A. (1977). *The visible hand.* Cambridge, MA: Harvard University Press.

Chomsky, N. (1965). *Aspects of the theory of syntax.* Cambridge: MIT Press.

Clawson, D., Neustadtl, A., & Bearden, J. (1986). The logic of business unity. *American Sociological Review, 51*, 797-811.

Clough, P. (1986). Understanding subjugation: The relation of theory and ethnography. *Studies in Symbolic Interaction, 7*, 3-11.

Coch, L., & French, J.R.P. (1948). Overcoming resistance to change. *Human Organization, 1*(4), 512-532.

Cohen, I. (1989). *Structuration theory.* New York: St. Martin's.

Cohen, S., & Zysmen, J. (1988). Manufacturing innovation and American industrial competitiveness. *Science, 239*, 1110-1115.

Collins, P. (1991). *Occupational inertia, radical technological change and the occupational structure of manufacturing establishments.* Unpublished paper, School of Business, University of Washington.

Collins, P., Hage, J., & Hull, F. (1988). Technical systems: A framework for the analysis of technology. In S. Bachrach & N. Di Tomest (Eds.), *Research in the sociology of organizations* (pp. 81-100). Greenwich, CT: JAI.

Collins, R. 1979. *The Credential Society.* New York: Academic Press.

Collins, R. (1981). On the micro-foundations of macro-sociology. *American Journal of Sociology, 86,* 984-1014.

Collins, R. (1988). *Theoretical sociology.* New York: Harcourt Brace Jovanovich.

Cook, K., & Emerson, R. (1978). Power, equity, and commitment in exchange networks. *American Sociological Review, 43,* 721-739.

Cook, K., Emerson, R., Gillmore, M., & Yamagishi, T. (1983). The distribution of power in exchange networks: Theory and experimental results. *American Journal of Sociology, 89*(2), 275-305.

Cooley, C. H. (1902). *Human nature and social order.* New York: Scribner.

Corwin, R. (1969). Patterns of organizational conflict. *Administrative Science Quarterly, 14,* 507-521.

Corwin, R. (1970). *Militant professionalism: A study of organizational conflict in high schools.* New York: Appleton-Century-Crafts.

Coser, L. (1956). *The functions of social conflict.* New York: Free Press.

Coser, L. (1969). *Greedy institutions.* New York: Free Press.

Coser, R. (1961). Insulation from observability and types of social conformity. *American Sociological Review, 26,* 28-39.

Crozier, M. (1964). *The bureaucratic phenomenon.* Chicago: University of Chicago Press.

Daft, R. (1989). *Organizational theory and design* (3rd ed.). St. Paul: West.

Daft, R., & Becker, S. (1978). *Innovation in organizations: Innovation adaption in school organization.* New York: Elsevier.

Degler, C. (1980). *At odds: Women and the family in America from the revolution to the present.* New York: Oxford University Press.

Delacroix, J., & Solt, M. (1987). Niche formation and foundations in the California wine industry 1941-1984. In G. Carrol (Ed.), *Ecological models of organization.* Cambridge, MA: Ballinger.

Denzin, N. (1991). *Postmodernism and the poverty of social theory.* Newbury Park, CA: Sage.

Dertouzas, M., Lester, R., & Solow, R. (1989). *Made in America.* Cambridge: MIT Press.

Deutsch, K. (1953). *Nationalism and social communication.* Cambridge, MA: MIT Press.

Dubin, R. (1979). Central life interests: Self-integrity in a complex world. *Pacific Sociological Review, 22,* 405-426.

Durkheim, E. (1964). *The division of labor in society,* (G. Simpson, Trans.). New York: Free Press. (Original work published 1893)

Erikson, K. (1986). On work and alienation. *American Sociological Review, 51,* 1-8.

Featherstone, M. (Ed.). (1988a). *Postmodernism.* Newbury Park, CA: Sage.

Featherstone, M. (1988b). In pursuit of the post-modern. *Theory, Culture, and Society, 5,* 195-216.

Feher, F. (1987). The status of post modernity. *Philosophy and Social Criticism, 13*(2), 195-206.

Fleming, L. (1989). *The one-minute commute*. Davis, CA: Acacia Books.

Florida, R., & Kenney, M. (1991). Transplanted organizations. *American Sociological Review, 56*, 381-399.

Forester, T. (1985). *The information technology revolution*. Cambridge: MIT Press.

Foucault, M. (1977). *Discipline and punishment*. New York: Pantheon.

Freeman, C. (1982). *The economics of industrial innovation* (2nd ed.). Cambridge: MIT Press.

Freudenberger, H., with Geraldine Richelson. (1981). *Burn out*. Toronto: Bantam.

Frey, S. (1990, Winter). Who takes care of the kids? *Santa Clara Magazine*, pp. 12-16.

Friday, P., & Hage, J. (1981). Youth crime in postindustrial societies: An integrated perspective. In L. Shelley (Ed.), *Readings in comparative criminology* (pp. 43-56). Carbondale: Southern Illinois Press.

Furstenberg, F., Jr. (1990). Divorce and the American family. *Annual Review of Sociology, 16*, 379-403.

Furstenberg, F., & Spanier, G. B. (1984). *Recycling the family*. Beverly Hills, CA: Sage.

Galbraith, J. R., & Kazanjian, R. K. (1986). *Strategy implementation: Structure, systems, and process*. St. Paul: West.

Garfinkel, H. (1967). *Studies in ethnomethodology*. Englewood Cliffs, NJ: Prentice-Hall.

Garson, B. (1975). *All the live long day: The meaning and demeaning of routine work*. New York: Penguin.

Gelber, S. (1983, June). Working at play: The culture of the workplace and the rise of baseball. *Journal of Social History, 16*, 3-22.

Gelber, S. (1991, June). A job you can't lose: Work and hobbies in the great depression. *Journal of Social History, 21*, 741-766.

Genevie, L., & Margolies, E. (1987). *The motherhood report*. New York: Macmillan.

Gerson, K. (1985). *Hard choices: How women decide about work and motherhood*. Berkeley: University of California Press.

Getzel, J., & Jackson, P. W. (1968). *Creativity and intelligence: Explorations with children*. New York: John Wiley.

Ghoshal, S., & Bartlett, C. (1990). The multinational corporation as an interorganizational network. *Academy of Management Review, 15*(4), 603-625.

Giddens, A. (1984). *The constitution of society*. Berkeley, CA: University of California Press.

Goffman, E. (1959). *The presentation of self in everyday life*. New York: Doubleday.

Goffman, E. (1967). *Interaction ritual*. New York: Doubleday.

Goode, W. J. (1960). A theory of role strain. *American Sociological Review, 25*, 483-496.

Granovetter, M. (1983). The strength of weak ties: A network theory revisited. *Sociological Theory, 1*, 201-233.

Granovetter, M. (1984). Small is beautiful: Labor markets and establishment size. *American Sociological Review, 49*(3), 323-334.

Gross, N., Mason, W. S., & McEachern, A. W. (1958). *Explorations in role analysis: Studies of the school superintendency role*. New York: John Wiley.

Habermas, J. (1968). *The philospheric discourse of modernity* (F. Lawrence, Trans.). Cambridge: MIT Press.

Habermas, J. (1984). *The theory of communicative action*. Boston: Beacon.

Hage, J. (1974). *Communication and organizational control: A cybernetics perspective in a health welfare setting*. New York: Wiley-Interscience.

Hage, J. (1980). *Theories of organizations: Form, process, and transformation*. New York: Wiley-Interscience.

Hage, J. (1988). *The futures of organizations*. Lexington, MA: D. C. Heath.

Hage, J., Collins, P., Hull, F., & Teachman, J. (1991). *Organizational form and the survival of American manufacturing plants*. Unpublished paper, Center for Innovation, University of Maryland.

Hage, J., & Marwell, G. (1969). Toward the development of an empirically based theory of role relationships. *Sociometry*, 200-212.

Hage, J., & Powers, C. (1990, August). *Co-Determination: The real meaning of agency in post-industrial society*. The German/American Theory Conference, College Park, Maryland.

Hall, R. (1987). *Organizations: Structures, processes and outcomes* (4th ed.). Englewood Cliffs, NJ: Prentice-Hall.

Hall, R., Clark, J., Giordano, P., Johnson, P., & van Roekel, M. (1977). Patterns of interorganizational relationships. *Administrative Science Quarterly, 22*(3), 457-474.

Hannan, M., & Freeman, J. (1989). *Organizational ecology*. Cambridge, MA: Harvard University Press.

Hanneman, R. (1988). *Computer assisted theory building: Modeling dynamic social systems*. Newbury Park, CA: Sage.

Harrington, A. (1958). *A day at the crystal palace*. New York: Knopf.

Harris, J. L. (1984). *Henry Ford*. New York: Franklin Watts.

Hauser, P. M. (1964). Labor force. In R.E.L. Faris (Ed.), *Handbook of modern sociology* (p. 183). Chicago: Rand McNally

Heise, D. (1979). *Understanding events: Affect and the construction of social experience*. New York: Cambridge University Press.

Hickson, D. J., Henning, C., Lee, C. A., Schoeck, R. E., & Pennings, J. M. (1971, June). A strategic contingencies theory of interorganizational power. *Administrative Science Quarterly, 16*(2), 216-229.

Hilbert, R. (1990). Ethnomethodology and the micro-macro order. *American Sociological Review, 55*(6), 794-808.

Hirsch, E. D. (1987). *Cultural literacy: What every American needs to know*. Boston: Houghton Mifflin.

Hodson, R., & Sullivan, T. (1990). *The social organization of work*. Belmont, CA: Wadsworth.

Hollingsworth, J. R., & Lindberg, L. (1989). *Patterns of governance in American industry*. Madison: University of Wisconsin Press.

Homans, G. (1950). *The human group*. New York: Harcourt.

Homans, G. (1974). *Social behavior: Its elementary forms*. New York: Harcourt Brace Jovanovich.

Hudson Institute. (1987). *Workforce 2000*. Washington, DC: Government Printing Office.

Hull, F., & Hage, J. (1982). Organizing for innovation: Beyond Burns and Stalker. *Sociology, 16*(4), 564-567.

Ihinger-Tallman, M. (1988). Research on stepfamilies. *Annual Review of Sociology, 14*, 25-48.

Impending U.S. jobs disaster: Workforce unqualified to work. (1989, September 25). *The New York Times*, pp. A1, B6.

Inkeles, A., & Smith, D. (1974). *Becoming modern: Individual change in six developing countries*. Cambridge, MA: Harvard University Press.

Janis, I. L. (1972). *Victims of group think*. Boston: Houghton Mifflin.

Juhasz, A. (1985). Measuring self esteem in early adolescence. *Adolescence, 20*, 877-887.

Kahn, R. L., Wolfe, D. M., Quinn, R. P., Snoeck, J. D., & Rosenthal, R. A. (1964). *Organizational stress: Studies in role conflict and ambiguity*. New York: John Wiley.

Katz, J. (1988). *Seductions of Crime*. New York: Basic Books.

Kelley, H., & Thibault, J. (1978). *Interpersonal relations: A theory of interdependence*. New York: John Wiley.

Kellner, D. (1990). The postmodern turn: Positions, problems, and prospects. In G. Ritzer (Ed.), *Frontiers of social theory* (pp. 255-286). New York: Columbia University Press.

Kemper, T. D. (1978). *A social interaction theory of emotions*. New York: John Wiley.

Kemper, T. D. (1989). *Research agendas in the sociology of emotions*. Albany, NY: S.U.N.Y. Press

Kidder, T. (1979). *The soul of a new machine*. New York: Avon.

Kidder, T. (1985). *House*. Boston: Houghton Mifflin.

Kimmel, M. (Ed.). (1987). *Changing men*. Newbury Park, CA: Sage.

Kinlaw, D. (1990). *Developing superior work teams*. Lexington, MA: Lexington Books.

Kohn, M. (1977). *Class and conformity* (2nd ed.). Chicago: University of Chicago Press.

Kohn, M., & Schooler, C. (1973). Occupational experience and psychological functioning: An assessment of reciprocal effects. *American Sociological Review, 38*, 97-118.

Kuhn, M. (1960). Self-attitudes by age, sex, and professional training. *Sociological Quarterly, 1*, 39-55.

Kuhn, M., & McPhartland, T. S. (1954). An empirical investigation of self-attitudes. *American Sociological Review, 19*, 68-76.

Kutscher, R. E. (1987). Overview and implications of the projections to 2000. *Monthly Labor Review, 107*(9), 6.

Landes, D. (1969). *The unbound Prometheus: Technological change and industrial development in western Europe from 1750 to present*. Cambridge, UK: Cambridge University Press.

Larson, C., & LaFasto, F. (1989). *Teamwork*. Newbury Park, CA: Sage

Lawrence, P., & Lorsch, J. (1967). *Organizations and environment*. Cambridge, MA: Harvard Graduate School of Business Administration.

Lenski, G. (1954). Status crystallization: A nonvertical dimension of social status. *American Sociological Review, 19*, 405-413.

Lenski, G. & Lenski, J. (1974). *Human societies: An introduction to macrosociology*. New York: McGraw-Hill.

Linton, R. (1936). *The study of man*. New York: Appleton.

Lipset, S. M., Trow, M., & Coleman, J. (1956). *Union democracy*. New York: Free Press.

Luhmann, N. (1986). *Love as passion: The codification of intimacy* (J. Gaines & D. Jones, Trans.). Cambridge, MA: Harvard University Press.

Lyotard, J-F. (1984). *The postmodern condition*. Minneapolis: University of Minnesota Press.

Mann, F. C., & Hoffman, R. (1960). *Social change in power plants*. New York: Holt.

Mann, F. C., & Williams, L. K. (1960, September). Observations on the dynamics of a change to electronic data processing equipment. *Administrative Science Quarterly, 5*, 217-510.

Manufacturing trade gap in equipment. (1987, May 16). *U.S. News & World Report*, pp. 38-39.

March, J., & Simon, H. (1958). *Organizations*. New York: John Wiley.

Marcus, A., & Segal, H. (1989). *Technology in America*. San Diego: Harcourt Brace Jovanovich.

Marsden, P., & Lin, N. (Eds.). (1982). *Social structure and network analysis*. Beverly Hills, CA: Sage.

Marwell, G., & Hage, J. (1970). The organization of role-relationships: A systematic description. *American Sociological Review, 35*, 884-900.

Marx, K. 1967. *Capital*. (3 vols.) New York: International Publishers. (Original work published 1867, 1885, & 1894)

Marx, K., & Engels, F. (1967). *The communist manifesto*. New York: Pantheon. (Original work published 1848)

Maslow, A. (1954). *Motivation and personality*. New York: Harper.

Mason, K., Czajka, J., & Arber, S. (1976). Change in U.S. women's sex role attitudes, 1964-1974. *American Sociological Review, 41*, 573-596.

McLanahan, S. (1985). Family structure and the reproduction of poverty. *American Journal of Sociology, 90*, 873-883.

McQuarrie, E. (1991). The customer visit. *Marketing Research, 3*, 15-28.

Mead, G. H. (1913). The social self. *The Journal of Philosophy, Psychology and Scientific Methods, 10*.

Mead, G. H. (1964). *Mind, self, and society* (C. Morris, Ed.). Chicago: University of Chicago Press. (Original work published 1934)

Merton, R. (1957). The role-set: Problems in sociological theory. *British Journal of Sociology, 8*(2), 106-120.

Merton, R. (1968). *Social theory and social structure* (3rd ed.). Glencoe, IL: Free Press.

Meyer, J., & Hannan, M. (Eds.). (1979). *National development and the world system: Educational, economic and political change, 1950-1970*. Chicago: University of Chicago Press.

Miner, A. S. (1987). Idiosyncratic jobs in formalized organizations. *Administrative Science Quarterly, 32*, 327-351.

Mintzberg, H. (1979). *The structuring of organizations*. Englewood Cliffs, NJ: Prentice-Hall.

Mintzberg, H., & McHugh, A. (1985). Strategy formation in an adhocracy. *Administrative Science Quarterly, 30*, 160-197.

Miyamoto, F., & Dornbush, S. (1956). A test of the symbolic interactionist hypothesis of self-conception. *American Journal of Sociology, 61*, 399-403.

Mizaruchi, M., & Koenig, T. (1986). Economic sources of corporate political con-
senses. *American Sociological Review, 51,* 797-811.

Mohr, W., & Mohr, H. (1983). *Quality circles.* Reading, MA: Addison-Wesley.

Morrissey, J., Tausig, M., & Lindsey, M. (1985). Network analysis methods for mental
health service system research (National Institute of Mental Health Series BN #6).
Washington, DC: Government Printing Office.

Moscovici, S. (1981). On social representations. In J. Forges (Ed.), *Social Cognition* (pp.
181-209). London: Academic Press.

Mullins, N. (1973). *Theory and theory groups in contemporary American sociology.* New
York: Harper & Row.

Munch, R., & Smelser, N. (1987). Relating the micro and macro. In J. Alexander, B.
Gresen, R. Munch, & N. Smelser, *The micro-macro link.* Berkeley: University of
California Press.

Nadel, S. F. (1942). *A black Byzantium.* London: Oxford University Press.

Nadel, S. F. (1956). *The theory of social structure.* London: Cohen and West.

Naisbitt, J. (1982). *Megatrends: Ten new directions transforming our lives.* New York:
Warner Books.

Naisbitt, J., & Aburdene, P. (1985). *Re-inventing the corporation: Transforming your job
and your company for the new information age.* New York: Warner Books.

Naisbitt, J., & Aburdene, P. (1990). *Megatrends 2000.* New York: William Morrow.

Nakashima, C. (1991). An invisible monster: The creation and denial of multi-racial
people. In M. Root (Ed.), *Mixed race people coming of age in America.* Newbury Park,
CA: Sage.

Neustadtl, A., & Clawson, D. (1988). Corporate political groupings. *American Sociological Review, 53*(2), 172-190.

New challenge in automation. (1986, October 30). *The New York Times.*

The New York Times Magazine. (1990, October 14). *[article on Robert Bly].*

Nisbet, R. (1970). *The social bond.* New York: Knopf.

O'Connor, J. (1973). *The fiscal crisis of the state.* New York: St. Martin's Press.

Ogburn, W. F. (1922). *Social change with respect to cultural and original nature.* New
York: B. W. Huebsch.

Ott, J. S. (1989). *The organizational culture perspective.* Chicago: Dorsey.

Ouchi, W. (1979). *Theory Z: How American business can meet the Japanese challenge.*
Reading, MA: Addison-Wesley.

Papanek, H. (1973). Men, women, and work: Reflections on the two-person career.
American Journal of Sociology, 78(4) 852-872.

Pareto, V. 1984. *The transformation of democracy* (C. Powers, Ed., R. Girola, Trans.).
New Brunswick, NJ: Transaction Books. (Original work published 1923)

Parsons, T. (1937). *The structure of social action* (2 vols.). New York: McGraw-Hill.

Parsons, T. (1951). *The social system.* Glencoe, IL: Free Press.

Parsons, T. (1966). *Societies, evolutionary and comparative perspectives.* Englewood
Cliffs, NJ: Prentice-Hall.

Parsons, T. (1967). Pattern variables revisited: A response to Robert Dubin. In T.
Parsons, *Sociological theory and modern society* (pp. 192-219). New York: Free Press.

Parsons, T., Bales, R., & Shils, E. (1953). *Working papers in the theory of action.* Glencoe,
IL: Free Press.

Parsons, T., & Platt, G. (1973). *The American university.* Cambridge, MA: Harvard University Press.

Parsons, T., & Shils, E.. (1951). *Toward a general theory of action.* Cambridge, MA: Harvard University Press.

Paulos, J. (1988). *Innumeracy.* New York: Hill and Wang.

Pelz, D., & Andrews, F. (1966). *Scientists in organizations: productive climates of research and development.* New York: John Wiley.

Perrow, C. (1967). A framework for the comparative analysis of organizations. *American Sociological Review, 32,* 194-209.

Perrow, C. (1979). *Complex organizations* (2nd ed.). Glenview, IL: Scott, Foresman.

Peters, T. J., & Waterman, R. H. (1982). *In search of excellence.* New York: Harper & Row.

Pfeffer, J., & Nowak, P. (1976). Joint ventures and interorganizational dependence. *Administrative Science Quarterly, 21*(3), 398-418.

Piore, C. F., & Sabel, M. J. (1984). *The second industrial divide: Possibilities for prosperity.* New York: Basic Books.

Pitt, R., & Hage, J. (1964). Patterns of peer interaction during adolescence as prognostic indicators in schizophrenia. *American Journal of Psychiatry,* 1089-1096.

Powers, C. H. (1981a). Role imposition or role improvisation: Some theoretical principles. *Economic and Social Review, 12*(4), 287-299.

Powers, C. H. (1981b, December). *Power and principles of social integration.* Unpublished doctoral dissertation, University of California at Riverside.

Powers, C. H. (1990, December). Five generalizations: One step on the road to the discovery of sociological laws. *Revue Europeenne des Sciences Sociales [European Review of the Social Sciences], 28*(88), 135-148.

Powers, C., & Hanneman, R. (1983). Pareto's theory of social and economic cycles: A formal model and simulation. *Sociological Theory, 1,* 59-89.

Ray, M., & Myers, R. (1989). *Creativity in business.* New York: Doubleday.

Redfield, R. (1941). *The folk culture of the Yucatan.* Chicago: Chicago University Press.

Riesman, D. (1961). *The lonely crowd.* New Haven, CT: Yale University Press.

Ritzer, G. (1988). *Contemporary sociological theory* (2nd ed.). New York: Knopf.

Rogers, E. (1983). *Diffusion of innovations* (3rd ed.). New York: Free Press.

Ronken, H., & Lawrence, P. (1952). *Administering change: A case study of human relations in a factory.* Boston: Harvard Graduate School of Business Administration.

Rosenberg, M. (1979). *Conceiving the self.* New York: Basic Books.

Rosenberg, M. (1990). Reflexivity and emotions. *Social Psychological Quarterly, 53*(1), 3-12.

Rosenberg, M., & Turner, R. (1981). *Social psychology.* New York: Basic Books.

Rubin, L. (1976). *Worlds of pain.* New York: Basic Books.

Ruddick, S. (1977). *Working it out.* New York: Pantheon.

Rutherford, J., & Ahlgren, A. (1990). *Science for all Americans.* New York: Oxford University Press.

Sacks, H., Schegloff, E., & Jefferson, G. (1978). The simplest systematics for the organization of turn taking for conversation. In J. Schenkein (Ed.), *Studies in the organization of conversational interaction.* New York: Academic Press.

Sault, N. (Ed.). (1992). *Body image and social relationships in anthropological perspective.* Philadelphia: University of Pennsylvania Press.

Schael, A., & Fassel, D. (1988). *The addictive organization.* New York: Harper & Row.

Scheff, T. (1979). Negotiating reality: Watson power in the assignment of reality. In D. Birsset & C. Edgley (Eds.), *Life as theater.* Chicago: Aldine.

Schien, E. (1985). *Organizational culture and leadership.* San Francisco: Jossey-Bass.

Science and Engineering Indicators. (1987). Washington, DC: Government Printing Office.

Science and Engineering Indicators. (1989). Washington, DC: Government Printing Office.

Scott, R. (1987). *Organizations: Rational, national and open systems.* Englewood Cliffs, NJ: Prentice-Hall.

Shaiken, H. (1985). *Work transformed: Automation and labor in the computer age.* New York: Holt, Rinehart & Winston.

Shibutani, T. (1978). *The derelicts of Company K: A sociological study of demoralization.* Berkeley: University of California Press.

Shinn, T. (1982). Scientific disciplines and organizational specialty: The social and cognitive configuration of laboratory activities. *Sociology of the Sciences, 4*, 239-264.

Shorter, E. (1975). *The making of the modern family.* New York: Basic Books.

Sidel, R. (1986). *Women and children last.* New York: Penguin.

Siljak, D. (1991). *Decentralized control of complex systems.* Cambridge, MA: Academic Press.

Simmel, G. (1950). The metropolis and mental life. In K. Wolff (Ed.), *The sociology of Georg Simmel* (pp. 409-424). Glencoe, IL: Free Press. (Original work published 1902)

Simmel, G. (1955). *Conflict and the web of group affiliations* (K. Wolff, Trans.). Glencoe, IL: Free Press. (Original work published 1908)

Simon, H. (1957). *Models of man, social and rational.* New York: John Wiley.

Smelser, N. (1959). *Social change in the industrial revolution.* Chicago: University of Chicago Press.

Snyder, M. (1987). *Public appearances, private realities: The psychology of self-monitoring.* New York: Freeman.

Sofranko, A., & Fliegel, F. (1977). Industrialism and modernity: Economic and non-economic orientations. *Rural Sociology, 42*, 496-516.

Stinchcombe, A. (1965). Social structure and organizations. In J. G. March (Ed.), *Handbook of organizations* (pp. 142-193). Chicago: Rand McNally.

Stolz, L. (1967). *Influences on parents' behavior.* Palo Alto, CA: Stanford University Press.

Stone, G. P. (1962). Appearance and the self. In A. Rose (Ed.), *Human behavior and social process* (pp. 86-118). Boston: Houghton Mifflin.

Strauss, A., Schatzman, L., Bucher, R., Ehrlich, D., & Sabshin, M. (1964). Negotiated order and the coordination of work. In A. Strauss, L. Schatzman, R. Bucher, D. Ehrlich, & M. Sabshin, *Psychiatric ideologies and institutions* (pp. 292-315). Glencoe, IL: Free Press.

Stryker, S. (1980). *Symbolic interactionism: A social structural version.* Menlo Park, CA: Benjamin/Cummings.

Stryker, S. (1990). Further developments in identity theory: Singularity versus multiplicity of self. In J. Berger & M. Zelditch (Eds.), *Sociological theories in progress* (Vol. 3). Newbury Park, CA: Sage.

Taylor, F. (1967). *The principles of scientific management.* New York: Norton. (Original work published 1911)

Teune, H. (1984). Intregration. In G. Sartori (Ed.), *Social science concepts* (pp. 235-264), Beverly Hills, CA: Sage.

The rise and rise of America's small firms. (1989, January 21). *The Economist.*

The takeover of American industry. (1989, May 28). *The New York Times,* Section 3.

Thibault, J., & Kelley, H. (1959). *The social psychology of groups.* New York: John Wiley.

Thoits, P. (1983). Multiple identities and psychological well-being: A reformulation and test of the social isolation hypothesis. *American Sociological Review, 48,* 174-187.

Thoits, P. (1989). The sociology of emotions. *Annual Review of Sociology* (pp. 317-342).

Tilly, C. (Ed.). (1975). *The transformation of the state.* Princeton, NJ: Princeton University Press.

Toennies, F. (1963). *Community and society.* New York: Harper & Row. (Original work published 1887)

Toffler, A. (1970). *Future shock.* New York: Bantam.

Toffler, A. (1981). *The third wave.* New York: Bantam.

Toffler, A., & Toffler, H. (1990). *Powershift.* New York: Bantam.

Tosi, H., & Carroll, S. (1982). *Management* (2nd ed.). New York: John Wiley.

Touraine, A. (1988). *Return of the actor.* Minneapolis: University of Minnesota Press.

Turner, J. (1972). *Patterns of social organization.* New York: McGraw-Hill.

Turner, J. (1987). Toward a sociological theory of motivation. *American Sociological Review, 52,* 15-27.

Turner, J. (1990). *The structure of sociological theory* (5th ed.). Belmont, CA: Wadsworth.

Turner, J., Beeghley, L., & Powers, C. (1989). *The emergence of sociological theory* (2nd ed.). Chicago: Dorsey Press.

Turner, J., & Maryanski, S. (1979). *Functionalism: An intellectual portrait.* Menlo Park, CA: Benjamin/Cummings.

Turner, R. (1968). Role: Sociological aspects. *International Encyclopedia of the Social Sciences, 13,* 552-557. New York: Macmillan.

Turner, R. (1978). The role and the person. *American Journal of Sociology, 84,* 1-23.

Turner, R. (1990). Role change. *Annual Review of Sociology, 16,* 87-110.

Tyebjee, T. (1991). The strategy of alliances. *Journal of Private Enterprise, 7*(1), 36-54.

U.S. Department of Commerce, Bureau of the Census. (1981). *Statistical abstract of the U.S.* Washington, DC: Government Printing Office.

U.S. Statistical Abstract. (1990). Washington, DC: Goverment Printing Office.

Useem, M. (1986). *The inner circle: Large corporations and the rise of business activity in the U.S. and the U.K.* New York: Oxford.

Van de Ven, A., Delbecq, A., & Koenig, R. (1976). Determinants of coordination: Modes within organizations. *American Sociological Review, 41,* 322-328.

Vogel, E. (1979). *Japan as number 1: Lessons for America.* New York: Harper & Row.

Walker, C. R. (1957). *Toward the automated factory: A case study of men and machines.* New Haven, CT: Yale University Press.

Walton, R., Dutton, J., & Cafferty, T. (1969). Organizational context and interdepartmental conflict. *Administrative Science Quarterly, 14*, 522-543.

Weber, M. (1958). *The Protestant ethic and the spirit of capitalism.* New York: Scribner. (Original work published 1905)

Weber, M. (1922). *The theory of social and economic organization.* New York: Oxford University Press.

Weber, M. (1923). *General economic history.* New Brunswick, NJ: Transaction Books.

Weber, M. (1946). *From Max Weber: Essays in sociology* (H. Gerth & C. W. Mills, Ed. & Trans.). New York: Oxford University Press.

Weber, M. (1968). *Economy and society* (G. Roth & C. Wittich, Eds.). Berkeley: University of California Press.

Weick, K. (1969). *The social psychology of organizing.* Reading, MA: Addison-Wesley.

Weick, K. (1976). Education organizations as loosely coupled systems. *Administrative Science Quarterly, 21*, 1-19.

Weiss, R. S. (1956). *Processes of organizations.* Ann Arbor, MI: Institution for Social Research.

Wellman, B., & Wortley, S. (1989). Brothers' keepers: Situating kinship relations in broader networks of social support. *Sociological Perspectives, 32*(3) 273-306.

Wells, E., & Marwell, G. (1975). *Self esteem: Its conceptualization and measurement.* Beverly Hills, CA: Sage.

White, H. (1970). *Chains of opportunity.* Cambridge, MA: Harvard University Press.

White, H. (1981). Where do markets come from? *American Journal of Sociology, 87*, 517-547.

White, H., Boorman, S., & Breiger, R. (1976). Social structure from multiple networks I. Blockmodels of roles and positions. *American Journal of Sociology, 81*, 730-780.

Whyte, W. F. (1981). *Steet corner society: The social structure of an Italian slum* (3rd ed.). Chicago: University of Chicago Press.

Williamson, O. (1975). *Markets and hierarchies: Analysis of antitrust implications.* New York: Free Press.

Wilson, S. (1955). *The man in the gray flannel suit.* New York: Simon & Schuster.

Womack, J., Jones, D., & Roos, D. (1990). *The machine that changed the world.* New York: Rawsen.

Woodward, J. (1965). *Industrial organization: Theory and practice.* London: Oxford University Press.

Wright, J. P. (1980). *On a clear day you can see General Motors.* New York: Avon.

Zaltman, G., Duncan, R., & Holbek, J. (1973). *Innovations and organizations.* New York: John Wiley.

Zuboff, S. (1984). *In the age of the smart machine.* New York: Basic Books.

Zurcher, L. (1977). *The mutable self: A self-concept for social change.* Beverly Hills, CA: Sage.

Zurcher, L. (1983). *Social roles: Conformity, conflict, and creativity.* Beverly Hills, CA: Sage.

NAME INDEX

Aburdene, P., x, 2, 26, 28
Adler, P., 145, 161
Ahlgren, A., 24
Aiken, M., 113, 171, 186
Alba, R., 80
Aldrich, H., 6, 36, 154, 162, 168
Alexander, J., 18n, 156, 162, 212
Alger, H., 78
Allen, S., xi, 177
Allison, P., 40
Alter, C., 78, 154
Ambry, M., 15
Andrews, F., 77
Apple, 191
Arber, S., 113
Aron, A., 103, 157
Ashby, E., 116
AT&T, 177
Atari, 36
Auster, E., 36, 168
Azumi, K., 76

Bales, R., 171
Bane, M. J., 23
Barley, S., 113
Bartlett, C., 183
Barton, C., 75
Bateson, G., 99
Bauman, Z., ix
Bearden, J., 154
Becker, S., 113
Bell, D., x, 2, 19n, 38, 39, 42
Biddle, B., 6-7, 139, 143
Birenbaum, A., 109n, 125
Blau, P., 49, 76
Blauner, R., 10, 30, 169
Blumer, H., 83, 89n, 126, 145, 161, 175, 198, 200, 210
Blumstein, P., 7, 161, 163
Bly, R., 106
Boeing, 47
Boje, D., 138, 153, 187
Boorman, S., 151

233

Bott, E., 149
Boyett, J., 179
Bradley, R., 103, 151, 152
Brayfield, A., 113, 116
Breiger, R., 151
Britain, 3, 23-24, 25, 32-33
Bucher, R., 109n, 164
Bullough, V., 118
Burawoy, M., 10
Burns, T., 6, 178, 185
Burr, W., 110n
Burt, R., 138, 153, 187
Burton, L., 15

Cafferty, T., 143
California, 3
Campbell, J., 183
Caplow, T., 141
Carnevale, A., 5, 36, 42, 57, 62n, 72, 78, 93, 169, 179
Carroll, G., 162, 168, 185
Chandler, A., 45, 46, 49, 56, 58, 172, 182
Chomsky, N., 65
Clawson, D., 153, 154, 187
Clough, P., 113
Coch, L., 76
Cohen, S., 32
Coleman, J., 171
Collins, P., 30, 37
Collins, R., 61n, 95, 102, 109n, 118, 122, 211
Columbia, 192n
Conn, H., 179
Cook, K., 153, 192n
Cooley, C. H., 66
Corning Glass, 183
Corwin, R., 143
Coser, L., 117, 141, 213
Coser, R., 141
Crozier, M., 142
Czajka, J., 113

Daft, R., 113, 185
Degler, C., 13

Delacroix, J., 192n
Delbecq, A., 179
Denzin, N., 111
Department of Defense, 23
Dertouzas, M., 23
Descartes, R., 198
Deutsch, K., 79, 80, 82
Diaghilev, S. P., 72
Dittmer, J., 15
DiVinci, L., 72
Dornbush, S., 67
Duncan, R., 113
DuPont, 35, 45, 56
Dubin, R., 10, 120
Durkheim, E., 12, 79, 138, 193n
Dutton, J., 143

Edison, T., 72, 75
Ehrlich, D., 109n, 164
Einstein, A., 72
Eliot, C., 75
Ellwood, D., 23
Emerson, R., 153, 192n
England, 44
Engles, F., 142, 176
Erickson, K., 10
Europe, 23, 35, 37
    Eastern, 34, 37
    Western, 34

Featherstone, M., ix, 19n
Feher, F., 19n
Fleming, L., 84
Fliegel, F., 82
Florida, R., 181
Forester, T., 40
Fortana, A., 145, 161
Foucault, M., 10
France, 23-24, 32-34, 46, 86
Freeman, C., 6, 36, 46, 162, 168, 173
French, J. P. R., 76
Freud, S., 103
Freudenberger, H., 87
Frey, S., 15

Redfield, R., 89n
Riesman, D., 78
Ritzer, G., 1
Rogers, E., 113
Ronken, H., 76, 78
Roos, D., 31
Rosenberg, M., xi, 18n, 67, 79, 81
Rosenthal, R. A., 143
Royal Dutch Shell, 182
Rubin, L., 14
Ruddick, S., 135n
Rutgers, 189
Rutherford, J., 24

Sabel, M. J., 4, 10, 19n, 31
Sabshin, M., 109n, 164
Sacks, H., 109n
Safeway, 24
Sault, N., 19n
Schatzman, L., 109n, 163
Scheff, T., 97, 103, 201
Schegloff, E., 109n
Schein, E., 109n
Schoeck, R. E., 164
Schoenherr, R., 49
Schooler, C., 65
Scott, R., 49, 76
Sears Roebuck, 57
Segal, H., 182
Shaiken, H., 23, 36
Shibutani, T., 163
Shils, F., 64, 171
Shinn, T., 177
Shorter, E., 118
Sidel, R., 25
Siljak, D., 186
Simmel, G., 2, 3, 117, 191n
Simon, H., 62n, 149
Singer Sewing Machine, 182
Sloan, A., 75
Smelser, N., 61n, 62n, 162, 214
Smith, D., 82
Snoeck, J. D., 143
Snyder, M., 67

Sofranko, A., 82
Solow, R., 23
Solt, M., 192n
Soviet Union, 34
Spanier, G. B., 26
Stalker, G. M., 6, 178, 185
Standard Oil of New Jersey, 56
Stinchcombe, A., 47
Stolz, L., 15
Stone, G. P., 85
Strauss, A., 109n, 163
Stryker, S., xi, 81, 85, 128, 141, 162
Sullivan, W., 27, 97
Sweden, 32
Swidler, A., 97

Tausig, M., 154
Taylor, F., 172
Teune, H., 149, 190
Thibault, J., 164
Thoits, P., 81, 95, 97, 100
Thomas, E., 6
Tilly, C., 62n
Tipton, S., 97
Toennies, F., 1, 89n, 161
Toffler, A., x, 2, 15, 16, 28, 32, 59
Tosi, H., 185
Touraine, A., 198
Toyota, 183
Trow, M., 162
Turner, J., x, 1, 98, 104, 149, 151, 200
Turner, R., x, xi, 6, 18n, 67, 81, 82, 88, 109, 110n, 111, 112, 115, 121, 122, 128, 130, 133, 138, 198, 216
Tyebjee, T., 182

U.S. Steel, 36, 182
United Kingdom. *See* Britain
Useem, M., 153

Van de Ven, A., 179
Vogel, E., 109

SUBJECT INDEX

Activities, in roles, 56, 156, 158, 163-164, 165, 166, 172
  integration of, 156, 158, 178, 180
  negotiation over, 181
  variety of, 117, 155-156, 158, 163, 166, 180
Actualization, self, 79, 107
Adaptiveness, 23, 36, 214
  in organizations, 5, 36
  of individuals, 17, 22, 80
Affect, 123, 164, 166.
  See also Emotions and feelings
Affective roles, 82
Agency, human, 89n, 198, 217n
  and co-determination, 211-212
  and group decision, 114
  and independence, 156, 158, 159
  and role change, 112, 133, 157
  and role-relationships, 120-121, 198
Alienation, 10, 126
Assembly-line, 36, 49, 172
Authority. *See* Hierarchy, Authority

Automation, 10, 14, 36, 42n
  and knowledge, 29, 36-37, 41, 206
  impact on roles, 14, 36-37, 54, 192n, 196, 206
Automobile industry, 45, 46, 49

Bio-tech industry, 3, 34, 35, 46
Bureaucracy, 4, 10, 49, 57, 79
  characteristics of, 6, 48, 172, 174-175
  vs. post-industrial organizations, 5-6, 174-175
Burnout, 9, 116, 143, 144.
  See also Stress

Centralization, 76.
  See also Hierarchy, Authority
Chemical industry, 24, 44, 35, 173
Codification, rules. *See* Rules, codification of
Commitment, 156, 157

ABOUT THE AUTHORS

Jerald Hage received his Ph.D. at Columbia University in 1963 and for some 30 years has been doing research and writing about organizations, including the book *Theories of Organizations*. During the past few years, he has published an edited book, titled *The Futures of Organizations*, and an analysis of the relevance of organizational theory to the developing world for U.S.A.I.D., titled *Organizational Change as a Strategy for Development* (with Finsterbusch). Most recently he has finished, with Cathy Alter, a book on systemic networks as a new form of institutional governance and is just completing a textbook designed to teach readers how to think in structural, political, ecological, and institutional terms about organizations.

Since the early 1980s, Hage has been increasingly shifting his attention to the problem of societal change, his long-time interest. He published two books relative to the theory of the state—*State Responsiveness and State Activism* (with Hanneman and Gargan) and *State Intervention in Medical Care* (with Hollingsworth and Hanneman)—both of which attempt to synthesize a number of different theoretical perspectives. Currently, he is analyzing the impact of state inter-

ventions on the growth of unionization, pathways of growth in welfare expenditures, state coupling of education to the economy, and
other issues that explore societal change.

Neither the study of organizations nor of society, however, represents Hage's major interest, which is writing general sociological
theories sensitive to both history and economics. This book represents the first in what he hopes will be a series of books designed to
provide a new synthesis.

Charles H. Powers is an Associate Professor at Santa Clara University in California's Silicon Valley, where he heads the Department
of Anthropology and Sociology's program in Business, Technology,
and Society. This program helps students apply specialized sociological knowledge in a business context. Stimulating organizational
innovation and capitalizing on the advantages of work-force diversity are two of the program's themes.

Powers is a sociological theroist who focuses on (a) role change,
which is one of the unifying threads of this book, and (b) the inter-
connection between economy and society. His earlier works on socio-
economics include *Vilfredo Pareto* and the second edition of *The Emergence of Sociological Theory* (co-authored with Jonathan Turner and
Leonard Beeghley). Powers also edited the English translation of
Vilfredo Pareto's last monograph, *The Transformation of Democracy*.
He is currently working on a compendium of axioms and principles that clarify the boundary between economics and sociology.

Dr. Powers received his B.A. and M.A. from the University of
Illinois at Urbana and his Ph.D. from the University of California at
Riverside. His previous teaching positions were at Talledega College in Alabama, and Indiana University at Bloomington. He also
taught in the M.B.A. program at Santa Clara University.